THE MILITARY MARRIAGE MANUAL

Military Life

Military Life is a series of books for service members and their families who must deal with the significant yet often overlooked difficulties unique to life in the military. Each of the titles in the series is a comprehensive presentation of the problems that arise, solutions to these problems, and resources that are of much further help. The authors of these books—who are themselves military members and experienced writers—have personally faced these challenging situations, and understand the many complications that accompany them. This is the first stop for members of the military and their loved ones in search of information on navigating the complex world of military life.

1. *The Wounded Warrior Handbook: A Resource Guide for Returning Veterans* by Don Philpott and Janelle Hill (2008).
2. *The Military Marriage Manual: Tactics for Successful Relationships* by Janelle Hill, Cheryl Lawhorne, and Don Philpott (2010).
3. *Combat-Related Traumatic Brain Injury and PTSD: A Resource and Recovery Guide* by Cheryl Lawhorne and Don Philpott (2010).
4. *Special Needs Families in the Military: A Resource Guide* by Janelle Hill and Don Philpott (2010).
5. *Life After the Military: A Handbook for Transitioning Veterans* by Janelle Hill, Cheryl Lawhorne, and Don Philpott (2011).

THE MILITARY MARRIAGE MANUAL

Tactics for Successful Relationships

JANELLE HILL, CHERYL LAWHORNE,
AND DON PHILPOTT

GOVERNMENT INSTITUTES
An imprint of
THE SCARECROW PRESS, INC.
Lanham • Toronto • Plymouth, UK
2010

**Government
Institutes**

Published by Government Institutes
An imprint of The Scarecrow Press, Inc.
A wholly owned subsidary of The Rowman & Littlefield Publishing Group, Inc.
4501 Forbes Boulevard, Suite 200, Lanham, Maryland 20706
http://www.govinstpress.com

Estover Road, Plymouth PL6 7PY, United Kingdom

British Library Cataloguing in Publication Information Available
The hardback edition of this was previously cataloged by the Library of Congress as follows:

Library of Congress Cataloging-in-Publication Data

Hill, Janelle.
  The military marriage manual : tactics for successful relationships / Janelle Hill, Cheryl
Lawhorne, and Don Philpott.
      p. cm.—(Military life ; no. 2)
  Includes index.
  1. Soldiers—Family relationships—United States—Handbooks, manuals etc. 2. Military
spouses—United States—Handbooks, manuals etc. 3. Marriage—United States—
Handbooks, manuals etc. 4. Married people—United States—Handbooks, manuals etc. 5.
United States—Armed Forces—Military life—Handbooks, manuals, etc. I. Lawhorne,
Cheryl, 1968– II. Philpott, Don, 1946– III. Title.
  U766.H55 2010
  355.1'29—dc22   2010019875
  ISBN: 978-1-60590-700-0 (cloth : alk. paper)
  ISBN: 978-1-60590-765-9 (pbk : alk. paper)

CONTENTS

Foreword

CONGRATULATIONS! YOU ARE EITHER MARRIED OR about to be married to a military service member. As such, you vow before the assembled family and friends to love and cherish your chosen one, in good times and in bad. Congratulations also because at least one of you wears the cloth of our nation and has sworn another oath to support and defend our Constitution against all enemies, foreign and domestic. Both allegiances are noble. Either oath by itself can prove challenging. To undertake these commitments and do both simultaneously and successfully are accomplishments that call for strategy, respect, and tact.

How were we to know, decades ago, that our military marriage would remain strong? Careful preparation, honest communication, and optimistic attitudes helped us enjoy the exciting twists and rise above the unexpected turns that every couple experiences. Our years together have been filled with the realities typical of military life—cross-country transfers, separations and deployments, tight finances, frequent school changes, new job searches. There have also been rewards—foreign travel, lifelong friendships, first-rate children, career accomplishments, and pride in our military.

Our strategies are not unique and can be learned. We bend so we don't break. We enjoy a loving relationship and laugh together often. We honor each other's talents. We maintain personal traditions with our children. We lean on our larger military family and its support services when help is needed.

The authors have drawn together valuable strategies for your successful military marriage in this accessible book. Within these pages are many issues that will confront and challenge you in the days ahead. All are surmountable—if you tackle them together. Just as continuous training is essential to military readiness, so is continued attention to your relationship. This book will remind you that you are not alone.

You love and need each other. Our nation and our military love and need both of you and are grateful that you have answered this special call. "God Speed, Fair Winds, and Following Seas" on the wonderful adventure that lies ahead of you—your military marriage.

Semper Fidelis (Always Faithful)
Jay and Debbie Paxton

LtGen J. M. Paxton, USMC, serves as director for operations, J-3, the Joint Staff

Mrs. Debbie Paxton is the mental health advisor, USMC Wounded Warrior Regiment

Author's Note

THIS GUIDE ASSISTS MILITARY COUPLES AND families by compiling and referencing information on how to be married, stay married, and deal with the unusual challenges of war, deployment, single parenting, constant moving, and all the other issues that have to be overcome in order to "live happily ever after."

Acknowledgments

The authors would like to thank all the people who generously gave of their time to assist us with this endeavor. Much of the information that we have used comes from federal and military websites and is in the public domain. These include the Department of Defense, American Forces Press Service, U.S. Army Medical Department, Department of Veterans Affairs, Department of Health and Human Services, and websites of all branches of the U.S. military. We have tried to extract the essentials. Where more information might be useful we have provided websites and resources that can help you. In particular we would like to thank Rod Powers for his permission to use some of his articles posted on the very informative www .usmilitary.about.com and Rich McCormack of *Military Spouse* magazine and www.milspouse.com for permission to quote extracts from articles that have appeared in both the magazine and on the website.

Getting Married   1

Thinking about Getting Married?

WHEN MOST PEOPLE GET MARRIED, THEY inherit a second family of in-laws. When you marry into the military, you get a very large third family. Your new third family—whether it is Army, Navy, Air Force, Marines, or Coast Guard—can also be quite a culture shock. They often speak what appears to be a different language and use expressions and acronyms that take a lot of getting used to. They tell time differently. They have rules and standards of conduct that you as a military spouse are expected to follow and ways of doing things that may be very strange to you at first. There is the chain-of-command structure, and you have to learn to recognize ranks and insignias. Living on base involves heightened levels of security. And this is all on top of getting married and setting up home.

The good news is that while it may all seem very strange and even daunting at first, there is a lot of help on hand. Other married couples will be quick to welcome you and help you get organized. There are support groups and clubs, social workers, chaplains, and a host of other people all waiting to help you get acclimated and familiar with your new third family.

First, it is useful to know a little about the military structure of the U.S. armed forces.

Who's Who and Who Does What?

There are five military branches: Army, Air Force, Navy, Marine Corps, and Coast Guard. The Army is commanded by a four-star general, known as the Army Chief of Staff. The Army Chief of Staff reports to the Secretary of the Army (for most matters). The top military member in the Air Force is the Air Force Chief of Staff. This four-star general reports (for most matters) to the Secretary of the Air Force. The Navy is commanded by a four-star admiral, called the Chief of Naval Operations. The Marine Corps is commanded by a four-star general called the Commandant of the Marine Corps. Both the Chief of Naval Operations and the Marine Corps Commandant report (for most matters) to the Secretary of the Navy.

Note how we indicated that they report "for most matters" to their respective service secretaries. These four flag officers also make up a group called the Joint Chiefs of Staff (JSC). The Joint Chiefs of Staff comprise the

A Little History . . .

The United States armed forces predate even the Declaration of Independence. In 1775, the Second Continental Congress created the Continental Army, and the establishment of the Continental Navy and Continental Marines soon followed. These forces were mostly disbanded in 1783 around the end of the Revolutionary War.

On June 14, 1784, the Congress of the Confederation created the United States Army, and in 1787, the Constitution granted Congress the power to "raise and support armies," to "provide and maintain a navy," and to declare war. It also made the president the military's commander-in-chief.

By 1785, all the remaining vessels of the Continental Navy had been sold. It was not until the Naval Act of 1794 that the United States rekindled efforts to develop a Navy. Tensions with France soon led to the Quasi-War in 1798, which was fought entirely at sea until 1800, and an act of Congress authorized a peacetime Navy shortly thereafter. The War of 1812 heightened awareness of the need for the expansion of the United States Navy. After the end of the war in 1815, funding for the Navy increased dramatically, and it grew rapidly.

Following the disbanding of the Continental Marines in 1783, the United States Marine Corps was established in 1798 at the beginning of the Quasi-War, and it largely developed alongside the Navy.

The United States Coast Guard traces its origin to the Revenue Cutter Service, which was founded in 1790, but it was formally established when the Revenue Cutter Service merged with the United States Life-Saving Service in 1915.

Beginning as a division of the U.S. Army in 1907, and after several changes in organization and title, the United States Air Force became an independent service under the National Security Act of 1947.

four service chiefs, the Vice Chairman of the Joint Chiefs of Staff, and the Chairman of the Joint Chiefs of Staff. The chairman is nominated by the president and approved by the Senate (as are other general and flag officer positions). For operational matters (such as war or conflict), the JCS by-passes the individual service secretaries and reports directly to the Secretary of Defense and the president.

That leaves the Coast Guard. The Coast Guard does not fall under the Department of Defense. Until recently, the Coast Guard was under the Department of Transportation. Recent legislation has moved the Coast Guard to the Department of Homeland Security. However, the Coast Guard is considered a military service, because during times of war or conflict the President of the United States can transfer any or all assets of the Coast Guard to the Department of the Navy. In fact, this has been done in almost every single conflict that the United States have ever been involved in. The Coast Guard is commanded by a four-star admiral, known as the Coast Guard Commandant.

So what are the different functions of the five branches of the military?

Army

The Army is the main ground force of the United States. The Army's main function is to protect and defend the United States (and its interests) by way of ground troops, armor (tanks), artillery, attack helicopters, tactical nuclear weapons, and so on. The Army is the oldest U.S. military service, officially established by the Continental Congress on June 14, 1775. The Army is also the largest U.S. military service. There are approximately 76,000 officers and 401,000 enlisted members in the active duty Army. The Army is supported by two reserve forces. The reserve forces can be tapped for trained personnel and equipment during times of need: the Army Reserves and the Army National Guard. The primary difference between the two is that the reserves are "owned" and managed by the federal government, and each state "owns" its own National Guard. However, the President of the United States or the Secretary of Defense can "activate" state National Guard members into federal military service during times of need.

The U.S. Army is made up of two parts: the active and reserve components. The active component consists of soldiers who are on full-time active duty. The reserve component consists of the Army National Guard and the Army Reserve. The reserve component receives military training and is ready to be called to active duty if necessary.

Army units can be organized several ways, but the following example is fairly typical:

- The squad is the smallest unit, consisting of eight to ten soldiers. The squad leader is a noncommissioned officer (NCO).
- The platoon includes the platoon leader (lieutenant) and two or more squads.
- The company includes the company commander (usually a captain, but sometimes a lieutenant), a headquarters, and two or more platoons.
- The battalion includes the battalion commander (a lieutenant colonel), his staff and headquarters, and several companies.
- The brigade includes the brigade commander (a full colonel), a headquarters, and several battalions.

Air Force

The Air Force is the youngest military service. As mentioned earlier, the Air Force was created under the National Security Act of 1947. Prior to 1947, the Air Force was a separate Corps of the Army. The primary mission of the Army Air Corps was to support Army ground forces. However, World War II showed that air power had much more potential than simply supporting ground troops, so the Air Force was established as a separate service. The primary mission of the Air Force is to defend the United States (and its interests) through exploitation of air and space. To accomplish this mission, the Air Force operates fighter aircraft, tanker aircraft, light and heavy bomber aircraft, transport aircraft, and helicopters (which are used mainly for rescue of downed aircrew and special operations missions). The Air Force is also responsible for all military satellites and controls all of our nation's strategic nuclear ballistic missiles. There are about 69,000 commissioned officers on active duty in the Air Force, and about 288,000 enlisted members. Like the Army, the active duty Air Force is supplemented by the Air Force Reserves, and the Air National Guard.

Navy

Like the Army, the Navy was officially established by the Continental Congress in 1775. The Navy's primary mission is to maintain the freedom of the seas. The Navy makes it possible for the United States to use the seas where and when our national interests require it. In addition, in times of conflict, the Navy helps to supplement Air Force air power. Navy aircraft carriers can often deploy to areas where fixed runways are impossible. An aircraft carrier usually carries about eighty aircraft. Most of these are fighters or fighter/bombers. Additionally, Navy ships can attack land targets from miles away (with very heavy guns and cruise missiles). Navy submarines (fast attack and ballistic missile subs) allow stealth attacks on our enemies from right off their shores. The Navy is also primarily responsible for transporting Marines to areas of conflict. The active duty Navy has about 54,000 officers and 324,000 enlisted personnel. The Navy is supported in times of need by the Naval Reserves. However, unlike the Army and Air Force, there is no Naval National Guard (although a few states have established Naval Militias).

Marine Corps

The Marines are often referred to as the Soldiers of the Sea. Marines specialize in amphibious operations. In other words, their primary specialty is to assault, capture, and control "beachheads," which then provide a route to attack the enemy from almost any direction. The Marines were officially established on November 10, 1775, by the Continental Congress to act as a landing force for the U.S. Navy. In 1798, however, Congress established the Marine Corps as a separate service. While amphibious operations are their primary specialty, in recent years, the Marines have expanded other ground-combat operations as well. The Marines are generally a "lighter" force when compared to the Army, so they can generally be deployed fast (although the Army has been making great strides in "rapid deployment" in the past few years). For combat operations, the Marines like to be self-sufficient as much as possible, so they also have their own air power, consisting primarily of fighter and fighter/bomber aircraft and attack helicopters. Even so, the Marines use the Navy for much of their logistical and administrative support. For example, there are no doctors, nurses, or enlisted medics in the Marine Corps. Even medics that accompany the Marines into combat are specially trained Navy medics. With the exception of the Coast Guard, the Marines are also the smallest service. There are approximately 18,000 officers and 153,000 enlisted personnel on active duty in the Marines. Like the Navy, there is no Marine Corps National Guard, but Marines are supported in times of need by the Marine Corps Reserves.

Coast Guard

The U.S. Coast Guard was originally established as the Revenue Cutter Service in 1790. In 1915, it was reformed as the U.S. Coast Guard under the Treasury Department. In 1967, the Coast Guard was transferred to the Department of Transportation. Legislation passed in 2002 transferred the Coast Guard to the Department of Homeland Security. In peacetime, the Coast Guard is primarily concerned with law enforcement, boating safety, sea rescue, and illegal immigration control. However, the President of the United States can transfer part or all of the Coast Guard to the Department of the Navy in times of conflict. The Coast Guard consists of ships, boats, aircraft, and shore stations that conduct a variety of missions. The Coast Guard is the smallest military service, with about 7,000 officers and 29,000 enlisted on active duty. The Coast Guard is also supported by the Coast Guard Reserves and a volunteer Coast Guard Auxiliary in times of need.

Organization/Chain of Command

Each of the services has its own unique organization. The Army is organized in squads, platoons, companies, battalions, brigades, divisions, and corps. The Air Force is organized in flights, squadrons, groups, wings, numbered air forces, and major commands. The Marine Corps is organized in teams, squads, platoons, companies, regiments, and divisions. The Navy has a somewhat complicated organizational structure.

Rank/Rate

There are three general categories of rank/rate (note that the Navy and Coast Guard call it *rate*, and the other services refer to it as *rank*): enlisted personnel, warrant officers, and commissioned officers.

Enlisted Personnel

Enlisted members are the "backbone" of the military. They perform the primary jobs that need to be done. Enlisted members are specialists. They are trained to perform specific specialties in the military. As enlisted personnel progress up the ranks (there are nine enlisted ranks), they assume more responsibility and provide direct supervision to their subordinates.

Enlisted personnel in certain grades have special status. In the Army, Air Force, and Marine Corps, this status is known as noncommissioned officer status, or NCO. In the Navy and Coast Guard, such enlisted are known as petty officers. In the Marine Corps, NCO status begins at the grade of E-4 (corporal).

In the Army and Air Force, enlisted personnel in the grades of E-5 through E-9 are NCOs. However, some Army E-4s are laterally promoted to corporal and are considered NCOs. Also in the Army and Air Force, personnel in the grades of E-7 to E-9 are known as senior NCOs.

In the Marine Corps, those in the grades of E-6 through E-9 are known as staff NCOs. In the Navy/Coast Guard, petty officers are those in the grades of E-4 through E-9. Those in the grades of E-7 to E-9 are known as chief petty officers.

To join the military today and become an enlisted member requires a high school diploma (although a very few—less than 10 percent each year—are accepted with "alternative credentials," such as a GED). However, a majority of enlisted members on active duty today have some college. Many have associate's and bachelor's degrees. Some even have higher-level degrees, such as masters and doctorates.

Warrant Officers

Warrant officers are very highly trained specialists. This is where they differ from commissioned officers. Unlike commissioned officers, warrant officers remain in their primary specialty to provide specialized knowledge, instruction, and leadership to enlisted members and commissioned officers alike.

With few exceptions, one must be an enlisted member with several years of experience, recommended by their commander, and pass a selection board to become a warrant officer. The Air Force is the only service that does not have warrant officers. The Air Force eliminated their warrant officer positions when Congress created the grades of E-8 and E-9 in the late 1960s. The other services elected to retain the warrant ranks and shifted the emphasis from a promotion process for E-7s to a highly selective system for highly skilled technicians. There are five separate warrant ranks. Warrant officers outrank all enlisted members. Warrant officers are not required to have college degrees (they are selected primarily based upon technical skills and experience), but many of them do.

Commissioned Officers

Commissioned officers are the "top brass." Their primary function is to provide overall management and leadership in their area of responsibility. Unlike enlisted members and warrant officers, commissioned officers do not specialize as much (with certain exceptions such as pilots, doctors, nurses, and lawyers). Let's take for example an infantry officer. An enlisted member in the Infantry Branch has a specific infantry specialty, such as infantryman (MOS 11B) or indirect fire infantryman (11C). Unless that enlisted member retrains, he will remain an 11B or 11C for his career. The officer, however, is designated to the Infantry Branch. He can start his career in charge of a light infantry platoon, then may move on to be in charge of a mortar platoon, then later in his career he may move on to become a company commander, commanding various types of infantry troops. As he moves up the ranks, he gets more and more experience in the different areas of his branch and is responsible for commanding more and more troops. All of this has the primary purpose of (ultimately) generating an experienced officer who can command an entire infantry battalion or division.

Commissioned officers must have a minimum of a four-year bachelor's degree. As they move up the ranks, if they want to get promoted, they will have to earn a master's degree. Commissioned officers are commissioned through specific commissioning programs, such as one of the military academies (West Point, Naval Academy, Air Force Academy, Coast Guard Academy), ROTC (Reserve Officer Training Corps), or OCS (Officer Candidate School), called OTS (Officer Training School) for the Air Force.

There are ten commissioned officer grades, ranging from the "lowly 2nd lieutenant" (or ensign for the Navy/Coast Guard) to the four-star general (or admiral in the Navy/Coast Guard). Commissioned officers outrank all warrant officers and enlisted personnel.

There are also two basic "types" of commissioned officers: line and non-line. A non-line officer is a non-combat specialist, which includes medical officers (doctors and nurses), lawyers, and chaplains. Non-line officers cannot command combat troops. For example, let's assume there was an infantry unit in combat, commanded by an infantry lieutenant. A captain who is a military chaplain is attached to the unit. The captain cannot issue any commands relating to the combat operation to the lieutenant or anyone else in the unit. If the lieutenant dies, command shifts to the highest-ranking warrant officer or enlisted member, not to the chaplain captain. The following is not an exact analogy, as it's not possible to accurately compare the military to a civilian company or corporation. However, it may help the layman to visualize the differences between enlisted, warrant officers, and commissioned officers.

Think of the enlisted member as the worker in a civilian company. The enlisted are the ones who hands-on perform the job. Within the "worker group," NCOs (Army, Air Force, and Marines) and petty officers (Navy and Coast Guard) are the foremen and line supervisors. They perform the job but also provide direct supervision to the other workers. Senior NCOs (Army, Air Force, and Marines) and chief petty officers (Navy and Coast Guard) are assistant managers who came up through the ranks of the corporation. They are valuable as managers because of their many years of experience but will never make it to the board of directors. Commissioned officers are the managers of the company. They have broad areas of responsibility for the management, organization, and efficiency of various departments of the corporation. Senior commissioned officers (generals and admirals) are the board of directors. Warrant officers can be thought of as the experienced technical specialists that the company hired to perform highly specialized functions.[1]

Getting Married

If You're Marrying Someone in the Military

As mentioned previously, marrying into the military can be a daunting task, but tens of thousands do it successfully every year and have happy marriages. Those who rush in without considering all the consequences are the ones who often face challenges down the road.

If you are marrying someone who is serving in the military, especially at a time when we are fighting a vicious enemy overseas on several fronts, several issues that a civilian couple doesn't even think about have to be addressed.

The most important question to ask is "Can I handle the demands of married life in the military?"

When you marry you will probably have to move away from home— away from your family and friends—to live on or close to the base where your partner is stationed. That is part of the commitment you make to the person you love. However, you will still be able to visit family and friends, and they can visit you—and within a short time you will have made lots of new friends as well.

The chances are that your partner will be deployed, and this can mean long and lonely separations. Deployment also brings with it the risk of injury or worse. You will worry all the time your partner is away, but you will still be able to communicate with each other, and there are strong support groups available if things get overwhelming. Many couples say that deployment made their marriages stronger because it helped focus what was really important and precious in their lives. As one army wife said, "Love isn't enough to make a marriage succeed. It also takes commitment and sacrifice. Your marriage will only be as successful as you want it to be."

Apart from the military considerations, there may be ethnic and cultural issues as well that have to be thought about. You and your partner may have different religions with different holidays and traditions. If you have children, in what religion will they be brought up? What holidays will you celebrate? You and your partner may have been born in different countries and have different primary languages. In some societies, younger relatives are expected to care for elderly members of the family when they become sick or can't look after themselves. What would you do if your partner asked that an elderly aunt move in with you?

These sorts of issues should not be an impediment to getting married, but they have to be discussed openly. Traditions that might seem unimportant to you might be extremely important to your partner. Talk about cultural traditions. Respect each other's position and point of view. Remember that talking problems over usually helps them go away.

There are lots of other things you can do to cement your relationship. You can each learn about your partner's history and cultural background through reading books or joining societies. If you were brought up speaking different languages, make a commitment to each other to become fluent in both. It will be a bond between you, and it will be invaluable when you each meet your partner's friends and family.

It is also important to talk about your plans to get married with your parents. If you are marrying someone in the military, your parents will probably be very concerned. No matter how supportive they are, they will be worry about what might happen if your partner is deployed and what might happen to you.

Talk it over with your parents, introduce your partner to them, and demonstrate through your love that this is the right thing to do. Family involvement can be an important part of a military spouse's support system, especially when a military member is often deployed.

If you're in the military and stationed in the United States, getting married as a member of the military is much the same as civilian marriages. You don't need advance permission, and there is no special military paperwork to fill out before the marriage. You simply get married according the laws of the state where the marriage is taking place after obtaining a marriage license.

If you are overseas and marrying a foreign national, it's a different story. There are tons of forms to complete; you must obtain counseling and your commander's permission (which is rarely withheld without very good reason); your spouse must undergo a security background check and pass a medical examination. Finally, the marriage has to be "recognized" by the United States Embassy. The entire process can take several months.

Regardless of where or who, once married, if the spouse is nonmilitary, the military member can bring a copy of the certified marriage certificate to the personnel headquarters on the base to receive a dependent ID card for the spouse and enroll the spouse in DEERS (Defense Eligibility Enrollment Reporting System) to qualify for military benefits such as medical coverage and commissary and base exchange privileges.

Timing can be important in a military marriage. If you have PCS (Permanent Change of Station) orders and get married before you actually make the move, you can have your spouse added to your orders and the military will pay for the relocation of your spouse and his or her property (furniture and such). However, if you report to your new duty assignment first and then get married, you will have to pay for the relocation of your spouse out of your own pocket.

Actually "making the move" means reporting in to your new base. So you can leave your old base, take leave (vacation), get married, report in to your new base, get your orders amended to include your new spouse, and the military might pay for the spouse's move. However, if you report to your new base and then take leave to get married, you're on your own when it comes to moving expenses for the spouse.

If you want to get married on base, the point of contact is the chaplain's office. Each military base has one (or more) chapels that are used for religious services. One can get married in a base chapel, just as one can get married in a church off base. Base chaplains offer a complete variety of marriage choices, including religious (almost any denomination), nonreligious, casual, civilian formal, and military formal.

If the wedding is conducted by a military chaplain, there is never a fee. By regulation, chaplains cannot directly accept donations. One can make a donation to the chaplain's fund, however, during a normal worship service.

MILITARY FORMAL WEDDINGS The military formal wedding would entail the following: An officer or enlisted personnel in the bridal party wear uniforms in accordance with the formality of the wedding and seasonal uniform regulations. For commissioned officers, evening dress uniform is the same as civilian white tie and tails. The dinner or mess dress uniform is equivalent to civilian "black tie" requirements. Dressing in uniform is optional for military guests who attend the wedding.

In the case of noncommissioned officers and other enlisted, dress blues or Army green uniforms may be worn at formal or informal weddings. A female military member (officer or enlisted) may wear a traditional bridal gown, or she may be married in uniform. A boutonniere is never worn with a uniform.

The arch of sabers is usually part of a military formal wedding. The arch of swords takes place immediately following the ceremony, preferably when the couple leaves the chapel or church, on the steps or walk. Since a church is a sanctuary, in case of bad weather, and with permission, the arch may be formed inside the chapel or church. Also, with permission, you may be allowed to have two arches of sabers, one in the church and one outside. White gloves are a necessity for all saber (sword) bearers.

If you are marrying someone in the military rather than a civilian, there's one primary difference, and that's in the area of housing benefits allowed after the marriage, rather than actual marriage procedures.

There are two basic types of housing allowance (monetary allowance paid to military members who live off base): single allowance and "with-dependent" allowance. Usually, single (nonmarried) military members who are allowed to live off base receive the single allowance. Those who have dependents (civilian spouse and/or children) receive a larger allowance called the with-dependent allowance.

If two military members marry (assuming there are no children), each receives the single allowance. The total of both of these single allowances is always more than the with-dependent allowance. For example, a military member in the rank of E-4, stationed at Fort McClellan, Alabama, who married a civilian would receive $525 per month for a housing allowance. If a military member married another military member, they would *each* receive the single rate, which would be $424 per month.

If a military member marries another military member and they have children, one member will receive the with-dependent rate, and the other member will receive the single rate. Usually the member with the most rank receives the with-dependent rate, because it means more money each month.

BEING POSTED TOGETHER Each of the services has a program called Join Spouse in which the services try as hard as they can to station spouses together, or at least within 100 miles of each other. However, there is absolutely no guarantee. In order for spouses to be stationed together, there have to be slots (job positions) available to assign them to.

For example, let's say that an Air Force B-1 aircraft mechanic married a Navy F-14 aircraft mechanic. Because the B-1 bomber is stationed only at certain Air Force bases, and because the F-14 Tomcat Fighter Aircraft is stationed only at certain Navy bases, this couple is probably never going to be stationed together. The best the services could do would be to try to find a B-1 base as close as possible to an F-14 base (and in this case, that would be at least 1,000 miles away).

If a military person marries a person in the same service, the chances of getting stationed together are better. Each of the services boasts about a 85 percent success rate with in-service Join Spouse (That sounds pretty good until you realize that 15 out of every 100 military couples in each service are not stationed together).

When one marries someone in a different service, it becomes more complicated, and the success rate of Join Spouse goes down dramatically to somewhere around 50 percent.

THE HONEYMOON Most military members get two weeks' or more notice before actually leaving on a deployment. So it's possible that a commander would grant a couple of days leave during those two weeks, but not much leave, as there is much to do before a unit can deploy.

Otherwise there are two primary ways to get time off in the military. The first is called a pass, which is basically normal time off (like holidays and weekends), and special time off that might be granted by a commander or supervisor (up to seventy-two hours). The second way is leave (vacation) time. Every military member gets thirty days of leave per year, earned at the rate of 2.5 days per month.

A commander and/or supervisor could grant a pass (up to three days) for a member to get married and/or honeymoon, or the military member could take up to thirty days' leave (assuming he or she had that much leave "saved up" and the unit can afford to lose him or her for that long of a period).

Make the most of your time. Spend as little of it traveling as possible; save the far-off journeys for when you can spare the days. Also, if you can afford to, splurge on one night in a great hotel rather than two in a mediocre one. And let the world (or at least the reservations clerk) know that you're on your honeymoon. It's true that "all the world loves a lover," and you never know what goodies or upgrades may come to you gratis.

Whether on a honeymoon or not, military members can travel "space available" for free on military aircraft to locations around the world. If available leave time is a factor, Space-A travel might not be viable. To travel Space-A, a military member must already be on leave. Sometimes it can take several days for a flight with space available to be going in your direction. Also, one wants to make sure he or she has adequate funds to buy a return ticket, in case the passenger can't find a Space-A flight going back to the originating base.

Check out the Armed Forces Vacation Club. This program allows military members to rent luxury condos around the world for $249 per week. In addition, many hotels and resorts offer military discounts; it always pays to ask. If money is an issue, military couples could stay in billeting on any military base, for about $16 to $70 per night—if you don't mind spending your honeymoon on a military base.

Consider the tradition of giving a wedding night gift to your new spouse. It doesn't have to be large or expensive (you can even make it yourself), just some object that can serve as a sentimental reminder of your first night together as a married couple. Then, if orders come through and you're separated for a time, you'll have something wonderful to hold on to until you're reunited.

If you are planning on joining the military and planning on getting married, there are certain advantages (as well as some disadvantages) to tying that knot before you leave for basic training.

However, it should be emphasized that one should not make a marriage decision based primarily on these factors. The divorce rate in the United States is about 50 percent, and that statistic follows over to the military. In fact, the military divorce rate may be even a little higher because of the difficulty of a military life (frequent moves, unaccompanied assignments, long working hours, combat deployments, etc.).

But if you've already made your decision to get married and are now just deciding whether it would be better to get married before or after joining the military, the following information may be of use to you.

HOUSING ALLOWANCE A married service member receives a housing allowance while in basic training and follow-on job training (technical school, AIT, A-School) in order to provide a household for his or her dependents, even though they are also living for free in government quarters (barracks). If you get married before joining the military, this tax-free housing allowance begins on the very first day of active duty (the first day of basic training).

If one waits until after joining the military to get married, the housing allowance becomes effective on the date of the marriage. However, one needs a "certified" copy of the marriage certificate to change their marital status, and (depending on the state) this can take a couple of weeks, or even a month to obtain. Even so, the housing allowance would be backdated to the date of the marriage.

MEDICAL CARE Dependents of active duty members are covered by the Military Medical System (TRICARE), effective the very first day of active duty. During basic training in-processing, the recruit completes paperwork to enroll their dependents in DEERS (Defense Eligibility Enrollment System), and for a military dependent ID card. The ID card paperwork is mailed to the spouse, who can then take it to any military installation and obtain a military dependent ID card. If medical care is needed before getting the ID card, the spouse can keep the medical receipts and then file for reimbursement later under the TRICARE Standard or TRICARE Extra program (depending on whether or not the medical provider is part of the TRICARE network).

FAMILY SEPARATION ALLOWANCE Married members are entitled to a Family Separation Allowance when they are separated from their dependents due to military orders. The tax-free allowance begins after separation of thirty days. This means married people in basic training and technical school (if the technical school duration is less than twenty weeks) begin to receive this pay thirty days after going on active duty. Single personnel do not receive this allowance.

MOVEMENT OF DEPENDENTS Unless the first duty assignment is an unaccompanied (remote) overseas tour, the married military member is entitled to move their dependents (and personal property) to the first duty station at government expense. Travel entitlements end when one signs in at their new duty station, so whether or not one can be reimbursed for dependent travel depends on the date of the marriage.

For example, Airman Jones graduates technical school (Air Force Job Training), then goes home on leave en route to his first duty assignment. While on leave, Airman Jones gets married. He then reports to his first duty station. He will be entitled to movement of dependents at government expense, because the date of the marriage was before he signed in at the duty station.

Another example: PFC Jackson finishes AIT (Army Job Training) and goes to his first duty assignment. A couple of weeks later, his fiancée flies down, and they get married. PFC Jackson cannot move his wife and her property to the duty assignment at government expense, because the marriage occurred after he completed his assignment move.

There is an exception to the above rule for certain overseas assignments. When a single person is assigned to a "long" overseas tour, the assignment length is generally twenty-four months (the unaccompanied tour length). For an accompanied married person, the tour length is usually thirty-six months. If a single person goes overseas on such a tour, then gets married during the tour, he or she can apply to move his dependents overseas if they agree to extend his tour length to the accompanied tour length.

In order to move dependents at government expense, one's "orders" must include authorization to do so. This means that if one gets married at the last minute before leaving job training, or if one gets married on leave en route to the first assignment, the orders won't have this authorization on them and will have to be amended after arrival. As the military rarely does paperwork very quickly, this amendment process can sometimes take several weeks. This will delay the reimbursement of dependent moving expenses. If the member had gotten married before joining the military, his or her orders would have had dependent moving entitlements annotated originally and would thereby avoid this delay in reimbursement.

JOB TRAINING If technical school, AIT, or A-School is twenty weeks or longer in duration (at a single location), one is entitled to move dependents to the school location at government expense. They are then (usually thirty days after arrival) allowed to live with their dependents after duty hours. Single members, of course, cannot move their girl/boyfriends at government expense, nor will they be allowed to live off base (even at their own expense) at job training locations.

In such cases, if the military member elects not to move his or her dependents, the Family Separation Allowance stops, because the member is not being forced to be separated (the dependents are allowed to move at government expense, so if they don't move, that's the member's choice). Of course, if the dependents do join the member, Family Separation Allowance stops as well, as the member is no longer separated from his or her dependents due to military orders.

If the job training is less than twenty weeks, a married person can still elect to move his or her dependents (at his or her own expense), but would (usually) be allowed to live with them, off base (beginning thirty days after arrival), with the school commander's permission (as long as the student is doing okay in class, such permission is routinely granted). If the dependents do move to the member's school location, Family Separation Allowance stops.

QUALIFICATIONS The services require additional paperwork, additional processing, and sometimes even waivers for members with dependents. For example, the Air Force requires a credit check for any member who is married or has ever been married. If you're in the Delayed Enlistment Program (DEP) and decide to get married before shipping out to basic training, you'll want to check with your recruiter to determine (depending on what additional processing is required, and when you're shipping out) if this would possibly delay your shipping date.

DEPENDENT SUPPORT All of the services have regulations that require military members to provide adequate support to their dependents. In fact, while in basic training and job school, you're being provided a housing allowance for the sole purpose of providing a place to live for your dependent family members. If your spouse makes an official complaint to your commander that you are failing or refusing to provide financial support, you could be in a heap of trouble.

While one doesn't want to think about divorce when they're anxious to get married, divorce is a real possibility (remember the 50 percent statistic). Military members should be aware that there is a special law that applies to them when it comes to divorce and retirement pay. The Uniformed Services Former Spouse Protection Act allows any state court to treat your *future* military retired pay as joint property, to be divided with your spouse, in the event of a divorce.[2]

The Newlyweds

The honeymoon may be over, but now is the time to get down to the serious business of organizing your new lives together. There are all sorts of procedures to be followed, benefits to sign up for, and special deals to take advantage of. There is health care, shopping at the Exchange stores and commissaries, as well as a wide range of facilities and activities to get involved with—from bowling and movie theaters to fitness centers and social clubs.

If you haven't done it already, you must notify your command that you are married and have a spouse. If you are the serving member, you become your spouse's sponsor and, as such, have to fill in a lot of paperwork on their behalf.

One of your next stops should be to the Family Support Center (FMS). It will have all the latest information and knowledgeable people ready to help you acclimatize. Many bases run orientations for newcomers, especially for spouses. The FMS will also be able to tell where to go to sign up for benefits, classes, orientations, and so on.

However, before you can start doing the paperwork you will have to assemble a number of important documents. You will need:

- An original copy of your marriage certificate, and make several copies of it

Each branch of the military has its own name for Family Support Centers and their own programs for new spouses. These are:

Army Community Service Center—Family Team Building
Airman and Family Readiness Center—Heartlink
Marine Corps Community Services Center—LINKS (Lifestyle, Insights, Networking, Knowledge, and Skills)
Navy Fleet and Family Support Center—COMPASS

Focus on Family Readiness Groups (FRG)

An FRG is a command-sponsored organization of family members, volunteers, soldiers, and civilian employees associated with a particular unit. They are normally organized at company and battalion levels and fall under the responsibility of the unit's commanding officer.

FRGs are established to provide activities and support to enhance the flow of information, increase the resiliency of unit soldiers and their families, provide practical tools for adjusting to military deployments and separations, and enhance the well-being and esprit de corps within the unit. The activities emphasized will vary depending on whether the unit is in pre/postdeployment, deployed, or in a training/sustainment period at home station. Since one of the goals of an FRG is to support the military mission through provision of support, outreach, and information to family members, certain FRG activities are essential and common to all groups and include member meetings, staff and committee meetings, publication and distribution of newsletters, maintenance of virtual FRG websites, maintenance of updated rosters and readiness information, and member telephone trees and e-mail distribution lists.

FRG Mission
1. Foster competent, knowledgeable, and resilient families
2. Act as an extension of the unit in providing official, accurate command information
3. Provide mutual support
4. Build soldier and family cohesion and foster a positive outlook
5. Advocate more efficient use of community resources
6. Help families solve problems at the lowest level
7. Reduce stress and promote soldier and family readiness
8. Contribute to the well-being and esprit de corps of the unit

FRG Goals
1. Gaining necessary family support during deployments
2. Preparing for deployments and redeployments
3. Helping families adjust to military life and cope with deployments
4. Developing open and honest channels of communication between the command and family members
5. Promoting confidence, cohesion, commitment, and a sense of well-being among the unit's soldiers

FRG Activities

Some activities that FRGs commonly sponsor, coordinate, or participate in that directly or indirectly foster unit family readiness goals include (but are not limited to):

- Classes and workshops
- Volunteer recognition
- Unit send-off and welcome-home activities
- FRG member, staff, or committee meetings
- Newcomer orientation and sponsorship

- Defense Enrollment Eligibility Reporting System (DEERS) enrollment form (see below); it is up to you to enroll—it is not automatically done for you
- Birth certificates for spouse and all children
- Social security cards for spouse and all children
- Photo ID

ID Cards

All spouses and children aged ten and over must have a military ID card. You apply for your ID card using Department of Defense Form 1172; an accompanying booklet explains how to fill it in. You will also have to produce a birth certificate, marriage license, and photo ID.

You will need your ID card to get on base, to use commissaries, and the like. You will also have to show it when getting medical treatment (see below).

Vehicle Registration

Remember to register your vehicle and get a sticker that will allow you to enter the base or installation. You normally register through the military police, and it is worth a call to them beforehand to see what documents you need to bring—usually your driver's license, proof of insurance, and registration document. Some military bases are migrating to alternate security policies for vehicles, so please be prepared to follow any procedural changes that may be base-specific and/or security-threat-level specific.

Legal Considerations

While it may be the last thing you want to think about, you should establish a durable power of attorney for your spouse, especially if they are likely to be deployed. This will allow you to make decisions on their behalf if they are unable to, and it is important that you talk through various scenarios so that you are absolutely sure you will be doing what they want. Some examples of uses for a power of attorney include changing utility accounts if you must move while your spouse is overseas, handling banking or insurance-related matters, and/or arranging passports for dependent children. Again, most bases have a Legal Assistance Office that can help you with this.

Health Benefits and Insurance

Legal Assistance

You and your dependents are eligible to receive military legal assistance. You can get most of the legal services you could get from a civilian attorney, except appearance in a civilian court. Among the available services are:

- Advice and assistance with personal problems of a civil nature, such as marriage, divorce, adoption, civil damage actions, insurance, indebtedness, and contracts
- Advice on tax matters and forms
- Preparation of wills and powers of attorney
- Notary public services
- Advice concerning sale or lease of real property
- Assistance in obtaining applications for certificates of citizenship and naturalization

Medical

All military spouses are entitled to medical benefits through the Defense Enrollment Eligibility Reporting System—DEERS. You enroll at the

Morale, Welfare, and Recreation (MWR)

Most bases offer MWR (sometimes referred to as Morale, Well-Being, and Recreation), and it is a way of staying active and healthy, meeting new friends, and having a fun time with your family and friends. MWR offers activities, programs, gear, and rentals at deep discounts to help families and couples have access to quality-of-life enrichment. Activities range from swimming lessons and keeping fit to auto repairs and fun camping weekends. The chances are that if you have an interest or hobby, there is an MWR program for you, and if there is not, you should approach them to start one.

uniformed services personnel office, and you can find the one nearest to you at www.militaryinstallations.dod.mil.

DEERS ENROLLMENT Proper registration in DEERS is key to receiving timely and effective medical benefits. DEERS is a worldwide, computerized database of uniformed services members (sponsors), their family members, and others who are eligible for military benefits, including TRICARE (for more information see below).

All sponsors (active duty, retired, National Guard, or Reserve) are automatically registered in DEERS. However, the sponsor must register eligible family members. After family members are registered, they can update personal information such as addresses and phone numbers.

To use TRICARE benefits, you must have a valid uniformed services or military ID card, which you can obtain from your nearest ID card office, and you must be listed in the DEERS database. The ID card states on the back, in the "medical" block, whether you are eligible for medical care from military or civilian sources.

When getting care, your provider will ask to see a copy of your ID card and will make copies for his or her records. Please ensure you have your ID card with you whenever you are getting care or having prescriptions filled.

CHILDREN Children under age ten can generally use a parent's or guardian's ID card, but they must be registered in DEERS. When the child is age ten, the sponsor must obtain an ID card for him or her. Children under age ten should have an ID card of their own when in the custody of a parent or guardian who is not eligible for TRICARE benefits or who is not the custodial parent after a divorce. If both parents are active duty service members, then either may be listed as the child's sponsor in DEERS.

Stepchildren and adopted children can also be enrolled provided they live with the service member and spouse and are not already the dependent of another service member. You will need birth certificates and final adoption decree in the case of an adopted child. If the child is from a former marriage, you will also need a copy of the divorce decree, or a death certificate if your former spouse is deceased, and any custody documents.

Health Benefits

You may want to make a change to a family health benefits enrollment. You may enroll or change enrollment from Self Only to Self and Family, from one plan or option to another, or make any combination of these changes during the period beginning thirty-one days before and ending sixty days after a change in your family status. Otherwise, you will have to wait until the next health benefits open season to make the change.

If you want to provide immediate coverage for your new spouse, you may submit an enrollment request during the pay period before the anticipated date of your marriage. If the effective date of the change is before your marriage, *your new spouse does not become eligible for coverage until the actual day of your marriage.*

If you enroll or change your enrollment before the date of your marriage and intend to change your name, you must note on your request: "Now: [Current Name] will be: [Married Name]." You must also give the reason for the change *and* the date of the marriage in your request.

SELF AND FAMILY A Self and Family enrollment provides benefits for you and your eligible family members. All of your eligible family members are automatically covered, even if you didn't list them on your Health Benefits Election Form (SF 2809) or other appropriate request. You cannot exclude any eligible family member and you cannot provide coverage for anyone who is not an eligible family member.

You may enroll for Self and Family coverage before you have any eligible family members. Then a new eligible family member (such as a newborn child or a new spouse) will be automatically covered by your family enrollment from the date he or she becomes a family member. When a new family member is added to your existing Self and Family enrollment, you do not have to complete a new SF 2809 or other appropriate request, but your carrier may ask you for information about your new family member. You will send the requested information directly to the carrier. Exception: If you want to add a foster child to your coverage, you must provide eligibility information to your employing office.

If both you and your spouse are eligible to enroll, one of you may enroll for Self and Family to cover your entire family. If you have no eligible children to cover, each of you may enroll for Self Only in the same or different plans. Generally, you will pay lower premiums for two Self Only enrollments.

Insurance

SERVICEMEMBER'S GROUP LIFE INSURANCE (SGLI) SGLI is a program of low-cost group life insurance for service members on active duty, ready reservists, members of the National Guard, members of the

TRICARE Programs

TRICARE Prime is a managed-care option, similar to a civilian HMO (health maintenance organization).

Prime is for active duty service members and is available to other TRICARE beneficiaries. Active duty service members (ADSMs) are required to be enrolled in Prime; they must take action to enroll, by filling out the appropriate enrollment form and submitting it to their regional contractor. There is no cost to the service member.

Other TRICARE beneficiaries may be eligible for Prime. Eligibility for any kind of TRICARE coverage is determined by the uniformed services. TRICARE manages the military health care program, but the services decide who is or is not eligible to receive TRICARE coverage.

Prime enrollees receive most of their health care at a military treatment facility (MTF) and their care is coordinated by a primary care manager (PCM). Prime is not available everywhere.

Prime enrollees must follow some well-defined rules and procedures, such as seeking care first from the MTF. For specialty care, the Prime enrollee must receive a referral from his/her PCM and authorization from the regional contractor. Failure to do so could result in costly point of service (POS) option charges. Emergency care is not subject to POS charges.

TRICARE Prime Remote is the program for service members and their families who are on remote assignment, typically fifty miles from a MTF.

The TRICARE Overseas Program delivers the Prime benefit to ADSMs and their families in the three overseas areas: Europe, the Pacific, and Latin America/Canada. The TRICARE Global Remote program delivers the Prime benefit to ADSMs and families stationed in designated "remote" locations overseas.

TRICARE Standard is the basic TRICARE health care program, offering comprehensive health care coverage for beneficiaries (not to include active duty members) not enrolled in TRICARE Prime. Standard does not require enrollment.

Standard is a fee-for-service plan that gives beneficiaries the option to see any TRICARE-certified/authorized provider (doctor, nurse-practitioner, lab, clinic, etc.). Standard offers the greatest flexibility in choosing a provider, but it will also involve greater out-of-pocket expenses for you, the patient. You also may be required to file your own claims.

Standard requires that you satisfy a yearly deductible before TRICARE cost sharing begins, and you will be required to pay copayments or cost shares for outpatient care, medications, and inpatient care.

TRICARE Extra can be used by any TRICARE-eligible beneficiary who is not active duty, not otherwise enrolled in Prime, and not eligible for TRICARE For Life (TFL).

TRICARE Extra goes into effect whenever a Standard beneficiary chooses to make an appointment with a TRICARE network provider. Extra, like Standard, requires no enrollment and involves no enrollment fee.

TRICARE Extra is essentially an option for TRICARE Standard beneficiaries who want to save on out-of-pocket expenses by making an appointment with a TRICARE Prime network provider (doctor, nurse-practitioner, lab, etc.). The appointment with the in-network provider will cost 5 percent less than it would with a doctor who is a TRICARE-authorized or TRICARE-participating provider.

Also, the TRICARE Extra user can expect that the network provider will file all claims forms for him. The Standard beneficiary might have claims filed for him, but the nonnetwork provider can decide to file on his behalf or not, on a case-by-case basis.

Under TRICARE Extra, because there is no enrollment, there is no Extra identification card. Your valid uniformed services ID card serves as proof of your eligibility to receive health care coverage from any TRICARE Prime provider.

TRICARE For Life (TFL) is a Medicare wraparound coverage available to Medicare-entitled uniformed service retirees, including retired guard members and reservists, Medicare-entitled family members and widows/widowers (dependent parents and parents-in-law are excluded), Medicare-entitled Congressional Medal of Honor recipients and their family members, and certain Medicare-entitled unremarried former spouses.

To take advantage of TFL, you and your eligible family members' personal information and Medicare Part B status must be up to date in the DEERS. You may update your information by phone (1-800-538-9552) or by visiting your nearest ID card–issuing facility. Visit www.dmdc.osd.mil/rsl to locate the nearest ID card facility.

Commissioned Corps of the National Oceanic and Atmospheric Administration and the Public Health Service, cadets and midshipmen of the four service academies, and members of the Reserve Officer Training Corps.

SGLI coverage is available in $50,000 increments up to the maximum of $400,000. SGLI premiums are currently $.065 per $1,000 of insurance, regardless of the member's age. SGLI is highly recommended to be carried at all times, and recommended to be carried at maximum benefit during wartime and/or during deployments.

FAMILY SERVICEMEMBERS' GROUP LIFE INSURANCE (FSGLI) FSGLI is a program extended to the spouses and dependent children of members insured under the SGLI program. FSGLI provides up to a maximum of $100,000 of insurance coverage for spouses, not to exceed the amount of SGLI the insured member has in force, and $10,000 for dependent children. Spousal coverage is issued in increments of $10,000, at a monthly cost ranging from $.55 to $5.20 per increment.

Service members should contact their Personnel Support Center, Personnel Flight, Payroll, and/or Finance Office for SGLI and Family SGLI premium payment information.

TRAUMATIC INJURY PROTECTION UNDER SERVICEMEMBERS' GROUP LIFE INSURANCE (TSGLI) The TSGLI program is a rider to Servicemembers' Group Life Insurance (SGLI). The TSGLI rider provides for payment to service members who are severely injured (on or off duty) as the result of a traumatic event and suffer a loss that qualifies for payment under TSGLI.

TSGLI payments are designed to help traumatically injured service members and their families with financial burdens associated with recovering from a severe injury. TSGLI payments range from $25,000 to $100,000 based on the qualifying loss suffered. Every member who has SGLI also has TSGLI effective December 1, 2005. TSGLI coverage is automatic for those insured under basic SGLI and cannot be declined. The only way to decline TSGLI is to decline basic SGLI coverage. It is not recommended to decline basic SGLI coverage under any circumstances during a time of war.

The premium for TSGLI is a flat rate of $1 per month for most service members. Members who carry the maximum SGLI coverage of $400,000 will pay $29.00 per month for both SGLI and TSGLI.

To be eligible for payment of TSGLI, you must meet all of the following requirements:

- You must be insured by SGLI when you experience a traumatic event.
- You must incur a scheduled loss, and that loss must be a direct result of a traumatic injury.
- You must have suffered the traumatic injury prior to midnight of the day that you separate from the uniformed services.
- You must suffer a scheduled loss within 2 years (730 days) of the traumatic injury.
- You must survive for a period of not less than seven full days from the date of the traumatic injury. (The seven-day period begins on the date and time of the traumatic injury, as measured by Zulu

[Greenwich Meridian] time and ends 168 full hours later.)

Exceptional Family Member Program (EFMP)

The EFMP is a mandatory enrollment program, based on carefully defined rules. EFMP works with other military and civilian agencies to provide comprehensive and coordinated medical, educational, housing, community support, and personnel services to families with special needs. EFMP enrollment works to ensure that needed services are available at the receiving command before the assignment is made.

An Exceptional Family Member is a dependent, regardless of age, that requires medical services for a chronic condition; receives ongoing services from a specialist; has behavioral health concerns/social problems/psychological needs; receives education services provided on an Individual Education Program (IEP); or a family member receiving services provided on an Individual Family Services Plan (IFSP). The military member is responsible for contacting the EFMP service office on base and enrolling family members who meet the above description, and for maintaining any and all updates to the EFMP paperwork. The EFMP program also has a coordinator who may be knowledgeable about local, military, or related community services that may benefit the EFMP family member(s).

Life Insurance

If you already have a family plan, your personnel office can assist you in getting your spouse (and if appropriate, stepchildren) added to your enrollment. Changes must be made within sixty calendar days of your marriage.

You must provide supporting documentation (e.g., a marriage certificate) for any "non-open season" change. Documentation should be submitted to your HR/personnel office.

Update Designations of Beneficiary

You may want to change your designations of beneficiary for life insurance or for retirement. New designations must be in writing and witnessed. Your agency can provide you with the appropriate forms, or you may print them using the links below. There can be no erasures or cross-outs on these forms. If the forms are incomplete or have errant marks, they will not be processed and will be returned to you.

When your beneficiary forms are filled in, be sure you have signed them. After obtaining witness signatures, submit your completed forms to the address or agency noted on the form.

Note: If you choose to complete beneficiary forms, it is your responsibility to keep them up to date. A marriage, divorce, or other change in family status does not automatically change a beneficiary form previously submitted, nor does it prevent the named beneficiary from receiving the death benefits.

Taxing Matters

Newlyweds should seek advice about whether to change their tax status with the IRS. Depending on the date that you got married, there may be advantages in still being taxed separately. Most bases have an income tax assistance program that you can turn to for advice.

Talk over finances with your spouse. If he or she is deployed, it is important to be able to manage finances in their absence. You can get a lot of information about pay and compensation from www.dod.mil/militarypay.

It is also important to familiarize yourself with your spouse's Leave and Earnings Statement (LES), which gives details about pay, allowances, and vacation time accrued.

Federal taxes must be paid on all income, including wages, interest earned on bank accounts, and so on. However, some tax benefits may arise as a result of a service member serving in a combat zone, while other benefits—such as exclusions, deductions, and credits—may arise as a result of certain expenses incurred by the service member. The Combat Zone Exclusion, for instance, is tax-free and does not have to be reported on tax returns.

The deadline for filing tax returns and paying any tax due is automatically extended for those serving in the Armed Forces in a combat zone, in a qualified hazardous duty area, or on deployment outside of the United States while participating in a contingency operation.

Combat zones are designated by an executive order from the president as areas in which the U.S. Armed Forces are engaging or have engaged in combat. There are currently three such combat zones (including the airspace above each):

Arabian Peninsula Areas, beginning January 17, 1991—the Persian
   Gulf, Red Sea, Gulf of Oman, the part of the Arabian Sea north of
   10° North latitude and west of 68° East longitude, the Gulf of
   Aden, and the countries of Bahrain, Iraq, Kuwait, Oman, Qatar,
   Saudi Arabia, and the United Arab Emirates.
Kosovo area, beginning March 24, 1999—Federal Republic of
   Yugoslavia (Serbia and Montenegro), Albania, the Adriatic Sea, and

the Ionian Sea north of the 39th Parallel.
Afghanistan, beginning September 19, 2001.

In general, the deadlines for performing certain actions applicable to taxes are extended for the period of the service member's service in the combat zone, plus 180 days after the last day in the combat zone. This extension applies to the filing and paying of income taxes that would have been due April 15.

Members of the U.S. Armed Forces who perform military service in an area outside a combat zone qualify for the suspension of time provisions if their service is in direct support of military operations in the combat zone, and they receive special pay for duty subject to hostile fire or imminent danger as certified by the Department of Defense.

The deadline extension provisions apply not only to members serving in the U.S. Armed Forces (or individuals serving in support thereof) in the combat zone, but to their spouses as well, with two exceptions. First, if you are hospitalized in the United States as a result of injuries received while serving in a combat zone, the deadline extension provisions would not apply to your spouse. Second, the deadline extension provisions for a spouse do not apply for any tax year beginning more than two years after the date of the termination of the combat zone designation.

Filing individual income tax returns for your dependent children is not required while your spouse is in the combat zone. Instead, these returns will be timely if filed on or before the deadline for filing your joint income tax return under the applicable deadline extensions. When filing your children's individual income tax returns, put "COMBAT ZONE" in red at the top of those returns.

Note: Most bases offer Volunteer Income Tax Assistance (VITA), where service members and eligible civilians can get help with their tax returns and have them filed electronically.

Tax Exclusions

THE COMBAT ZONE EXCLUSION If you serve in a combat zone as an enlisted person or as a warrant officer (including commissioned warrant officers) for any part of a month, all your military pay received for military service that month is excluded from gross income. For commissioned officers, the monthly exclusion is capped at the highest enlisted pay, plus any hostile fire or imminent danger pay received.

Military pay received by enlisted personnel who are hospitalized as a result of injuries sustained while serving in a combat zone is excluded from

Military Spouses Relief Act

The Military Spouses Residency Relief Act (MSRRA) (Public Law 111-97) was signed into law on November 11, 2009, and is effective for taxable years 2009 and after. The new law affords spouses of active duty military service members similar income tax benefits that the service members themselves enjoy. Previously, when a military spouse moved with his or her active duty spouse to a new state, the spouse would have become a resident of that new state and income earned there would be taxable by the state. However, this new law allows, but does not require, the spouse of the military member to keep his or her previous residency in certain situations. By so doing, the spouse pays taxes in the state where he or she formerly lived and maintains residency, and not where he or she is actually living with the service member.

To avoid being taxed in the state where he or she is currently living, the spouse of the military member must, at a minimum, meet the following four factors:

1. The spouse of the military member must claim a state of residency that is different from the state where he or she resides with the service member.
2. The spouse must presently live in the state solely in order to live with the service member.
3. The service member must be present in the state in compliance with military orders.
4. The spouse and service member must both have the same state of residency.

If the spouse meets these requirements, he or she is entitled to a refund of any taxes already paid to such state through withholding and estimated payments in 2009. The spouse will then pay tax to the state of legal residency for 2009, assuming that state has an income tax.

Some important notes to keep in mind:

- Like service members themselves, spouses cannot choose their state of legal residency.
- The spouse does not "inherit" the residency of the service member upon marriage.
- State laws and regulations that are now being written will vary on what circumstances validate having established a residency in another state, and what proof is sufficient to show that it has been done.

It is important to remember that under the new law, a spouse will still have to pay state income tax in the state where they currently live if they haven't already established residency there. The spouse may claim his or her former residency for tax purposes only if he or she first reestablishes legal residency and contacts in that state.

gross income for the period of hospitalization, subject to the two-year limitation provided below. Commissioned officers have a similar exclusion, limited to the maximum enlisted pay amount per month. These exclusions from gross income for hospitalized enlisted personnel and commissioned officers end two years after the date of termination of the combat zone.

Annual leave payments to enlisted members of the U.S. Armed Forces upon discharge from service are excluded from gross income to the extent the annual leave was accrued during any month in any part of which the member served in a combat zone. If your wife is a commissioned officer, a portion of the annual leave payment she receives for leave accrued during any month in any part of which she served in a combat zone may be excluded. The annual leave payment is not excludable to the extent it exceeds the maximum enlisted pay amount for the month of service to which it relates less the amount of military pay already excluded for that month.

The reenlistment bonus is excluded from gross income even if received in a month that you were outside the combat zone, because you completed the necessary action for entitlement to the reenlistment bonus in a month during which you served in the combat zone.

A recent law change makes it possible for members of the military to count tax-free combat pay when figuring how much they can contribute to a Roth or traditional IRA. Before this change, members of the military whose earnings came from tax-free combat pay were often barred from putting money into an IRA, because taxpayers usually must have taxable earned income. Taxpayers choosing to put money into a Roth IRA don't need to report these contributions on their individual tax return. Roth contributions are not deductible, but distributions, usually after retirement, are normally tax-free. Income limits and other special rules apply.

Changing Tax Withholdings

You may want to change your income tax withholdings. You can do this using myPay or by contacting your HR/pay office and letting them know how much you want withheld.

Savings

Thrift Savings Plan (TSP)

The TSP is a retirement savings plan with special tax advantages for federal government employees and service members. Participation is optional, and service members must join TSP while they are still serving in the military. TSP is similar to traditional 401(k) plans often sponsored by private employers; contributions to TSP accounts are not taxed at the time they are made, but distributions from the accounts generally are subject to income tax at the time the distributions are withdrawn. Veterans who did not sign up for TSP while in service cannot join the plan after leaving the military. Contributions to TSPs are subject to certain limitations. Detailed information about TSP is available at www.tsp.gov.

USMC Key Volunteer Network is an official Marine Corps family readiness program. The network consists of Marine spouses called key volunteers (KVs), and they serve in both active duty and reserve units. KVs receive formal training and a certificate of completion of their training either from classes on base or online and are appointed by the unit commander.

The KVN structure includes a Key Volunteer Advisor (KVA) who is usually the commanding officer's spouse (or spouse of another senior officer), a key volunteer coordinator (KVC) who is the executive officer's spouse (or spouse of another senior officer), as well as a number of KVs who are spouses of other marines within the unit.

The commanding officers (COs) of individual active duty units rely on the KVN to provide additional support and resource referrals to the Marine families of that unit. Reserve units also utilize the KVN. However, if a unit is widely geographically dispersed, the CO may appoint a parent to serve as a KV or KVC. Marine Forces Reserve parents that are local often have insight into resources and assistance that are available and helpful to unit families.

The goal of the KVN is to help families achieve and maintain family readiness. This means that they communicate official command information as directed, serve as a communication link between the command and families, and provide information to Marine families through resource referrals as needed. During deployments, the KVN is especially important because they are further utilized as a communications tool to keep families of Marines better informed about mission(s) and tasks of individual units. The Marine Corps believes that if marines feel their families are supported and taken care of, they are better able to perform efficiently, effectively, and safely.

Pets

Check your base's policy, because some don't allow pets—other than aquarium fish or small caged birds—in on-base housing. Others have strict regulations governing the keeping of pets—such as requiring microchipping—and a limit on the number of pets per household. If pets are allowed, a pet deposit is normally required to cover potential damage.

If you do have pets, ensure that special arrangements are in place in case you are relocated overseas and your spouse moves with you. If you are unable to take your pets, make sure that a family member or friend will look after them or make arrangements with the local animal adoption or humane society. A number of organizations can also provide foster homes for pets, looking after them until you relocate back to the United States.

Despite all the problems, it is still worth having a pet dog or cat. They make wonderful companions and can provide great comfort to you and your children if your partner is deployed. If you think a pet would be a wonderful addition to your family, please check with your base shelter to consider adopting an animal that had to be left behind by another military family or by a deployed single service member. The deployment rate is extremely high during wartime, and many on-base animals need homes or need on-base foster care until a loved one returns home.

Notes

1. Rod Powers, "United States Military Information," About.com, http://usmilitary.about.com.

2. Rod Powers, "United States Military Information."

Challenges

2

Communicating

THE SECRET TO A SUCCESSFUL MARRIAGE IS GOOD communication—being able to talk freely about any subject; able to share secrets, fears, and fantasies; and able to offer advice if asked and discuss problems when they arise as partners. It takes effort to be a good listener. It is not hiding behind your newspaper eating your breakfast as your wife speaks and mumbling "yes, dear." A good listener will put down the newspaper, look his wife in the eye, and focus on what she is saying. What sort of message does it send if your partner is talking and you walk away and turn on the television?

With busy lives to lead it is important that couples make time to talk to each other. If you are together, you can do this whenever you want. If your partner is deployed, the time you have to communicate is even more precious.

Keeping this communication going during deployment may be difficult, but you can keep in touch through precious phone calls, through e-mails and the Internet, letters, videotapes, and so on.

Good communication is also part of the intimacy of marriage and a loving relationship. Saying "I love you" to your partner every day is part of that. It is such an easy thing to say and takes only a moment, but so often it doesn't get said. It doesn't matter how long you have been married; you can still do little things to communicate to your partner how much you still love him or her and how important your spouse is to you. You can send e-mail messages (where appropriate), leave love notes for your partner to find, send flowers with a loving message, and just be encouraging and supportive at all times. Sometimes active duty spouses facing imminent deployment will prearrange flower deliveries once or twice to surprise a spouse while the soldier is gone, with a loving message or simply a "thinking of you" message. Spouses on active duty will often work with children in the family to send a deployed spouse "care packages" of things he or she may need that would be difficult to obtain outside the United States.

Good communication keeps a marriage alive. It is when we stop communicating with each other that relationships tend to drift apart. If couples are not speaking to each other, other emotions can fill that void—anger, resentment, indifference—all negatives that can lead to marriage breakup.

It is as important to be a good communicator as it is to be a good listener. The good communicator will consider carefully what he or she says so as not to hurt or offend the partner. If there is an issue, it is better to say "What can we do . . ." rather than "Why did you let this happen . . ." When you start a sentence with "You . . ." it sounds as if you are attacking that person. Pointing fingers is never a good way to start a conversation. You need to spell out the problem and concentrate on ways of resolving it.

Start instead with "I think . . ." or "I am concerned about . . ." because this immediately tells your partner that these are your feelings and opens the door for your partner to respond with how he or she feels. Once you both know how the other feels, you are better able to work out a solution that suits both. Remember that you are both entitled to your opinion and you must respect your partner's right to hold it. Sometimes it is better to agree not to agree—but always do it with love and a hug.

The good communicator will be clear and to the point so there is little chance for misunderstanding. Arguments often result from misunderstandings—you said something and your partner totally misunderstood it.

How you say it is also important. If you are discussing something intimate or difficult, take hold of your partner's hand to show that you are in this together and that you care for him or her. Even if the subject matter is very serious, it doesn't hurt to smile at your partner every now and then. It is a reassuring gesture that says "I love you. We are in this together and we will work it out together."

The good listener will focus on what is being said and then think before replying. As you are listening, you are not thinking about what time the game starts or what you are doing tomorrow. Your partner deserves your full attention—and should get it.

Body language is every bit as important as the words you say. The wrong body language can send strong, antipathetic signals. If your arms are folded or you are leaning away from your partner, you are building a barrier between you and distancing yourself from him or her. Leaning toward your partner as he or she speaks demonstrates genuine interest in what your partner saying and a desire to be close to him or her. Eye contact is critical because it creates a bond. If your eyes start to wander, it shows you are not concentrating. Even eye movements can convey subtle messages. You should always break eye contact by looking down. Turning your eyes upward might convey impatience (as in, that was a stupid thing to say), whereas looking up can signal thoughtfulness and nonaggression. If your eyes flicker to the left and right it indicates you are uncomfortable; that is, looking for a way to get out of here.

Set aside a time during the day to talk to each other—face to face and eye to eye. It can be over breakfast or dinner or just before you go to sleep. Several studies show that the more a couple speaks to each other, the stronger their marriage is likely to be, while conversely, couples that hardly speak at all are likely to break up.

If you have a particularly difficult subject to discuss, set aside a time especially for it. Don't try to have the conversation while you are cooking dinner or trying to put the children to bed, or over the television, or while simultaneously texting from your phone. Find a time when you can sit down quietly and devote all your attention to the matter at hand and each other.

There may be times when your partner may not want to communicate. He or she may have returned from a particularly harrowing deployment and may need "downtime" to reassimilate back into "normal" life. You may be having an issue at work or issues with the children. Try to assess a good time for good communication—perhaps not toward the end of the day when both spouses are very tired.

If you have a strong relationship, don't assume that the lack of communication is because you have done something wrong. With soothing and sympathetic words such as "I'm always here for you if you want to talk," or "Is there anything I can do to help?" your partner should eventually open to you, and your relationship should be right back on track. If not, suggest that counseling may help. Your Family Support Center can offer advice and recommend counselors.

Building Successful Relationships

When you first get married, you do everything you can to please your partner. You buy each other little gifts, you help each other with the chores and the shopping, and you enjoy doing these things together.

Once you have been married a little while, these little intimacies might become less and less frequent for a number of reasons. You might both have jobs and be so tired when you get home that all you want to do is eat and go to bed. You may have children who are very demanding and time consuming. You might work different shifts, so you pass each other in the hallway—as one comes home the other is going to work.

Whatever the circumstances, you have to work at the relationship to make it successful. Your relationship is like a fire. It needs fuel to make it burn, and without it, the flames will die down until there is nothing left. Despite all the other pressures on your time, you have to keep that fire burning. And you can do lots of things to make that fire burn strongly.

The most important thing is to find time to spend together—when the children are in bed, when the chores have been done, when there are no other distractions to stop you from focusing on each other. Set aside this time as your special time to do what you want to do together. It can be once a week or once a month, but make it happen.

Find time to talk honestly about the things that are important to you both—what are your goals and aspirations? Do you both have the same dreams for the future? It is much easier to achieve these goals when you are both on the same page.

This honest talking should include your sex life as well. You both have needs—are these being met? Would you like more intimacy? Discuss what you would both like without embarrassment or guilt. Unless you talk about it, neither of you will know what is important to the other—and who knows? It could lead to all sorts of new and exciting things.

With that in mind, keep the magic alive. Just because you are married doesn't mean that you can't still go on dates with your partner. Go to your special restaurant for an intimate candlelit dinner; hold hands. Do not spoil the occasion by talking about work, problems, or the children. Talk about each other, funny things that have happened to you, things you'd like to do, where you would like to go on vacation, and so on. It is all about you as a couple. If your budget is tight, have an intimate dinner at home. Light some candles, dress up for the occasion, play your favorite music—and have fun.

Like a good bottle of wine, a marriage changes as it ages. If handled correctly a fine bottle of wine becomes more complex yet more harmonious, and so it is with a good marriage. The honeymoon may be over, but the love, like the wine, should be nurtured so that it develops and grows into something more beautiful.

Remember the little things—the kiss as you leave for work or when you come home, the hug for no other reason than to show that you care, sending flowers even though it is not a birthday or anniversary. It is these little things that show you still care.

If you ask couples who have been happily married for a long time, they will often say that they are not just lovers but best friends as well. They are able to talk to each other about anything, they share jokes, and they enjoy doing things together as a couple.

Sharing a common interest—everything from jogging to bird watching and singing in the church choir to being on the same trivia team at the local pub helps cement that bond and develop a much broader relationship. Find things that you enjoy doing together—from volunteering to gardening—and really enjoy doing them together.

At the same time, everyone needs his or her own space—time to do his or her own thing. It is important that you make time for this as well.

Never take anything for granted, especially in a relationship. We all need reassuring from time to time. If you suddenly stop saying "I love you," your partner may well wonder why but be afraid to ask. It is so easy to prevent those situations from arising by simply saying those three small but important words.

Disagreements Do Happen

At some time or other every couple has an argument. How they handle that argument is a testimony to how strong their marriage is. If one partner loses control and storms out of the house, that is not a good sign.

One piece of advice that used to be handed down to newly married couples was "never go to bed on an argument"—that is, kiss and make up so that whatever you were arguing about doesn't fester overnight and resurface in another row.

You are bound to have disagreements, and sometimes over the silliest little things, although at the time they may not have appeared to be so silly and little. The important thing is that when you do have an argument, you have to make sure that it does not escalate out of control.

There are several ways of doing this. First stay in control of your emotions. Something has clearly annoyed you or your partner, so try to discuss it objectively. Never make it personal with name calling or deliberately hurtful remarks. No matter how much you want to hurt your partner in the heat of that particular moment, words spoken can never be taken back. Apologies afterward for saying such things don't work; your partner will remember exactly what you said and may come to resent you for it.

If you do have a disagreement, argue only about what has upset you. Don't use it as an excuse to bring in all sorts of other issues you may have with your partner.

Stay in control of your words and actions—don't sneer, don't shout or point fingers.

If things are getting too heated, leave the room—don't storm out, but just say that you think a time-out would be a good idea. It gives you both a chance to cool down.

Apologies for having the argument, however, are a good idea provided they are sincere. It allows you both to kiss and make up, and having cleared

Useful Tips from MilSpouse.com: Rekindle the Spark in Your Marriage by Jennifer Murphy

Reinvigorating the romance in a marriage takes time and will take a little effort from the both of you. Both you and your spouse need to set aside time to rekindle and maintain a romantic relationship.

If work and family never seem to give enough time for just the two of you, consider going on a vacation together. Getting away for a week or more is a wonderful way to rekindle the romance, but for military families getting even just a week off is a feat. If getting that much time off is impossible, contemplate getting away for just the weekend. Try a weekend trip to the nearest big city or even just renting a room in a nice hotel in your current town and enjoy the alone time you two rarely have.

Even a day date is a nice alternative when vacations are out of the question. Removing yourselves from the familiar atmosphere of your home can work wonders in bringing spouses back together on a romantic level. New surroundings help to create a new mood for you and your spouse.

Try not planning anything. Spontaneity is a surefire way to create a spark that may have dimmed. This is the first thing to do when you have a family and a demanding military schedule, but the fun is in throwing the routine out the window. The same excitement felt when breaking the rules will carry over into the relationship.

In order to make a relationship last for years, willful efforts to romance each other must be made. Relationships left to monotony will generate into relationships in which partners begin to take each other for granted. Firing up the relationship and finding exciting new ways to enjoy each other's company are necessary to keep a good marriage strong.

Jennifer Murphy, "Rekindle the Spark in Your Marriage," *Military Spouse*, www.milspouse.com/article.aspx?id=10068. Used with permission.

the air, move on. If there are still issues to be resolved, set a time to sit down and talk about them. Some couples prefer to do this on "neutral" territory—at a café or on a walk. Practice the skills mentioned in the communications section earlier—listen carefully to what your partner is saying, respect his or her position, and then let him or her know how you feel and perhaps suggest ways you can work together to resolve the problem.

Sometimes couples have issues that they cannot sort out themselves, and they should then seek help. You can approach a trusted mutual friend or a chaplain, or seek advice from the Family Service Center.

Sharing Responsibilities in the Home

Sharing household chores is one of the most important factors in a happy marriage—and far more significant than having children, a study has found.

The findings, from an American survey of more than 2,000 people, show the extent to which couples no longer see parenthood as central to their relationship, instead favoring "personal satisfaction," said researchers.

Having a good sex life, a nice house, and shared tastes and interests were also put ahead of raising a family in the study of couples' priorities by the Pew Research Center in Washington, D.C. Overall, having children came eighth out of a list of nine factors seen as contributing to a successful marriage—a drop of five places on the same survey in 1990.

Top was "faithfulness," followed by "a happy sexual relationship," with "sharing household chores" in third.

However, fighting over domestic duties and chores around the house is second only to conflict over money in a marriage.

Most men do not pull their weight when it comes to chores around the house, and this can lead to resentment, especially if the wife has a job outside the home as well. Resentment then turns to anger, and you are on a slippery, downhill slope.

Even if the wife is at home with the children all day, there is no reason why the husband should not help out. After all marriage is a partnership.

One way to resolve issues is to sit down together and write down everything that needs to be done and then agree who will do what. One advantage of the list is that it may well come as a surprise just how much needs to be done.

You could agree to alternate cooking the nightly meal or take turns to do the weekly wash. Some chores you could agree to do together, like the weekly grocery shopping or tidying up the yard.

Once you have decided who is doing what, that person must be allowed to get on with it his or her way. Nothing is likely to cause friction more than you popping your head around the door and telling your spouse how you would do it.

If you have children and they are old enough, they should help in the

Useful Tips from MilSpouse.com:
Tips for Arguing by Anita Tedaldi

No one wants to fight, especially when we see a recurring issue that's a flashpoint. Diane Sollee, founder of Smart Marriages, a marriage education center based in Washington, D.C., explained that "psychologists have found that all couples disagree about the same amount—it's the way they manage conflict that distinguishes satisfied partners from miserable ones."

Before an argument: Avoid keeping all frustrations inside and then letting them out at once, in a big, unproductive explosion. Another major mistake is constantly nagging and trying to force the other partner into a confrontation. Choose the issues that will benefit you most to address and keep quiet about other things that you can live with.

During an argument: Both individuals should be able to explain their different points of view and ideas. Stay somewhat focused on the issue at hand; it's not "kitchen sink" time to dump every negative thing you can think of on the other person. The couple should focus on reaching a compromise. Arguments are not debates—there is no "winner" and no "loser." Strive for a compromise. If you can inject humor and recognize that you still love your spouse, chances are the fight won't extend into other aspects of your life together.

Sit down: If possible—it forces us to focus on our partner, and it's more difficult to use dominating body gestures.

Don't interrupt: Try to let your mate finish a thought. If you don't, you can quickly wind up in an unconstructive fight that has little to do with the original issue.

Don't be judgmental: Rather than criticize, state your opinions as concerns or fears. Ask for specific changes.

Don't correct your partner: Don't tell them how they are feeling and why they should feel a completely different way.

Consider counseling: This shouldn't be seen as a last resort. If you feel that you could benefit from a neutral third party, go for it. There is no shame in seeking help, and one or two appointments can help you get on the right track.

Anita Tedaldi, "Tips for Arguing," *Military Spouse*, www.milspouse.com/article.aspx?id=3312. Used with permission.

chores as well. Start with little things like helping to lay the table and putting toys away. As they become older and more responsible, they can take on more chores and earn their allowance.

Balancing Work and Life as a Dual Military Couple

Being a senior personnel NCO married to a ranger, Sgt. Maj. Jennifer Pearson knows a thing or two about deployments and separations. She spent a year in Bosnia.

Her husband, Sgt. Maj. James Pearson, was in Afghanistan at the beginning of Operation Enduring Freedom. "We've probably been separated more than we've been together," she said.

Despite that, Pearson, who at the time of writing was a student in the

Useful Tips from MilSpouse.com: Prioritizing Your Life by Krista Wells, The Military Spouse Coach

As military wives, we have the responsibility of supporting our service members while maintaining a focused commitment to that which makes our hearts sing. We can accomplish a great deal if we manage our behavior, attitude, and obligations with regard to our goals in life and our established purpose.

You might have heard of the 80/20 rule in business—80 percent of your results come from 20 percent of your efforts. I would suggest that this goes for our personal lives, as well. So often I see spouses pushing themselves, scheduling busier and busier lives, creating unnecessary stress and pressure on themselves as things pile up at work and home. If we structure our lives and align our energy toward what is most important, we find the energy to push worry aside and deal with issues more efficiently.

Have you set priorities for your life? One of my workshop participants identified her priorities as maintaining physical health, spending quality time with her children, and being outdoors. She no longer felt obligated to participate in activities that were not in alignment with her values, which created new space in her schedule. She decided not to watch television in the mornings and instead started an early-morning running club with other mothers in her neighborhood. She made a decision to identify her "big rocks" and shift priorities to align with what really mattered in her life.

Krista Wells, "Prioritizing Your Life," *Military Spouse*, www.milspouse.com/article.aspx?id=982&LangType=1033. Used with permission.

Sergeants Major Course Class 54 at the U.S. Army Sergeants Major Academy (USASMA), Fort Bliss, Texas, swears being a member of a dual-military couple is a great experience.

"I believe it's been very positive. The deployments are small stuff," she said. "Sure we're away from each other a lot, but we have a good relationship and our strengths complement each other's weaknesses."

Being a member of a dual-military couple presents a unique set of challenges. Still, many choose to endure the hardships, finding a balance between their marriages and their careers. More than 20,000 dual-military couples currently serve in the U.S. Army. The majority of these couples—79 percent—enjoy joint domicile assignments, but that doesn't mean they won't endure long separations and domestic difficulties.

For soldiers contemplating trying to marry up matrimony and the military, veteran dual-military couples stationed throughout the Army have plenty of advice to share on the subject.

"Being in the military has strengthened our relationship because every day is a test," said Pearson, whose husband, she added, also a Class 54 student, has been a valuable resource for training and motivation. Being a ranger, he's been able to help keep her tactical skills up to speed. She, in turn, has been able to provide him with personnel and finance information.

"We're a team," she said. "He'll use me in a heartbeat, just like I'll use him. We're both professional soldiers and we believe the Army is where we should be," she said.

"You don't have to make a choice whether you want to stay in the military or stay together with your family," said Master Sgt. Yolanda Choates, public affairs chief for the U.S. Army Maneuver Support Center, Fort Leonard Wood, Missouri. Her husband, Sgt. 1st Class Meco Choates, is the Protective Services Training Branch course manager for Company A, 701st Military Police Battalion.

"It's possible to do both; it's challenging. It's not easy, but anything worth striving for is never easy."

Doing both, keeping a family together while accomplishing the missions set forth by the Army, is something many dual-military couples face. One way to meet the challenge is by enrolling in the Married Army Couples Program (MACP). Established in August 1983, the MACP is a program designed to help ensure soldiers married to other soldiers are considered for joint domicile assignments.

"The hardships associated with maintaining a family while being a soldier are compounded in a married Army couple," said Lt. Col. Patrick Sedlack, chief of Plans, Procedures and Operations Branch, Army Human

Resources Command. "The MACP was established to help alleviate some of the problems by trying, when possible, to assign married couples at the same location. The goal of the program is to ensure that MACP Soldiers are considered for assignment together as often as possible."

To enroll in the MACP, married couples need to submit a Department of the Army Form 4187, Request for Personnel Action, to their local military personnel office. The personnel office will then process the information and enroll the soldiers. If the soldiers are assigned to separate duty stations, each soldier must submit a DA Form 4187 to his or her personnel office.

"The Married Army Couples Program works, but it doesn't guarantee you will be assigned together," said Staff Sgt. William Herold, a paralegal assigned to headquarters and Headquarters Company, 173rd Airborne Brigade, Vicenza, Italy. His wife, Sgt. Antoinette Herold, is a paralegal assigned to Headquarters Support Company, Southern European Task Force, Vicenza, Italy.

A number of things can make it difficult for the MACP to station a couple together, said Sedlack. If two soldiers have the same low-density MOS, they may be more difficult to station together, he explained. Or if a soldier has an MOS in which most available assignments are outside the continental United States (CONUS)—for example, a soldier who's a Korean linguist is married to a soldier with an MOS in which most available assignments are in CONUS—it may be difficult to station them together.

MACP also applies to soldiers married to members of other services or to Army Reserve or National Guard soldiers, but it is more difficult for assignments managers to station them together, Sedlack said. In addition to the difficulties inherent in stationing soldiers from different career fields together, there are also problems stationing soldiers together when they volunteer for special duty.

"There are no specific restrictions on the MACP, but some programs and situations are much more difficult to accommodate a [joint domicile] assignment," said Sedlack. For assignments such as drill sergeant and recruiter, selectees enrolled in MACP are required to provide a written statement saying he or she understands a joint-domicile assignment may not be possible due to restrictions pertaining to the duty.

"The assignments managers will still consider [joint domicile] for those couples but want to make sure the soldiers understand that it is very difficult to provide [it] due to the demands and locations of those assignments," said Sedlack.

"If it meant being separated for a long period of time, I don't think either one of us could [provide] such a [written statement]," said Herold. "Our branch manager has worked very hard to ensure we stay together, and I think signing a [written statement] wouldn't stop our branch from working just as hard to keep our family together."

While some, like Herold, place a lot of faith in their branch managers, others recommend that couples take a more proactive hand in their careers.

"You have to plan properly and manage your own career," said Sgt. Maj. Henry Garrett. Garrett is the Human Resources sergeant major for Fort Bliss, Texas. His wife, Sgt. Maj. Shirley Garrett is a student in Sergeants Major Course Class 54 at USASMA.

For example, Garrett said when he knew he was due for an assignment outside CONUS, he volunteered for duty in Korea with the hope that his wife would be able to follow.

When Shirley became the tactical NCO at the U.S. Military Academy at West Point, New York, Henry called his branch manager to find out what was available for him at the same location.

The Choateses have made similar sacrifices. "When we moved here from the [Washington] D.C. area, [Yolanda] had only one position available here," said Sgt. 1st Class Choates. "If she had to choose a position, this probably wouldn't be it, but she made that choice for the family."

"I would rather have been a first sergeant in Korea, but that's not what was best for my family," said Master Sgt. Choates. "We do these things because, being in the Army, you don't always have a choice."

Unfortunately, this strategy also has some drawbacks.

"We had to decline appointments to command sergeant major for the last five years because as command sergeants major it would be harder to station us together," Garrett said. He added that the key to a successful dual-military marriage is consideration for each other's career goals.

"I really didn't want to go to West Point, but I knew Shirley needed something that would help her stand apart from her peers," he said.

"If a couple is not in the same career management field, I recommend they learn as much as they can so they know what it takes to advance each other's careers."

Communication, said the Choateses, is another important factor in maintaining a successful dual-military marriage.

"You have to communicate," said Sgt. 1st Class Choates. "If you don't let each other know what's going on or how you feel, you're not going to succeed."

"You have to talk about schedule requirements and needs," added Master Sgt. Choates. She said it's important to coordinate things like picking up children from school, parent/teacher conferences, and medical and dental appointments.

Another challenge dual-military couples must tackle are family care plans—written instructions for the care of family members in the event of deployments, temporary duty, or field exercises. Dual-military couples have thirty days after arriving at a new unit to produce a valid family care plan, which includes naming both a short-term and long-term care provider.

In some cases, finding a short-term care provider at a new duty station can be difficult.

"[Early in our careers,] we didn't really know anybody at our next duty stations. We had thirty days to find someone we'd trust enough to take care of our kids, who was willing to do it," said Master Sgt. Choates.

"Now that we're older and we've been in a while, we know people at most of our duty stations when we get there."

Master Sgt. Choates added that those who haven't been in the Army long enough to know someone at every duty station should look among their coworkers for short-term care providers, because the people a soldier works with on a daily basis are the ones he or she gets to know first.

"Family readiness groups [FRGs] are another good source of information," said Sgt. 1st Class Choates. "But you have to go to the FRG meetings. They won't come to you."

Many soldiers married to other soldiers agree that being a member of a dual-military couple involves a lot of sacrifice. Some, however, find the sacrifice to be too much. Being a soldier is something Staff Sgt. Alison Kempke enjoys. A technical engineer assigned to Company A, 94th Engineer Battalion, Hohenfels, Germany, she is currently deployed in Iraq. And though she's a dedicated soldier in the War on Terrorism, her husband and two children waiting for her in Germany are never far from her thoughts. Kempke said she finds her job both rewarding and challenging, but she'll be ending her military career after only eight years.

"I love the military and I'd love to stay in, but the separations are hard, especially this one, because you don't know when you're coming back," she said. "I'd also like to be around to raise my kids."

Her current deployment is one of many separations she and her husband, Kenneth, a cavalry scout assigned to the Combat Maneuver Training Center, Hohenfels, Germany, have been forced to endure. Still other dual-military couples said while there are difficulties, there are also a number of benefits.

"When things happen that are beyond my control, [my husband] understands because he knows how things are in the military," said Sgt. 1st Class Regina Jamerson, a medic assigned to Headquarters Support Company, 94th Engineer Battalion, currently deployed in Iraq.

She's been deployed in support of Operation Iraqi Freedom since May. This is the first time in her eight-year marriage that she's been separated from her husband, Sgt. 1st Class Gregory Jamerson, a medic assigned to 7th Army Training Command, Grafenwoehr, Germany.

"We can relate to each other because we understand how things happen in the Army," she said. "Also, my husband can pack my duffle bag when I have [a field training exercise]. How many civilian spouses can do that?"

Marriage and Stress

All marriages undergo stress from time to time. This can be a result of emotional strains, work or financial problems, children, and so on. For military families there are many other situations that can be very stressful—coping with deployment and separation and frequent moves being at the top of the list.

When people are stressed they react differently. It is difficult for them to eat and sleep. They become irritable and short tempered. They may say things in the heat of the moment they would not otherwise say. As couples tend to react differently under stress, one partner may be affected far more than the other, and so the relationship gets out of kilter. The answer is to identify the source of stress and see what can be done about it. First you must accept that you are under stress and that this is causing problems in the relationship. Then sit down together and talk about the issues. That alone is often enough to relieve some of the stress. Whatever the cause of the stress, it is not likely to be resolved easily or quickly, but just recognizing it and having some sort of plan to tackle it is reassuring. Much more important, by sitting down with your partner and talking about it you can work together to resolve it. There is a lot of truth in the saying "A problem shared is a problem halved."

Talking about the problem is half the battle; showing that you care is the other half. Be supportive and loving. Buy your partner something special—it doesn't have to be expensive—but it does show that you are thinking of them and are there for them.

Remember: Help is always at hand. Marriage counseling, support, retreats, and assistance are widely available in the military. Check with Family Readiness, LINKS, your chaplain's office or militaryonesource.com for resources. Resources available include access to professionals trained to provide help on challenges unique to the military.

Housing

3

EVERYONE IN THE MILITARY GETS "FREE" (or almost free) housing; funds for housing are allocated in the overall benefit entitlements of every active duty service person. How the military chooses to provide this to you depends mostly upon your marital (dependency) status or your rank. If you are married and living with your spouse and/or minor dependents, you will either live in on-base housing or be given a monetary allowance called BAH (Basic Allowance for Housing) to live off base. The amount of BAH is dependent upon your rank, your location, and whether you have dependents.

If you are in the Guard or Reserves and entitled to a housing allowance, you will receive a special, reduced BAH, called BAH Type II, anytime you are on active duty for less than thirty days. If you are on orders to serve on active duty for thirty days or more, you'll receive the full housing allowance rate (the same as active duty).

If you have dependents, you will receive the housing allowance, even when staying in the barracks at basic training and/or technical school/AIT/A-School. This is because the military makes it mandatory for you to provide adequate housing for your dependents. This will be included as part of your regular paycheck. (*Note:* In the military, your monthly pay entitlements are paid twice per month—half on the first of the month and half on the last duty day of the month.) For basic training and/or technical school/AIT/A-School, you will receive the BAH amount for the location where your dependent(s) are residing.

However, if you are not married and/or divorced and are paying child support, you do not receive full-rate BAH while living in the barracks. In this case, special rules apply, and the member receives BAH-DIFF. Unlike basic pay, BAH is an "allowance," not a "pay," and is therefore not taxable.

If you are single, you can expect to spend a few years of your military service residing on base in the dormitory, or "barracks." Policies concerning single military members living off base at government expense vary from service to service, and even from base to base, depending on the occupancy rate of the barracks/dormitories on the particular base.

Army policy allows single members in the pay grade of E-6 and above to live off base at government expense. However, at some bases, E-5s are allowed to move off base at government expense, depending on the barracks' occupancy rates of that base.

The Air Force policy generally allows single E-4s with more than three years of service and above to reside off base at government expense.

The Navy policy allows single sailors in the pay grades of E-5 and above and E-4s with more than four years of service to reside off base and receive a housing allowance.

The Marines allow single E-6s and above to reside off base at government expense. On some bases, depending on the barracks' occupancy rate, single E-5s and even some E-4s are authorized to reside off base.

There are certain unique stipulations for rank and on-base housing for military assignments outside the continental United States.

Dormitories

If your recruiter promised you condos, you're out of luck (remember the movie *Private Benjamin*?). However, all of the services have implemented plans to improve single housing (dormitories/barracks) for enlisted personnel.

The Air Force was the first service to get started on the program and is arguably ahead of the other services. All airmen outside of basic training and technical school are now entitled to a private room. The Air Force started with remodeling barracks into a concept called one-plus-one, which provided a private room, a small kitchen, and a bathroom/shower shared with one other person. The Air Force has now upgraded its program using a concept called Dorms-4-Airmen. All new Air Force dormitories (except basic training and technical school) are now designed using this concept. Dormitories under this program are four-bedroom apartments. Airmen have a private room and private bath and share a kitchen, washer and dryer, and living room with three other airmen.

The Army's standard is a two-bedroom apartment, designed for two soldiers. Each soldier gets a private bedroom and shares a kitchen, bathroom, and living room.

The Navy had a serious problem when this initiative started. Thousands of their junior sailors were living on ships, even when their assigned ships were in port. To construct enough barracks on a Navy base to provide single rooms for all of these sailors would cost a fortune. The Navy solved this problem by getting permission from Congress to use private industry to construct and operate privatized housing for lower-ranking single sailors. As with the Army, this design is a two-bedroom apartment. Each sailor will have a private bedroom and a private bathroom, and share a kitchen, dining area, and living room with another sailor. However, under the Navy's Homeport Ashore initiative, sailors assigned to ships that are in port must share a bedroom until additional funding becomes available to build new complexes. As in privatized family housing, the sailor would pay the complex management monthly rent (which is equal to their housing allowance). The "rent" covers all utilities and rental insurance. The plan calls for the apartment complexes to include fitness facilities, media centers, wi-fi lounges, and technology centers. The first two contracts were awarded for the Navy's two largest fleet areas (San Diego and Norfolk). Additional projects are projected for Hampton Roads, Virginia, and Mayport, Florida.

The Marines have taken a different route. The Marine Corps believes that lower-ranking enlisted marines living together is essential to discipline, unit cohesion, and esprit de corps. Under the Marine Corps program, junior marines (E-1 to E-3) share a room and a bathroom. Marines in the dormitory rooms are normally subject to two types of inspections: First, there is the normal or periodic inspection, which may or may not be announced in advance. This is where the commander or first sergeant (or other designated person) inspects your room to make sure you are abiding by the standards (bed made, trash empty, room clean, etc.). The second type of inspection is called a Health and Welfare Inspection (HWI). This type of inspection is always unannounced, often occurs about 2:00 AM, and comprises an actual search of the dormitory rooms for contraband (drugs, guns, knives, etc.). At times, these HWIs are accompanied by a "random" urinalysis test, looking for evidence of drug abuse.

Some services/bases allow you to use your own furniture. Others are very strict about using the provided government furniture only. Even if you are required to use government furniture, you can have your own stereo, television, or computer system.

Moving Out

At most locations, single members can elect to move out of the dormitory and get a place off base at their own expense. That means the government will not give them BAH (housing allowance), nor will the government give them a food allowance (discussed in the next chapter). Unless you get a roommate (or two) it can be hard to make ends meet living off base, with just your base pay.

By law, the services cannot allow single members to move off base at government expense, unless the base-wide dormitory occupancy rate exceeds 95 percent. That means over 95 percent of all dormitory rooms on the base must have people living in them before anyone can be allowed to move out of the dormitories and receive a housing allowance.

Unfortunately, dormitory/barracks spaces are usually allocated to specific units (squadrons, divisions, companies, etc.), and commanders are notoriously against allowing members of their units to live in other units' dormitories/barracks. Therefore, it's entirely possible for your particular unit to be overcrowded in the dormitory (thereby mandating that you have a roommate), while another unit has plenty of space. Unfortunately, unless the *base-wide* occupancy rate exceeds 95 percent, your commander can't authorize you to move off base at government expense.

When the base-wide occupancy rate does exceed 95 percent, the way it is usually done is that the base offers the chance to move off base to dormitory residents, based on rank. That is, the person (base-wide) with the most rank is offered the chance to move out first, followed by the person (base-wide) who has the next most rank, and so on, until the base-wide occupancy rate falls below 95 percent.

That means it's entirely possible that your particular dorm may be overcrowded, but the person given the chance to move off base may be in another dorm, which is not nearly so crowded, and there you are—stuck with a roommate because your commander won't let you move to another unit's uncrowded dormitory. The solution to this problem is to periodically reallocate dormitory spaces, but this is a major hassle, and most bases are reluctant to tackle the project more often than every five years or so. This system is the source of much frustration among single military members.

On-Base Housing

Most places have limited on-base housing, so there is usually a waiting list (sometimes more than one year!). To qualify for on-base housing, you must be residing with a dependent (in most cases, that means spouse or minor children). Exceptional family members may be put ahead on the waiting list based upon category and medical need. The number of bedrooms you'll be authorized depends on the number and age of the dependents residing with you. Some bases have very nice housing—on other bases the housing barely qualifies for slum status. Utilities (trash, water, gas, electric) are normally free. Cable TV and phones are not. Furniture is normally not provided (although many bases have "loan closets," which will temporarily loan you furniture). Appliances, such as stoves and refrigerators, are usually provided. Many on-base houses even have dishwashers.

Clothes washers and dryers are usually not provided, but most units—at least in the states—have hookups. Additionally, many bases have laundromats located close to the housing area. Overseas, many housing units are "condo-style," and a laundry room with washers and dryers is located in each "stairwell."

Government Family Housing

The insides of occupied housing units are not normally inspected as dormitories are (although they may be inspected no-notice if the commander receives any kind of safety or sanitary problem reports). The outside of housing is an entirely different matter. All of the services are pretty strict about dictating exactly how the outside of the house (yard) must be maintained. Most of them employ personnel who will drive by each and every housing unit once per week and write "tickets" for any discrepancies noted. Receive too many tickets in too short a period of time, and you will be requested to move off base.

In the United States, most on-base family housing units are duplexes, or sometimes four-plexes. For officers and more senior enlisted members, on-base family housing in the United States are usually either duplexes or single dwellings. Sometimes there are fenced-in backyards, and at other bases there are not. Usually, if the housing unit has a backyard but no fence, you can get permission to install a fence at your own expense (though you have to agree to take the fence down when you move out if the next occupant decides he or she doesn't want a fence).

The same is true of almost any "improvement" you wish to make to on-base family housing. Usually you can get permission to do "self-help" improvements, but you must agree to return the house to its original state if the next person to move in doesn't want to accept your "improvement."

Overseas, on-base family housing units are generally in the form of high-rise apartment buildings—kind of like condominiums.

Moving out of base housing is a lot harder than moving in. This is the one time when the inside of the house *will* be inspected, and it is expected to be in immaculate condition (many people hire professional cleaners prior to checkout). However, many bases now have programs where the base itself hires professional cleaners when an occupant moves out, making the process much easier.

More and more military bases are moving to privatized family housing. This housing is maintained and managed (and sometimes built) by private industry. The "rent" for these privatized units is paid to the housing management agency by military pay allotment and is equal to the member's housing allowance.

Off-Base Housing

Instead of living in the dormitories or residing in on-base housing, you may be authorized to live off base. In this case, the military will pay you BAH. The amount of this nontaxable allowance is dependent upon your rank, marital (dependency) status, and the area you (or your dependents) live in. Once per year, the military hires an independent agency to survey the average housing costs in all of the areas where significant numbers of military personnel live. The Per Diem, Travel and Transportation Allowance Committee uses this data to compute the amount of BAH you will receive each month (currently designed to cover about 96.5 percent of the total average housing costs, but scheduled to increase so that it covers 100 percent of average housing costs).

One of the nice features about the BAH law is that the amount of BAH you receive may never go down while you are living in an area, even if the average cost of housing in that area goes down. Of course, once you move to a different base, your BAH will be recalculated for the current rate in the new location.

An interesting aspect of BAH is the type of housing that the entitlement is based upon. BAH is based on acceptable housing for an individual (or an individual with dependents). For example, a married E-5 is reimbursed based on what the Department of Defense (DoD) considers minimum acceptable housing, a two-bedroom townhouse or duplex. For an O-5 it is a four-bedroom detached home. While whether one has dependents is a factor, the number of dependents is not.

If you move into off-base housing overseas, your monthly entitlement is called OHA (Overseas Housing Allowance) and is recalculated every two weeks. This is because currency rates can fluctuate dramatically overseas, causing housing expenses to go up and down. In addition to OHA, those overseas are entitled to some additional allowances, such as an initial move-in expense allowance and reimbursement for costs to improve the security of the off-base residence.

If you are authorized to reside off base, it's very important that you ensure your lease contains a "military clause." A military clause allows you to break your lease in case you are forced to move on official orders, without penalty.

Special Considerations

If you are married to a nonmilitary member and/or you have children, your spouse and children are considered to be dependents by the military.

The military requires you to provide adequate support (which includes housing) to your dependents. Because of this, if you are married, you receive a housing allowance at the "with-dependent" rate, even if you are living in the single dormitories/barracks.

Because living in the barracks/dormitories is mandatory during basic training and job school, and because your dependents are not allowed to travel to basic training and/or job school (unless the job school is over twenty weeks long at a single location) at government expense, during these periods you live in the barracks/dormitories and receive BAH for the area where your dependents reside.

When you move to your first permanent duty station, the rules change. Your dependents are allowed to move there at government expense. If they don't move there, that is considered your choice. In such cases, you receive BAH (at the with-dependent rate) for the amount of your duty station, regardless of where your dependent is actually living.

As long as you are still married, to give up BAH, you would have to reside in on-base family housing. However, unless your dependents move to your duty location, you are not authorized to reside in on-base family housing, because the rules say to qualify, your dependents must be living with you.

If there is extra space available in the barracks/dormitories, you are allowed to live there and still receive your BAH. However, now that the military is trying to give all single people living in the dormitories their own room, most bases do not have any extra space available in their dormitories. Therefore, as a married person who has voluntarily elected not to be accompanied by their dependents, you will likely be required to live off base. You will receive BAH for the area you are assigned to. If you are allowed to live in the dormitory/barracks, space available, you must be prepared to move out, with little or no notice, in case the space is needed (although most commanders/first sergeants will try to give at least two weeks' notice, if possible).

The rules change for overseas assignments. If you are assigned overseas and elect not to be accompanied by your dependents, you can live in the barracks/dormitories on base and still receive BAH in order to provide adequate housing support in the States for your dependent(s).

Military Married to Military

There are about 84,000 military-married-to-military couples in the U.S. armed forces. These days, it seems that more and more married couples are joining the military together or—very common—"falling in love" in job training or during the first assignment and getting married. So what trials do these couples face that aren't faced by a military member married to a civilian? Does the military guarantee to assign such couples together? If they live off base, how much housing allowance do they receive?

Join Spouse

Each of the services has an assignment program called Join Spouse. Basically, under this program the military will try as hard as it can to station military spouses at the same base or within 100 miles of each other. Note there is no guarantee—the military just agrees to try. The services will not create a new slot for Join Spouse. There has to be an existing slot in the rank/job that the member(s) can be assigned against.

DoD-wide, about 80 percent of military-married-to-military couples are assigned within 100 miles of each other. That sounds pretty good until you realize that means 20 percent of military couples are not assigned close to each other. I knew one military couple who did an entire twenty-year career in the military without once being assigned together (special case— she was a naval officer, and he was an Air Force test pilot).

One of the primary factors to consider when contemplating a military-couple marriage is if both members are in the same service. Obviously, it's easier for the services to assign couples together when both are in the same branch. For one thing, it takes less coordination, as only one branch assignment division is involved. Also remember that it was indicated that the services will not create a job slot just to assign couples together. Well, there just aren't that many Air Force airmen assigned to Marine Corps bases, nor many marines assigned to Air Force bases except where joint forces commands exist. Additionally, there aren't that many Air Force bases and Marine Corps bases that are close together. So marrying someone in your same branch of service obviously increases your chance of a successful Join Spouse assignment.

In order for Join Spouse to work, both members must apply. If only one member applies for a Join Spouse, the assignment system won't process it. Then it's up to the military to determine who should move (or whether both should move), based on the needs of the service and funding constraints.

One thing worth mentioning that confuses folks when it comes to Join Spouse—normal time-on-station rules apply. For example, in general, in order for a first-termer (a military member on his or her first enlistment), assigned to a CONUS (Continental United States) base, to move overseas, he or she must have twelve months' time-on-station. In order for the first-termer to move from one CONUS base to another, he or she must have twenty-four months' time-on-station.

For "careerists," (those who have reenlisted at least once), the time-on-station requirements are greater. For a careerist to move from CONUS to overseas requires twenty-four months' time-on-station, and to move from CONUS to CONUS requires thirty-six months' time-on-station.

When one is assigned to an overseas tour, there is a set tour length, generally (for most tours) twenty-four months for a single person and thirty-six months for a married person who is accompanied by his or her spouse and/or dependents.

So let's say that Private Jones and Private Smith meet and fall in love at AIT (job training). When they finish AIT, Private Jones gets assigned to Washington, D.C., and Private Smith gets assigned to California. After a month, they decide they can't stand to be apart, so they arrange to go on leave and get married. Guess what? Neither one can move to the other's CONUS base for two whole years! Of course, they could both put in for overseas and apply for Join Spouse and hope they get picked up for an overseas assignment, and can then both move after twelve months' time-on-station.

Another scenario: Jack and Jill are engaged and join the Air Force at the same time. They agree to wait until they make it through basic training and technical school (job training) to get married. While in technical school, Jack gets a two-year assignment to Japan, and Jill gets an assignment to Florida. If they wait until after they leave technical school (on leave and on their way to their respective assignments), it's going to be too late for Join

Spouse. Join Spouse can take several weeks to process, and by that time, they will both be at their new assignments. Then, time-on-station applies. Jack is ineligible to move until his rotation date two years down the road, and Jill isn't eligible to move overseas until she's been at her CONUS assignment for twelve months.

Military couples stationed together can live off base and receive a housing allowance, or can give up the housing allowance and live free in on-base family housing, just as members married to a civilian can. If there are no other dependents (children), each member is treated as "single" (for housing allowance purposes), and each will receive the single-rate Basic Allowance for Housing (BAH) for their rank and assignment location. If there are children, one member receives the with-dependent rate, and the other member receives the single rate. In most cases, the couples choose the senior-ranking member to receive the with-dependent rate, as it means more money.

If there are no dependents, each member is considered "single" (as far as housing allowance) when not stationed together. For example, if a married couple (with no children) join the military together, neither will receive a housing allowance while undergoing basic training and job training (because each one is living in the barracks at basic and job training locations). If there are dependents (children), one of the members would receive a with-dependent housing allowance while in basic/job training, in order to provide a household for the dependents. (*Note:* This scenario is unlikely, as it requires a very-hard-to-get waiver for a couple with children to both join the military.)

Another example: The Markets (both PFCs in the Army) are assigned together at an Army post in Texas. They have no children and are living off base. Both are receiving single-rate housing allowance. One of the members, Sally, gets orders for a twelve-month remote (unaccompanied) tour to Korea. While in Korea, Sally loses her housing allowance (because she is living in the barracks there). John, still stationed in Texas and living in their off-base house while she is gone, will continue to receive his single-rate housing allowance.

Family Separation Allowance

Family Separation Allowance (currently $250 per month) is normally paid anytime a military member is separated from his or her dependents for longer than thirty days, due to military orders. For example, members with dependents attending basic training and job training (if the job training is less than twenty weeks and dependents are not authorized to relocate to the training base) receive $250 per month, beginning thirty days after separation.

The same applies to military-married-to-military, except:

1. The members must be residing together immediately prior to the departure.
2. Only one member can receive the allowance.

Payment shall be made to the member whose orders resulted in the separation. If both members receive orders requiring departure on the same day, then payment will go to the senior member.

Care of Children (Dependents)

Military couples with children must develop a "family care plan" that details exactly what the care arrangements are in the event that both members must deploy. Failure to develop and maintain a workable family care plan can result in discharge.

Note: If you are a wounded warrior, there are lots of ways of getting housing grants and assistance for yourself and your family. There are grants for remodeling homes to make them disability-friendly. Habitat for Humanity has an extensive building program for combat-disabled veterans and their families. See the "Wounded Warrior" chapter for more information.

Buying Your First Home

Buying your own home is always a sound investment, but it can be difficult if you frequently have to relocate. It is also a major investment and one that many young couples have to think seriously about, although with the present housing market there has never been a better time to buy, and as a military couple you are eligible for special mortgage rates.

A lot of things have to be considered. Buying a home is not only a big investment, it is an ongoing one with upkeep and maintenance, property taxes, and other fees and services that have to be paid. There is no doubt, however, that if you can afford to buy a house now and perhaps rent it out if you are posted elsewhere, it will steadily appreciate in value and be a valuable nest egg in years to come.

Some of the advantages of buying your own home are that you save on your income tax because your mortgage interest payments are deductible every year and you own the place, so you are not paying rent every month with nothing back in return. If you own your home, you can customize it to your liking—something most landlords don't encourage—and anyhow, why would you spend money on upgrading a property you do not own? Another major advantage is that your house will appreciate in value and as it does so, so your equity in the property increases. In a few years if you need extra cash—to start a family, for instance—you can take out a loan against that equity.

There are downsides as well. Buying a home is an expensive initial investment, although buyers can exert a lot of leverage at the moment, such as getting the seller to pay all or some of your closing costs. If the seller is anxious to sell, this might be acceptable to them in order to close the deal. There are other costs such as legal fees, surveys, deposits, and so on. There are then the ongoing payouts for mortgage, taxes, and homeowner's insurance.

If you buy, you will become responsible for upkeep and maintenance—if something goes wrong, you have to fix it. Housing association fees may have to be paid.

To buy or not to buy has to be a decision taken together after much thought. Do you both want to be tied down with home ownership and everything that goes with it? Can you afford to buy a property—do you earn enough to pay the mortgage every month and not get into arrears?

If you expect to get a new posting in a couple of years, it is unlikely that the house will have appreciated sufficiently for you to recoup your buying costs, and it is probably better to rent. If you think you are not going to move for four or five years, then buying becomes a serious option.

If you buy a house near a base and are relocated, it may be easier to rent your home to another military couple rather than sell it. If you plan on selling each time you move on, you can always move into rented accommodations on a short lease rather than make a snap decision to buy after only a short time of looking at what is available. Rushed decisions are seldom the right ones.

If you purchased a home as a result of a Permanent Change of Station (PCS) assignment during the peak of the housing market and then had to sell your home at a loss at the trough of the housing market resulting from a second PCS assignment, you may be entitled to recoup a substantial portion of your housing loss through a provision in the American Recovery and Reinvestment Act of 2009 (ARRA).

Frequently Asked Questions

Why should I buy instead of rent?
A home is an investment. When you rent, you write your monthly check and that money is gone forever. But when you own your home, you can

deduct the cost of your mortgage loan interest from your federal income taxes, and usually from your state taxes. This will save you a lot each year, because the interest you pay will make up most of your monthly payment for most of the years of your mortgage. You can also deduct the property taxes you pay as a homeowner. In addition, the value of your home may go up over the years. Finally, you'll enjoy having something that's all yours—a home where your own personal style will tell the world who you are.

What are HUD homes, and are they a good deal?

HUD homes can be a very good deal. When someone with a HUD-insured mortgage can't meet the payments, the lender forecloses on the home, HUD pays the lender what is owed, and HUD takes ownership of the home. Then it is sold at market value as quickly as possible. Read all about buying a HUD home.

Can I become a home buyer even if I've had bad credit and don't have much for a down payment?

You may be a good candidate for one of the federal mortgage programs. Start by contacting one of the HUD-funded housing counseling agencies that can help you sort through your options. Also, contact your local government to see if any local home-buying programs might work for you. Look in the blue pages of your phone directory for your local office of housing and community development, or, if you can't find it, contact your mayor's office or your county executive's office.

Should I use a real estate broker? How do I find one?

Using a real estate broker is a very good idea. All the details involved in home buying, particularly the financial ones, can be mind-boggling. A good real estate professional can guide you through the entire process and make the experience much easier. A real estate broker will be well acquainted with all the important things you'll want to know about a neighborhood you may be considering—the quality of schools, the number of children in the area, the safety of the neighborhood, traffic volume, and more. He or she will help you figure the price range you can afford and search the classified ads and multiple listing services for homes you'll want to see. With immediate access to homes as soon as they're put on the market, the broker can save you hours of wasted driving-around time. When it's time to make an offer on a home, the broker can point out ways to structure your deal to save you money. He or she will explain the advantages and disadvantages of different types of mortgages, guide you through the paperwork, and be there to hold your hand and answer last-minute questions when you sign the final papers at closing. And you don't have to pay the broker anything! The payment comes from the home seller—not from the buyer.

By the way, if you want to buy a HUD home, you will be required to use a real estate broker to submit your bid. To find a broker who sells HUD homes, check your local Yellow Pages or the classified section of your local newspaper.

How much money will I have to come up with to buy a home?

Well, that depends on a number of factors, including the cost of the house and the type of mortgage you get. In general, you need to come up with enough money to cover three costs: *earnest money*—the deposit you make on the home when you submit your offer, to prove to the seller that you are serious about wanting to buy the house; the *down payment*, a percentage of the cost of the home that you must pay when you go to settlement; and *closing costs*, the costs associated with processing the paperwork to buy a house.

When you make an offer on a home, your real estate broker will put your earnest money into an escrow account. If the offer is accepted, your earnest money will be applied to the down payment or closing costs. If your offer is not accepted, your money will be returned to you. The amount of your earnest money varies. If you buy a HUD home, for example, your deposit generally will range from $500 to $2,000.

The more money you can put into your down payment, the lower your mortgage payments will be. Some types of loans require 10 to 20 percent of the purchase price. That's why many first-time home buyers turn to HUD's FHA for help. FHA loans require only 3 percent down—and sometimes less.

Closing costs—which you will pay at settlement—average 3 to 4 percent of the price of your home. These costs cover various fees your lender charges and other processing expenses. When you apply for your loan, your lender will give you an estimate of the closing costs, so you won't be caught by surprise. If you buy a HUD home, HUD may pay many of your closing costs.

How do I know if I can get a loan?

Use simple mortgage calculators to see how much mortgage you could pay—that's a good start. If the amount you can afford is significantly less than the cost of homes that interest you, then you might want to wait a while longer. But before you give up, why don't you contact a real estate broker or a HUD-funded housing counseling agency? They will help you evaluate your loan potential. A broker will know what kinds of mortgages the lenders are offering and can help you choose a lender with a program that might be right for you. Another good idea is to get prequalified for a loan. That means you go to a lender and apply for a mortgage before you actually start looking for a home. Then you'll know exactly how much you can afford to spend, and it will speed the process once you do find the home of your dreams.

How do I find a lender?

You can finance a home with a loan from a bank, a savings and loan, a credit union, a private mortgage company, or various state government lenders. Shopping for a loan is like shopping for any other large purchase: you can save money if you take some time to look around for the best prices. Different lenders can offer quite different interest rates and loan fees; and as you know, a lower interest rate can make a big difference in how much home you can afford. Talk with several lenders before you decide. Most lenders need three to six weeks for the whole loan approval process. Your real estate broker will be familiar with lenders in the area and what they're offering. Or you can look in your local newspaper's real estate section— most papers list interest rates being offered by local lenders. You can find FHA-approved lenders in the Yellow Pages of your phone book. HUD does not make loans directly—you must use a HUD-approved lender if you're interested in an FHA loan.

In addition to the mortgage payment, what other costs do I need to consider?

Well, of course you'll have your monthly utilities. If your utilities have been covered in your rent, this may be new for you. Your real estate broker will be able to help you get information from the seller on how much utilities normally cost. In addition, you might have homeowner association or condo association dues. You'll definitely have property taxes, and you also may have city or county taxes. Taxes normally are rolled into your mortgage payment. Again, your broker will be able to help you anticipate these costs.

So what will my mortgage cover?

Most loans have four parts: principal (the repayment of the amount you actually borrowed); interest (payment to the lender for the money you've borrowed); homeowner's insurance (a monthly amount to insure the property against loss from fire, smoke, theft, and other hazards required by most lenders); and property taxes (the annual city/county taxes assessed on your property, divided by the number of mortgage payments you make in a year). Most loans are for thirty years, although fifteen-year loans are available, too. During the life of the loan, you'll pay far more in interest than you will in principal—sometimes two or three times more! Because of the way loans are structured, in the first years you'll be paying mostly interest in your monthly payments. In the final years, you'll be paying mostly principal.

What do I need to take with me when I apply for a mortgage?

Good question! If you have everything with you when you visit your lender, you'll save a good deal of time. You should have (1) social security numbers for both your and your spouse, if both of you are applying for the loan; (2) copies of your checking and savings account statements for the past six months; (3) evidence of any other assets like bonds or stocks; (4) a recent paycheck stub detailing your earnings; (5) a list of all credit card accounts and the approximate monthly amounts owed on each; (6) a list of account numbers and balances due on outstanding loans, such as car loans; (7) copies of your last two years' income tax statements; and (8) the name and address of someone who can verify your employment. Depending on your lender, you may be asked for other information.

I know there are lots of types of mortgages—how do I know which one is best for me?

You're right—there are many types of mortgages, and the more you know about them before you start, the better. Most people use a fixed-rate mortgage. In a fixed-rate mortgage, your interest rate stays the same for the term of the mortgage, which normally is thirty years. The advantage of a fixed-rate mortgage is that you always know exactly how much your mortgage payment will be, and you can plan for it. Another kind of mortgage is an adjustable-rate mortgage (ARM). With this kind of mortgage, your interest rate and monthly payments usually start lower than a fixed-rate mortgage. But your rate and payment can change either up or down, as often as once or twice a year. The adjustment is tied to a financial index, such as the U.S. Treasury Securities index. The advantage of an ARM is that you may be able to afford a more expensive home because your initial interest rate will be lower. There are several government mortgage programs, including the Veterans Administration's programs. Most people have heard of FHA mortgages. FHA doesn't actually make loans. Instead, it insures loans so that if buyers default for some reason, the lenders will get their money. This encourages lenders to give mortgages to people who might not otherwise qualify for a loan. Talk to your real estate broker about the various kinds of loans before you begin shopping for a mortgage.

When I find the home I want, how much should I offer?

Again, your real estate broker can help you here. But you should consider several things: (1) Is the asking price in line with prices of similar homes in the area? (2) Is the home in good condition or will you have to spend a substantial amount of money making it the way you want it? You probably want to get a professional home inspection before you make your offer. Your real estate broker can help you arrange one. (3) How long has the home been on the market? If it's been for sale for a while, the seller may be more eager to accept a lower offer. (4) How much mortgage will be required? Make sure you really can afford whatever offer you make. (5) How much do you really want the home? The closer you are to the asking price, the more likely your offer will be accepted. In some cases, you may even want to offer more than the asking price, if you know you are competing with others for the house.

What if my offer is rejected?

They often are! But don't let that stop you. Now you begin negotiating. Your broker will help you. You may have to offer more money, but you may ask the seller to cover some or all of your closing costs or to make repairs that wouldn't normally be expected. Often, negotiations on a price go back and forth several times before a deal is made. Just remember—don't get so caught up in negotiations that you lose sight of what you really want and can afford!

So what will happen at closing?

Basically, you'll sit at a table with your broker, the broker for the seller, probably the seller, and a closing agent. The closing agent will have a stack of papers for you and the seller to sign. While he or she will give you a basic explanation of each paper, you may want to take the time to read each one and/or consult with your agent to make sure you know exactly what you're signing. After all, this is a large amount of money you're committing to pay for a lot of years! Before you go to closing, your lender is required to give you a booklet explaining the closing costs, a "good faith estimate" of how much cash you'll have to supply at closing, and a list of documents you'll need at closing. If you don't get those items, be sure to call your lender *before* you go to closing. It will help you understand your rights in the process. Don't hesitate to ask questions.

Moving

Being married in the military has more than its fair share of challenges, and frequent moves are one of them. No sooner have you gotten used to one base and met lots of new friends, you receive Permanent Change of Station (PCS) orders and have to pack up all over again. It is even more difficult if you have children in school and family nearby.

Planning every detail of the move is the secret to success. First treat the move as a new adventure—something to look forward to as a new, exciting chapter in your marriage. If your partner is deployed and still receives PCS orders, you will need power of attorney to get things done.

Start making lists—lists of bills to be paid, utilities and services to be cancelled or transferred, people to be informed, important telephone numbers, and so on.

Gather together documents that you may need—such as orders, medical records, birth certificates, marriage certificates, powers of attorney, living wills, and insurances.

Create a countdown calendar and enter everything that needs doing three months ahead of time (if you have that luxury of planning time); everything that needs doing one month out; one week out; and on the day. Keep referring to this calendar and add to it as you think of new things that have to be done.

Check out your new base and what facilities and services are available. One of the great things about the military is that you may well have friends at the new base who can give you useful tips.

Check out the local Chamber of Commerce and Convention and Visitors Bureau if there is one—for job opportunities and to familiarize yourself with your new home area.

Stay in touch with family and friends—they will be a great support group during move.

Your Relocation Office should be your first stop when you are considering a move or when you actually receive orders. This office is staffed by trained professionals who will help manage your move. Their goal is to connect you to the right resources at the right time so that you can execute an efficient and cost-effective move within the military system.

Your Installation Relocation Office can help you:

- determine your PCS allowances
- connect with your new installation's relocation office
- create and customize a moving calendar
- connect with important installations agencies
- create a customized booklet of resources
- access a loan closet
- understand out-processing requirements
- obtain a sponsor

Permanent Change of Station (PCS) Allowances

Various allowances are associated with most moves within the continental United States (CONUS) and outside the continental United States (OCO-NUS). *Do not assume* that you will receive any of these allowances. Allowances change periodically. Check with the finance office on your installation to determine the exact amount of your allowances. For additional information, you can visit the Per Diem, Travel and Transportation Allowance Committee website, the official source for the most up-to-date changes to benefits and allowances.

Housing Office

Your Installation Housing Office can help you with:

- determining your housing allowances
- determining availability of government housing at your new location
- understanding your housing privatization options at your new location
- finding local community housing at your new location
- arranging for temporary lodging

The DoD's Automated Housing Referral Network (www.ahrn.com) can help you look for housing.

Household Goods (HHG)

HHG include items associated with the home and all personal effects belonging to a member and dependents on the effective date of the member's PCS or temporary duty (TDY) order that legally may be accepted and transported by an authorized commercial transporter. HHG also include professional books, papers, and equipment (PBP&E); spare privately owned vehicle (POV) parts and a pickup tailgate when removed; integral or attached vehicle parts that must be removed due to their high vulnerability to pilferage or damage (e.g., seats, tops, winch, spare tires, portable auxiliary gasoline can(s), and miscellaneous associated hardware); vehicles other than POVs (such as golf carts, motorcycles, mopeds, jet skis, hang gliders, snowmobiles) and their associated trailers; boats and single-occupant ultra-light vehicles for recreation or sport purposes (weighing less than 155 pounds if uncovered or less than 254 pounds if powered; having a fuel capacity not to exceed (NTE) 5 gallons; airspeed NTE 55 knots; and power-off stall speed NTE 24 knots).

HHG do not include:

- personal baggage when carried free on an airplane, bus, or train
- automobiles, trucks, vans, and similar motor vehicles
- airplanes, mobile homes, camper trailers, and farming vehicles
- live animals including birds, fish, and reptiles
- cordwood and building materials
- items for resale, disposal, or commercial use rather than for use by the member and dependents
- privately owned live ammunition
- articles that otherwise would qualify as HHG but are acquired after the effective date of PCS orders except bona fide replacements for articles that have become inadequate, worn out, broken, or unserviceable on/after the effective date of orders

Personally Owned Vehicle (POV)

One POV belonging to you or your family member may be shipped at government expense overseas. It must, however, be for you or your family member's personal use only. If you desire to make your own arrangements and ship an additional POV, consult your Transportation Office for any restrictions that may apply. You may be required to pay an import duty on a second POV. At the option of the member shipping a vehicle overseas, a motorcycle or moped may be considered a POV if the member does not ship a vehicle with four or more wheels under the same set of military orders. A vehicle under a long-term lease (twelve months or longer) may be shipped if you obtain written permission from the leasing company.

The POV should be delivered to the port prior to the departure of the member on whose orders the shipment is to be made. This includes dependent travel authorizations when no POV has been previously shipped on the sponsor's orders. The member must have a minimum of twelve months remaining on overseas tour at the time the vehicle is delivered to the loading port. If a military spouse delivers the vehicle to the loading port, he or she must have a special power of attorney.

Personally procured transportation moves (do–it–yourself moves) allow you to personally move household goods and collect an incentive payment up to 95 percent of the government's estimate to move your household goods. You can do a personally procured move (PPM) when you have PCS orders, temporary duty assignment, separation or retirement, or assignment to, from, or between government quarters. You can use certain vehicles to move your household goods instead of having the government ship them. You may use this option to move all or a portion of their authorized JFTR weight allowance. All of the details can be found at www.move.mil.

Exceptional Family Member Program rules allow a vehicle to be shipped at the military's expense under certain circumstances.

Transportation Office (TO)

Move.mil is DoD's worldwide moving website. All moving transactions are to be handled through this website. The first thing you should do is to log on and create an account. You will then be prompted to research your allowances and to send a message to your TO. Move.mil is the system that you will use to manage your move. On Move.mil, you will work through your allowances and you can book your shipment, track your shipment, and file claims if necessary for your move. You will also be prompted at the end of the move to fill in a customer satisfaction survey. It is a one-stop, self-help program designed to put you in charge of the shipment and storage process for your personal property.

Alternatively, you can set up an appointment with your TO as soon as you have a copy of your PCS orders. The earlier you call or visit your TO, the greater your chances of moving on your desired date. The counselor will explain your PCS move allowances in detail. He or she will also walk you through the pros and cons of having the government move you or managing the move yourself. If you choose a government move, the counselor will book your shipment and let you know the exact dates the movers will come. If you choose to move yourself, the counselor will give you recommendations and tips for making that personal move as smooth as possible. The TO can also give you information about HHG allowances, shipping a pet, and shipping your POV.

Unaccompanied Baggage (UAB)

If you are moving overseas, your shipment allowance for personal property will probably include a surface shipment and a UAB shipment that will be sent by air. The air shipment is coordinated so that it is available to you when you arrive at your destination. The UAB shipment should include items that you need upon arrival, such as clothes, linens, and baby or medical equipment. You will arrange for the UAB shipment when you arrange for your move either through Move.mil (DoD's self-counseling and shipment management system) or with your local transportation office. Your installation will also have a loan closet available to borrow items you might need when you arrive. This is especially important if you were not authorized a UAB shipment.

Other resources:

- Army—Army Community Service Center
- Air Force—Airman and Family Readiness Center
- Navy—Fleet and Family Support Center
- Marine Corps—Marine Corps Community Services

Moving with Children

Moving is particularly hard on children, especially if they are at school, have made lots of friends, and have favorite teachers. It is important to talk to them as soon as you know you are moving so that you address any fears they may have and get them used to the idea. They may well resent having to move, but spend time with them on the computer exploring your new home area—looking at the schools, attractions, sports facilities, and so on. If possible, try to make a quick visit so that you and they will have a clear idea of where they are moving to.

Get them involved in the planning but try to carry out your family routine as normal so that there is as little disruption as possible. These will help reassure them. Sudden changes to their routine will make them anxious.

Younger children are more able to take a move in their stride because their lives are constantly changing anyhow, but teenagers will need to be handled carefully. As teens they are already going through all sorts of emotional and developmental issues, and this is the last thing they want, especially if they have started dating or just won a place on one of the school's sports teams. Get them involved from day one and keep them involved throughout the process. Many bases run relocation briefings, and it is a good idea to encourage your teenager to attend these with you.

If you have a special-needs child within the Exceptional Family Member Program, you should talk to your advisor or EFMP coordinator so that things are in place on your arrival at your new home—such as the right school, medical specialists, support groups, and so on.

Useful Tips from MilSpouse.com: Preparing for Your Move—After You Arrive by MSM Staff

- Meet the movers at your new home. Supervise unloading until everything is inside.
- Check for damaged or missing belongings (refer to the bill of lading). If anything is missing or damaged, be sure to note this information on the inventory, both your copy and the movers'.
- Celebrate your arrival. Order a pizza. Take a walk in your new neighborhood. If an older relative has moved with you, find a restaurant she would enjoy and take her out for dinner. Help her find social activities she might enjoy at a local senior center, church, or synagogue.
- Spend some time with your family getting to know the new neighborhood. Take your child to a local ice cream shop. Visit the new school when classes aren't in session. Go for walks together. Explore a local park. Arrange play dates with other children who live nearby.
- If possible, unpack your child's things first, together with your child.
- Check your new home for safety. Make sure you have a smoke alarm on each floor, and that you have two exits from each floor in case of fire. Unpack your first-aid kit and make sure everyone knows where it is. Check for local emergency numbers (fire, police, ambulance, poison control) and post them near the phone.
- Transfer your driver's license and vehicle registration after you have settled in.
- If you've moved away from older relatives, make an effort to call or write. Tell them how the move is going and find out how they are.
- Make some time for yourself. This is especially hard when you're unpacking and settling into a new home, but it's as important now as ever. Order takeout food occasionally. Take some time off from unpacking to go for a walk by yourself, read a good book, or rent a movie you've wanted to see.

Military Spouse, "Preparing for Your Move: After You Arrive," www.milspouse.com/article.aspx?id=184&LangType=1033. Used with permission.

Counseling 4

Marriage Counseling

LOVE AND MARRIAGE HAVE BECOME MORE complex in the past few decades as the pressures of daily living take their toll on relationships. The military lifestyle creates additional pressures on couples who may already be struggling with communication and intimacy.

When couples have difficulty resolving these relationship problems, they often turn to family and friends for guidance. If that doesn't work, the next step is to see a marriage counselor. Many military couples seek free and confidential counseling through their Family Support Centers.

Of course, there has to be a commitment on both sides to try to make it work. If one partner doesn't want to go or goes very reluctantly, the counseling is not likely to work.

And don't expect it to be a speedy process. It could have taken many years for your marriage to deteriorate to the level where you need this sort of help, so it may take many sessions, some of them emotionally very painful, before you both understand where things have been going wrong and hopefully, what needs to be done to make things right again.

Counseling works only if you are honest. You both have to speak from the heart, and some of the things said may be hurtful, but if it helps in the healing process, it is all for the good. The sessions alone won't mend your marriage. You both have to put into practice the things you have learned at the sessions and really work at making it work.

Counselors can help couples clarify obstacles and develop solutions to their marital problems. By using some of the tips listed here and other

Relationship counseling is the process of counseling the parties of a relationship in an effort to recognize and to better manage or reconcile troublesome differences and repeating patterns of distress. The relationship involved may be between members of a family or a couple, employees or employers in a workplace, or between a professional and a client.

Couples therapy (or relationship therapy) is a related and different process. It may differ from relationship counseling in duration. Short-term counseling may be between one and three sessions, whereas long-term couples therapy may be between twelve and twenty-four sessions—an exception being brief or solution-focused couples therapy. In addition, counseling tends to be more "here and now," and new coping strategies the outcome. Couples therapy is more about seemingly intractable problems with a relationship history, where emotions are the target and the agent of change.

Marriage counseling or marital therapy can refer to either or some combination of the above.

available resources, many couples have strengthened the quality of the relationships.

Communicate clearly and specifically with each other about expectations, needs, and feelings. Check out assumptions and ask questions to clarify. Many arguments occur as a result of simple misunderstandings that can easily be avoided with clear communication.

Build a strong sense of commitment, trust, honesty, and openness. Keep your promises and be able to count on each other. Be loyal to one another to create a sense of safety and security in the relationship. Accept that conflict is normal. Work toward resolution with a spirit of teamwork rather than as a battle to be won. Negotiation, compromise, and give and take can help create a win–win situation. Respect your partner's right to have a different opinion and agree to disagree when necessary.

Make a point of saying or doing something supportive or affirming for your partner daily. Often the little things are taken for granted over time but are helpful in maintaining a happy relationship. Always be respectful and courteous. Good manners still apply when you are married. Don't interrupt or dominate the discussion. Say "please" and "thank you."

Anger is normal, and how it is expressed is important. Don't attack your partner. Stick to one issue at a time. Begin statements with "I feel . . ." rather than "You always . . ." or "You never . . ."

Make time for sharing and discussing. Maintain respect and give the discussion full attention. Turn off the TV or radio when discussing important issues. Unconditional love and acceptance are important. Whereas some behaviors cannot be tolerated in a healthy marriage, learning to tolerate smaller faults or personality differences can help. Don't try to change your partner into someone they are not.

According to the American Association for Marriage and Family Therapy (AAMFT, www.aamft.org), almost every couple can benefit from some help at times with their marriage. Premarital preparation and marital enrichment programs such as the Prevention and Relationship Enhancement Program (PREP) and the Relationship Enhancement Program are available in many localities, and most people find them helpful regardless of how well their relationship is going. And many people seek couples counseling with a trained therapist to improve their marriages even when their marriages are not unduly distressed. You don't need to be in a distressed marriage to be in marital therapy. Many people with very solid marriages choose this path to enhance their relationships.

Experiencing marital distress, however, represents a different state from the ups and downs of life in marriage that most people experience. In distressed marriages, people feel fundamentally dissatisfied with their marriages. Disappointment in the relationship doesn't just come and go; it is a constant companion. Most frequently, couples with high levels of marital distress fight a good deal, and their fights don't lead to resolution but simply a sense of being worn out. Or they may not fight, but simply feel completely disconnected. People stop doing nice things for each other, they stop communicating, and things tend to go from bad to worse. Frequent arguments that don't get resolved, loss of good feelings, and loss of friendship, sex, and vitality are other signs that a marriage is distressed. Other signs, such as contempt, withdrawal, violence, and a complete loss of connection signal that a marriage is in desperate trouble and that it is at high risk for divorce. And you need not be legally married to have "marital distress." Serious, long-term, committed relationships can experience these kinds of major problems, too.

Sometimes marital problems are purely about aspects of the relationship such as communication, solving problems, arguing, intimacy, and sex. These kinds of problems often begin with partners simply not having a good sense of how to be married and how to communicate and provide support. Other times couples may do well for a while, particularly in the earliest stages of their romance, but they are not ready for the longer-term tasks in marriage. Studies of couples show that while the risks for marital distress and divorce are highest early in marriage, these risks also grow just after the transitions that occur when couples begin to have children and when the children reach adolescence.

Other times, marital problems are directly the result of individual problems, such as substance abuse. And marriages can even seem to be going well, but one shattering event like an extramarital affair will throw a marriage into distress.

Marital distress has powerful effects on partner, often leading to great sadness, worry, a high level of tension, and problems such as depression. If prolonged, it even has been shown to have direct effect on physical health. The effect on families is also profound, especially when conflict is high. Children raised in high-conflict homes tend to have many more problems than other children. And once marriages are distressed, a progression begins that easily becomes a cascade downward, ultimately leading to the ending of a marriage.

The Kinds of Help That Work

The good news is that there are effective treatments for marital distress. Given a willingness to work on a marriage, most people can make their marriages satisfying again.

No one begins as a perfect partner. Marriage depends on a number of skills, such as being able to understand yourself, understand your partner, fight well, problem solve, and negotiate differences. Sometimes patterns we learned in our families growing up aren't effective, but are carried over to a marriage. And sometimes the stresses of life make it difficult to stay happily married.

Treatment for marital distress is in part building or rebuilding the skills that work in marriage, such as learning to communicate and problem solve, and how to fight without engaging in too much hurt. Partly, marital therapy is about partners working to see each other as people, to understand where they are coming from, and to negotiate those differences that can be negotiated and accept those differences that cannot. Couples all have issues that stay with them; the key is to build a process that can help find a way to talk about those issues, to find solutions, and not have the problems that emerge in life become overwhelming.

Couples therapists have special training. They know how to help couples have a sense of progress even as they struggle with difficult issues. There are many kinds of effective couples therapy. Some promote skills and practice, others look more at the past and how things got this way; most combine the two. If you have a marital problem, call a couples therapist and make an appointment. Finding a couples therapist is easy, but use caution. Be sure the person has specific experience in couples therapy, as marriage and family therapists do.

Beginning couples therapy is not easy. For most people, it's hard to begin to share with a person you don't know about marital difficulties, and it's hard not to be discouraged as you argue about these issues at first in front of a therapist. Couples with marital distress are often discouraged and have trouble believing that couples therapy can help. But couples who begin marital therapy begin to create a process for overcoming their difficulties. Sometimes the resolution of problems happens very quickly, though more typically a longer period is needed. For most, it's hard to work on these problems at first, but ultimately that becomes easier and problems are resolved.

What Should You Do If Your Partner Won't Go to Therapy?

Some people with marital problems won't seek help even when it is essential. If your partner won't go to therapy, try to encourage him or her. It's hard to fix a distressed marriage on your own. Still, if your partner won't go, you can begin to do some things yourself. A marriage and family therapist is likely to have some useful ideas about how to improve the relationship without both of you getting into therapy and about how to find better ways to approach your partner about the idea of entering treatment together.

It is important to honestly explore feelings—both yours and your partner's—about how various issues impact your overall family generally and your marriage specifically. Until you do this and come to some conclusions, you cannot move on.

Explore these issues within the context of your family of origin:

- Expressing anger
- Showing affection
- Spending money
- Male or female roles
- Education
- Dealing with crises
- Things important to mother
- Things important to father

Discuss these values within *your* marriage:

- Time—alone, with others, and as a couple
- Careers and education
- Housecleaning and home maintenance
- Money—save/spend; how to prioritize
- Sexuality—frequency; inside/outside the marriage

- Parenting issues
- Spirituality—church/other organizations
- In-laws

Communication Skills Assessment

Read each statement and decide if it applies to you 51 percent of the time. Give yourself a point for each skill you use 51 percent of the time or more.

Positive Communication Skills

☐ I repeat back what others say.
☐ I express my feelings about an issue.
☐ I tell others what I want to happen when discussing an issue.
☐ I acknowledge what another person is feeling or thinking about an issue.
☐ I encourage others to explain their point of view.
☐ I ask what another person is thinking, feeling, and wanting during a discussion.
☐ I propose a good time and place to discuss important issues.
☐ I summarize the messages I receive to ensure accuracy.
☐ I settle a conflict by compromising—trading something for something.
☐ I work to resolve problems by building agreements.
☐ I have pleasant, fun conversations.
☐ I explore possible causes of a problem.
☐ I brainstorm solutions to problems.
☐ I send clear, complete, and straightforward messages.
_____ Total Score

Negative Communication Skills

☐ I often put words into someone's mouth.
☐ I listen briefly, and then begin talking.
☐ I avoid talking about some subjects.
☐ I force decisions on others.
☐ I give in to others' decisions even when it is not required.
☐ I talk about problems but leave them unresolved.
☐ I direct or instruct others even when it is not required.
☐ I argue and fight.
☐ I directly blame or verbally attack others.
☐ I make indirect, spiteful, and undercutting remarks.
_____ Total Score

Add up the number of boxes you check for both positive and negative communication skills. Hopefully, you checked more positive communication skills than negative.

Substance Abuse

Dependence on alcohol and drugs is our most serious national public health problem. It is prevalent among rich and poor, in all regions of the country, and all ethnic and social groups.

Millions of Americans misuse or are dependent on alcohol or drugs. Most of them have families who suffer the consequences, often serious, of living with this illness. If there is alcohol or drug dependence in your family, remember you are not alone.

Most individuals who abuse alcohol or drugs have jobs and are productive members of society creating a false hope in the family that "it's not that bad."

The problem is that addiction tends to worsen over time, hurting both the addicted person and all the family members. It is especially damaging to young children and adolescents.

People with this illness really may believe that they drink normally or that "everyone" takes drugs. These false beliefs are called denial; this denial is a part of the illness.

Drug or alcohol dependence disorders are medical conditions that can be effectively treated. Millions of Americans and their families are in healthy recovery from this disease.

Resources

The following websites have advice and guidelines on confidential counseling:

www.militaryonesource.com
www.tricare.mil
CREDO—the Chaplains Religious Enrichment Development Operation—runs enrichment and relationship courses; you can get information from the base chaplain.
The FOCUS Project (Families Overcoming Under Stress) is a resiliency-training program for military families and children to help them meet the challenges of combat operational stress during wartime. Resiliency is the ability to effectively cope with, adapt to, and overcome adversity, stress, and challenging experiences. www.focusproject.org

Substance Abuse and the Military

Substance abuse is a growing problem in the military because of the tremendous strains both on military personnel themselves and their families.

Some have experienced devastating consequences, including family disintegration, mental health disorders, and even suicide. Research conducted by RAND has shown that 25 to 30 percent of Iraq and Afghanistan war veterans have reported symptoms of a mental disorder or cognitive impairment. Posttraumatic stress disorder (PTSD) is the most common, and traumatic brain injury may be a causal factor in some reported symptoms. Although less common, substance use is also a large concern, with aggregated data from the Substance Abuse and Mental Health Services Administration's annual household survey revealing that from 2004 to 2006, 7.1 percent of veterans (an estimated 1.8 million persons eighteen or older) met criteria for a past-year substance use disorder.

Problems with alcohol and nicotine abuse are the most prevalent and pose a significant risk to the health of veterans as well as to reserve component and National Guard soldiers. At greatest risk are deployed personnel with combat exposures, as they are more apt to engage in new-onset heavy weekly drinking, binge drinking, and to suffer alcohol-related problems, as well as smoking initiation and relapse. Within this group, reserve and National Guard personnel and younger service members are particularly vulnerable to subsequent drinking problems. And although alcohol problems are frequently reported among veterans, few are referred to alcohol treatment.

The military today have a number of things working against them, causing them to return home addicted to drugs or alcohol or suffering from mental illness. The military today regularly prescribes medication to help ease stress and anxiety, to help with physical pain, or to keep them alert when they need to be. These kinds of prescription drugs, while they might be necessary in a war situation, become addicting, and on return to normal life, soldiers can't do without them. Many other members of the military are self-medicating and becoming addicted in the process.

To gain a fuller understanding of these burgeoning issues, the Millennium Cohort Study—the largest prospective study in military history—is following a representative sample of U.S. military personnel from 2001 to 2022. Early findings highlight the importance of prevention in this group, given the long-term effects of combat-related problems and the ensuing difficulties experienced in seeking or being referred to treatment, likely because of stigma and other real and perceived barriers. To fill this need, a host of government agencies, researchers, public health entities, and others are working together to adapt and test proven prevention interventions, as well as drug abuse treatments, for potential use with military and veteran populations and their families.

To address the social problems both caused by and contributing to drug use, the Department of Defense (DoD) and partners are developing and testing novel treatment approaches with veterans. For example, Rosen's Money Management Intervention trains those in drug treatment to better manage their money by linking access to funds to treatment goal completion. For relapse prevention, McKay's telephone treatment approach delivers counseling at home for several months once a veteran has completed an initial face-to-face treatment episode.

While NIDA is striving to expand its portfolio of research related to trauma, stress, and substance use and abuse among veterans and their families, a number of promising projects are already being funded. These include studies on smoking cessation and PTSD, behavioral interventions for the dually diagnosed, substance use and HIV progression, and virtual reality treatment of PTSD and substance abuse. Additionally, NIDA's National Drug Abuse Treatment Clinical Trials Network (CTN) is developing, in conjunction with researchers from the Veterans Administration, a protocol concept on the treatment of PTSD/SUD in veteran populations.

Further, efforts are under way to make it easier for veterans to access treatments. Research on drug courts, for example, is now being applied to developing courts for veterans, the former having demonstrated their effectiveness in addressing nonviolent crimes by drug abusers and ushering them into needed treatment instead of prison. Because the criminal justice system is a frequent treatment referral source for veterans, such specialized courts may give them the opportunity to access the services and support they may not otherwise receive. While New York has the only court that exclusively handles nonviolent crimes committed by veterans, other states are considering establishing such courts.

If someone close to you misuses alcohol or drugs, the first step is to be honest about the problem and to seek help for yourself, your family, and your loved one.

Treatment can occur in a variety of settings, in many different forms, and for different lengths of time. Stopping the alcohol or drug use is the first step to recovery, and most people need help to stop. Often a person with alcohol or drug dependence will need treatment provided by professionals just as with other diseases. Your doctor may be able to guide you.

Warning Signs

Not all drinking is harmful, and moderate drinking (such as an occasional glass of red wine) might even be good for you. However, at-risk or heavy drinkers can face serious risks unless they take action.

INJURIES Drinking too much increases your chances of being injured or even killed. Alcohol is a factor, for example, in about 60 percent of fatal burn injuries, drowning, and homicides; 50 percent of severe trauma injuries and sexual assaults; and 40 percent of fatal motor vehicle crashes, suicides, and fatal falls.

HEALTH PROBLEMS Heavy drinkers have a greater risk of liver disease, heart disease, sleep disorders, depression, stroke, bleeding from the stomach, sexually transmitted infections from unsafe sex, and several types of cancer. They may also have problems managing diabetes, high blood pressure, and other conditions.

BIRTH DEFECTS Drinking during pregnancy can cause brain damage and other serious problems in the baby. Because it is not yet known whether any amount of alcohol is safe for a developing baby, women who are pregnant or may become pregnant should not drink.

Alcohol Use Disorders

Generally known as alcoholism and alcohol abuse, alcohol use disorders are medical conditions that doctors can diagnose when a patient's drinking causes distress or harm. In the United States, about 18 million people have an alcohol use disorder.

See if you recognize any of these symptoms in yourself or a loved one.

- In the past year, have you had times when you ended up drinking more, or longer, than you intended?
- More than once wanted to cut down or stop drinking, or tried to, but couldn't?
- More than once gotten into situations while or after drinking that increased your chances of getting hurt (such as driving, swimming, using machinery, walking in a dangerous area, or having unsafe sex)?
- Had to drink much more than you once did to get the effect you want? Or found that your usual number of drinks had much less effect than before?

- Continued to drink even though it was making you feel depressed or anxious or adding to another health problem? Or after having had a memory blackout?
- Spent a lot of time drinking? Or being sick or getting over other aftereffects?
- Continued to drink even though it was causing trouble with your family or friends?
- Found that drinking—or being sick from drinking—often interfered with taking care of your home or family? Or caused job troubles?
- Given up or cut back on activities that were important or interesting to you, or gave you pleasure, in order to drink?
- More than once gotten arrested, been held at a police station, or had other legal problems because of your drinking?
- Found that when the effects of alcohol were wearing off, you had withdrawal symptoms, such as trouble sleeping, shakiness, restlessness, nausea, sweating, a racing heart, or a seizure? Or sensed things that were not there?

If you or a loved one has any symptoms, then alcohol may already be a cause for concern. The more symptoms you have, the more urgent the need for change. A health professional can look at the number, pattern, and severity of symptoms to see whether an alcohol use disorder is present and help you decide the best course of action.

Alcoholism is chronic alcohol abuse that results in a physical dependence on alcohol and an inability to stop or limit drinking.

Family Intervention

Getting a loved one to agree to accept help and finding support services for all family members are the first steps toward healing for the addicted person and the entire family.

When an addicted person is reluctant to seek help, sometimes family members, friends, and associates come together out of concern and love, to confront the problem drinker. They strongly urge the person to enter treatment and list the serious consequences of not doing so, such as family breakup or job loss.

This is called "intervention." When carefully prepared and done with the guidance of a competent, trained specialist, the family, friends, and associates are usually able to convince their loved one—in a firm and loving manner—that the only choice is to accept help and begin the road to recovery.

People with alcohol or drug dependence problems can and do recover. Intervention is often the first step.

Children in families experiencing alcohol or drug abuse need attention, guidance, and support. They may be growing up in homes in which the problems are either denied or covered up.

These children need to have their experiences validated. They also need safe, reliable adults in whom to confide and who will support them, reassure them, and provide them with appropriate help for their age. They need to have fun and just be kids.

Families with alcohol and drug problems usually have high levels of stress and confusion. High-stress family environments are a risk factor for early and dangerous substance use, as well as mental and physical health problems.

It is important to talk honestly with children about what is happening in the family and to help them express their concerns and feelings. Children need to trust the adults in their lives and to believe that they will support them.

Children living with alcohol or drug abuse in the family can benefit from participating in educational support groups in their school student assistance programs. Those aged eleven and older can join Alateen groups, which meet in community settings and provide healthy connections with others coping with similar issues. Being associated with the activities of a faith community can also help.

If you're considering changing your drinking, you'll need to decide whether to cut down or to quit. It's a good idea to discuss different options with a doctor, a friend, or someone else you trust. Quitting is strongly advised if you try cutting down but cannot stay within the limits you set, have had an alcohol use disorder, or now have symptoms.

Help is available on base and in your local community. Look in the Yellow Pages under "alcoholism" for treatment programs and self-help groups. Call your county health department and ask for licensed treatment programs in your community. Keep trying until you find the right help for your loved one, yourself, and your family. Ask a family therapist for a referral to a trained interventionist, or call the Intervention Resource Center at 1-888-421-4321.

Self-Help Groups

Al-Anon Family Groups
www.al-anon.org
Alateen

www.alateen.org
Alcoholics Anonymous
www.aa.org
Adult Children of Alcoholics
www.adultchildren.org

Drugs

Each year, drug and alcohol abuse contributes to the death of more than 120,000 Americans. According to the Office of National Drug Control Policy, drugs and alcohol cost taxpayers more than $328 billion annually in preventable health care costs, extra law enforcement, auto crashes, crime, and lost productivity.

Drug abuse is the use of drugs to get "high." It is a voluntary act unlike drug addiction, which is involuntary. The addict is not able to stop using drugs unless there is intervention. Like alcoholism, drug addiction is a disease for which there is no cure.

Drug addiction can occur extremely easily and very quickly, leaving the addict suffering from the severe effects of the drugs and strong withdrawal effects if he or she does not take the drug. In order to cease the addiction a lot of support, help, and willpower is needed from both the addict and those around him or her.

The physical signs of a drug addiction can be quite varied depending on the drug used, the amount taken, and the environment in which it is taken. The early signs of a drug addiction can include mixed moods, sleepiness or excessive or unusual tiredness during the day, agitation, and paranoia. As the dependency develops, the signs can change to being frequently distracted, depression, mixed mental states including psychosis, and a decrease in the ability to coordinate or perform tasks that are normally easy to complete. The degree of effect is variable between users and also on the substance of choice. Other very obvious signs are needle marks on the arms (though these can appear on other areas of the body once the veins in the arms have deteriorated and cannot be used any longer), but this only occurs in those who have been injecting the drugs. People who are normally nonsmokers are likely to suffer from breathlessness or coughing if they have been smoking drugs for long periods.

Although they are cheaper than they were a few decades ago, drugs are still an expensive commodity, and most users struggle to keep up financially with their demand for their habit.

Quitting Techniques

Several proven treatment approaches are available. One size doesn't fit all, however. It's a good idea to do some homework on the Internet or at the library to find social and professional support options that appeal to you, as you are more likely to stick with them (see also the resources section). Chances are excellent that you'll pull together an approach that works for you.

Social Support
One potential challenge when people stop drinking is rebuilding a life without alcohol. It may be important to educate family and friends, develop new interests and social groups, and find rewarding ways to spend your time that don't involve alcohol. Ask for help from others. When asking for support from friends or significant others, be specific. This could include not offering you alcohol, not using alcohol around you, giving words of support and withholding criticism, not asking you to take on new demands right now, or going to a group like Al-Anon. Consider joining Alcoholics Anonymous or another mutual support group (see Resources). Recovering people who attend groups regularly do better than those who do not. Groups can vary widely, so shop around for one that's comfortable. You'll get more out of it if you become actively involved by having a sponsor and reaching out to other members for assistance.

Professional Support
Advances in the treatment of alcoholism mean that patients now have more choices and health professionals have more tools to help.

Medications to Treat Alcoholism
Newer medications can make it easier to quit drinking by offsetting changes in the brain caused by alcoholism. These options (naltrexone, topiramate, and acamprosate) don't make you sick if you drink, as does an older medication (disulfiram). None of these medications are addictive, so it's fine to combine them with support groups or alcohol counseling. A major clinical trial recently showed that patients can now receive effective alcohol treatment from their primary care doctors or mental health practitioners by combining the newer medications with a series of brief office visits for support. See Resources for more information.

Alcohol Counseling

"Talk therapy" also works well. Several counseling approaches are about equally effective—twelve-step, cognitive-behavioral, motivational enhancement, or a combination. Getting help in itself appears to be more important than the particular approach used, as long as it offers empathy, avoids heavy confrontation, strengthens motivation, and provides concrete ways to change drinking behavior.

Specialized, Intensive Treatment Programs

Some people will need more intensive programs. If you need a referral to a program, ask your doctor.

As the drug addiction develops, the person is likely to become isolated from their usual family and friends and may get quite agitated when approached about this.

What Happens to Your Brain When You Take Drugs?

Drugs are chemicals that tap into the brain's communication system and disrupt the way nerve cells normally send, receive, and process information. Drugs are able to do this in at least two ways: (1) by imitating the brain's natural chemical messengers and/or (2) by overstimulating the "reward circuit" of the brain.

Some drugs, such as marijuana and heroin, have a similar structure to chemical messengers, called neurotransmitters, that are naturally produced by the brain. Because of this similarity, these drugs are able to "fool" the brain's receptors and activate nerve cells to send abnormal messages.

Other drugs, such as cocaine or methamphetamine, can cause the nerve cells to release abnormally large amounts of natural neurotransmitters, or prevent the normal recycling of these brain chemicals, which is needed to shut off the signal between neurons. This disruption produces a greatly amplified message that ultimately disrupts normal communication patterns.

Nearly all drugs, directly or indirectly, target the brain's reward system by flooding the circuit with dopamine. Dopamine is a neurotransmitter present in regions of the brain that control movement, emotion, motivation, and feelings of pleasure. The overstimulation of this system, which normally responds to natural behaviors that are linked to survival (eating, spending time with loved ones, etc.), produces euphoric effects in response to the drugs. This reaction sets in motion a pattern that "teaches" people to repeat the behavior of abusing drugs.

As a person continues to abuse drugs, the brain adapts to the over-whelming surges in dopamine by producing less dopamine or by reducing the number of dopamine receptors in the reward circuit. As a result, dopamine's impact on the reward circuit is lessened, reducing the abuser's ability to enjoy the drugs and the things that previously brought pleasure. This decrease compels those addicted to drugs to keep abusing drugs in order to attempt to bring their dopamine function back to normal. And, they may now require larger amounts of the drug than they first did to achieve the dopamine high—an effect known as tolerance.

Long-term abuse causes changes in other brain chemical systems and circuits as well. Glutamate is a neurotransmitter that influences the reward circuit and the ability to learn. When the optimal concentration of glutamate is altered by drug abuse, the brain attempts to compensate, which can impair cognitive function. Drugs of abuse facilitate nonconscious (conditioned) learning, which leads the user to experience uncontrollable cravings when they see a place or person they associate with the drug experience, even when the drug itself is not available. Brain imaging studies of drug-addicted individuals show changes in areas of the brain that are critical to judgment, decision making, learning and memory, and behavior control. Together, these changes can drive an abuser to seek out and take drugs compulsively despite adverse consequences—in other words, to become addicted to drugs.

Why Do Some People Become Addicted, While Others Do Not?

No single factor can predict whether a person will become addicted to drugs. Risk for addiction is influenced by a person's biology, social environment, and age or stage of development. The more risk factors an individual has, the greater the chance that taking drugs can lead to addiction. For example:

Biology. The genes that people are born with—in combination with environmental influences—account for about half of their addiction vulnerability. Additionally, gender, ethnicity, and the presence of other mental disorders may influence risk for drug abuse and addiction.

Environment. A person's environment includes many different influences—from family and friends to socioeconomic status and quality of life in general. Factors such as peer pressure, physical and sexual abuse, stress, and parental involvement can greatly influence the course of drug abuse and addiction in a person's life.

Development. Genetic and environmental factors interact with critical developmental stages in a person's life to affect addiction vulnerability, and adolescents experience a double challenge. Although taking drugs at any age can lead to addiction, the earlier that drug use begins, the more likely it is to progress to more serious abuse. And because adolescents' brains are still developing in the areas that govern decision making, judgment, and self-control, they are especially prone to risk-taking behaviors, including trying drugs of abuse.

Treatments

Before deciding on a program of drug treatment and support, the individual must be able to admit he or she has an addiction and actually wants to overcome it. Positive thinking, willpower, and determination are fundamental to the success of following a drug treatment plan.

Consideration should be given to whether a support group, individual counseling, or a combination of both will be beneficial. These types of therapy are useful, as the therapists know what addiction is about, will help you to determine the cause, and will have a vast amount of advice regarding craving control, managing withdrawal, and restructuring life without the addiction.

Find out about help lines and when they can be accessed, who runs them, and what can be offered using them. Keep the list in close proximity at all times during the initial period of withdrawal and use these help lines when cravings are becoming too strong or anxieties are building up.

Allow for the "cold turkey" period. Warn family and close friends of what is happening and explain that it may cause distress to all those concerned. Exercise helps to ease symptoms of withdrawal, so plan an exercise regime.

Overcoming an addiction is a very individual experience, and a wide variety of resources may be needed to help break the drug addiction.

Anger Management

Violence

Domestic violence happens so much in the military that the DoD has made it an item of specific concern. First sergeants and military police hate domestic call-outs because the solutions are never clear cut. More often than not, the victims of domestic violence refuse to cooperate because they perceive a threat to their spouse's career.

In most cases, husbands abuse wives, but that's not always true. If the abuser is a civilian, the military has no control over the matter. In most cases, all the military can do is turn the information over the civilian authorities. Installation commanders do have the power to bar civilians from military installations, and will exercise that power to protect military members from abusive civilian spouses, if necessary.

If the abuser is a military member, domestic violence situations are handled on two separate tracks: the military justice system and the Family Advocacy system. It's important to realize that these are two separate systems, not connected. Family advocacy is an identification, intervention, and treatment program—not a punishment system. It's entirely possible that the Family Advocacy Committee will return a finding of "substantiated abuse," but there will be insufficient legally admissible evidence to allow punishment under the provisions of military justice.

On the other hand, one should realize that the Family Advocacy system does not enjoy the right of "confidentiality" under military law (such as chaplains and attorneys), and evidence gathered and statements made during Family Advocacy investigations may be used in military justice proceedings.

If the incident(s) happen off base, civilian agencies may be given jurisdiction on the legal side, but Family Advocacy should still be notified. Off base, local police may or may not report the incident to base officials. DoD officials are currently working to develop memoranda of understanding with civilian law enforcement authorities to establish such reporting procedures.

Regulations require military and DoD officials to report any suspicion of family violence to Family Advocacy, no matter how small. This includes commanders, first sergeants, supervisors, medical personnel, teachers, and military police.

In many cases, when responding to a domestic situation, the commander or first sergeant will order the military individual to reside in the dormitory/barracks until the Family Advocacy investigation is completed. This may be accompanied by a "military protective order," which is a written order prohibiting the military member from having any contact with the alleged victim. Many bases have an "abused dependent safeguard" system, where the first sergeant or commander can place the family members in billeting under an assumed name.

When domestic violence is reported to Family Advocacy, the agency will assign a caseworker to assess the victim's safety, develop a safety plan, and investigate the incident. Throughout the process, victims' advocates ensure that the victim's medical, mental health, and protection needs are being met. Family Advocacy officials will also interview the alleged abuser. The alleged abuser is informed of his or her rights under the provisions of

Article 31 of the UCMJ, and does not have to speak to the investigation officials if he or she chooses not to.

If child abuse is involved, regulations require that local child protection agencies be notified and participate in the process.

After the investigation, the case is then presented to a multidisciplinary case review committee with representatives from the Family Advocacy Program, law enforcement, staff judge advocate, medical staff, and chaplain. The committee decides whether the evidence indicates abuse occurred and arrives at one of the following findings:

Substantiated. A case that has been investigated and the preponderance of available information indicates that abuse has occurred. This means that the information that supports the occurrence of abuse is of greater weight or more convincing than the information that indicates that abuse did not occur.

Suspected. A case determination is pending further investigation. Duration for a case to be "suspected" and under investigation should not exceed twelve weeks.

Unsubstantiated. An alleged case that has been investigated and the available information is insufficient to support the claim that child abuse and/or neglect or spouse abuse did occur. The family needs no family advocacy services.

In making these determinations, the committee uses the following definitions for abuse:

Child abuse and/or neglect. Includes physical injury, sexual maltreatment, emotional maltreatment, deprivation of necessities, or combinations for a child by an individual responsible for the child's welfare under circumstances indicating that the child's welfare is harmed or threatened. The term encompasses both acts and omissions on the part of a responsible person. A "child" is a person under eighteen years of age for whom a parent, guardian, foster parent, caretaker, employee of a residential facility, or any staff person providing out-of-home care is legally responsible. The term "child" means a natural child, adopted child, stepchild, foster child, or ward. The term also includes an individual of any age who is incapable of self-support because of a mental or physical incapacity and for whom treatment in a military treatment facility is authorized.

Spouse abuse. Includes assault, battery, threat to injure or kill, other act of force or violence, or emotional maltreatment inflicted on a partner in a lawful marriage when one of the partners is a military member or is employed by the DoD and is eligible for treatment in an MTF. A spouse under eighteen years of age shall be treated in this category.

Based on the committee's recommendations, the commander decides what action to take regarding the abuser. The commander determines whether to order the individual into treatment and/or to seek to impose disciplinary procedures under the Uniform Code of Military Justice. The commander may also seek to obtain the discharge of the service member from the military.

Victims often hesitate to report abuse because they fear the impact it will have on their spouse's career. A recent DoD study found that service members reported for abuse are 23 percent more likely to be separated from the service than nonabusers and somewhat more likely to have other than honorable discharges. The majority who remain in the military are more likely to be promoted more slowly than nonabusers.

Many military spouses don't know that federal law gives financial protection to the spouse if the member is discharged for an offense which *"involves abuse of the then-current spouse or a dependent child."* It doesn't matter if the discharge is a punitive discharge imposed by a court-martial or an administrative discharge initiated by the commander. The key is that the reason for the discharge must be for a "dependent abuse" offense.

The term "involves abuse of the then-current spouse or a dependent child" means that the criminal offense is against the person of that spouse or a dependent child. Crimes that may qualify as "dependent-abuse offenses" are ones such as sexual assault, rape, sodomy, assault, battery, murder, and manslaughter.

You can check to see what the current authorized payment is. If the spouse has custody of a dependent child or children of the member, the amount of monthly compensation is increased for each child. If there is no eligible spouse, compensation paid to a dependent child or children is paid in equal shares to each child.

The duration of the payments cannot exceed thirty-six months. If the military member had less than thirty-six months of obligated military service at the time of the discharge or imposition of the court-martial sentence, then the duration of the payments will be the length of the member's obligated service, or twelve months, whichever is greater.

If a spouse receiving payments remarries, payments terminate as of the date of the remarriage. Payment shall not be renewed if such remarriage is terminated. If the payments to the spouse terminate due to remarriage and there is a dependent child not living in the same household as the spouse or member, payments shall be made to the dependent child.

If the military member who committed the abuse resides in the same household as the spouse or dependent child to whom compensation is otherwise payable, payment shall terminate as of the date the member begins residing in such household.

If the victim was a dependent child, and the spouse has been found by competent authority designated by the secretary concerned to have been an active participant in the conduct constituting the criminal offense or to have actively aided or abetted the member in such conduct against that dependent child, the spouse, or a dependent child living with the spouse, shall not be paid transitional compensation.

In addition to the transitional benefits, if the military member was eligible for retirement and was denied retirement because of the criminal offense, the spouse can still apply to a divorce court for a division of retired pay under the provisions of the Uniformed Services Former Spouse Protection Act, and the military will honor the payments. (*Note:* Under this provision, such payments terminate upon remarriage.)

Even if a domestic violence case is handled off base via the civilian criminal court system, criminal conviction of even a misdemeanor involving domestic violence can end a service member's military career. The 1996 Lautenberg Amendment to the Gun Control Act of 1968 makes it unlawful for anyone who has been convicted of a misdemeanor of domestic violence to possess firearms. The law applies to law enforcement officers and military personnel.

Stress

Recognizing the stresses military life and multiple deployments put on families, the services are stepping up their efforts to help their members strengthen their family relationships and avoid the divorce courts.

A full range of outreach programs—from support groups for spouses of deployed troops to weekend retreats for military couples—aims to help military families endure the hardships that military life often imposes.

Specific service-by-service statistics about divorce rates within the military weren't available, but the rates for the Army give a snapshot of what are believed to be a military-wide trend.

Army officials reported 10,477 divorces among the active duty force in fiscal 2004, a number that's climbed steadily over the past five years. In fiscal 2003, the Army reported fewer than 7,500 divorces; in 2002, just over 7,000, and in 2001, about 5,600.

During the past two years, the divorce rate has been higher among Army officers than their enlisted counterparts, reversing the previous trend, officials said. In fiscal 2003, the Army reported almost 1,900 divorces among its 56,000 married officers. The following year, that number jumped to more than 3,300—an increase of almost 1,500.

These statistics reflect a general trend in American society, Army chaplain (Col.) Glen Bloomstrom, director of ministry initiatives for the Army's Office of the Chief of Chaplains, pointed out. Bloomstrom commented that 45 to 50 percent of all first marriages end in divorce nationwide, and the failure rate is even higher for second marriages: a whopping 60 to 70 percent.

Divorce rates run even higher in specific occupations, particularly those that expose people to traumatic events and danger, as well as heavy responsibilities and public scrutiny, Army officials noted. Police officers, for example, face a divorce rates averaging between 66 and 75 percent, they said.

Despite the nationwide trends, Bloomstrom was quick to point out that the numbers represent far more than just statistics. "These are people we're talking about," he said. "When a marriage ends, it's the end of a dream."

The toll goes beyond the human side and affects military operations as well, he said. Service members in happy marriages tend to be more focused on their jobs and less likely to become disciplinary problems, Bloomstrom said. They're also more likely to remain in the military.

To help reverse the statistics, the services have introduced new programs and pumped up existing ones, offered through their family support, chaplain, and mental-health counseling networks.

For example, the Army's offerings include:

- The new Deployment Cycle Support Program, which includes briefings for service members on how their absence and return may affect their family relationships and how they can cope with the inevitable changes
- A family support group system that provides both practical and emotional support for spouses of deployed service members
- The Building Strong and Ready Families Program, a two-day program that helps couples develop better communication skills, reinforced by a weekend retreat
- The Strong Bonds marriage education program that focuses specifically on issues that affect Reserve and National Guard couples
- The Pick a Partner program that helps single soldiers make wise decisions when they choose mates

The Army is not alone in offering programs to help its families survive the rigors of deployments and strengthen their relationships in the process.

The Marine Corps' Prevention and Relationship Enhancement Program is a two-day workshop that teaches couples how to manage conflict, solve problems, communicate effectively, and preserve and enhance their commitment and friendship, Marine officials said.

Participants begin the program by taking a marriage survey, developed by a retired Navy chaplain, to help them evaluate their relationship and identify problems before they become serious. The four top problems generally involve communication, children and parenting, money, and sexual intimacy, according to a Navy chaplain involved in the program.

The Marine Corps program focused on what the chaplain calls "the mother lode of all issues" that can affect marriages: communication. "If you don't have good communication skills, you can't talk about the rest of the issues," he said.

The Navy has a similar program in its Marriage Enrichment Retreat. This weekend getaway is designed to give Navy couples the tools they need to help strengthen their marriages, according to Rachelle Logan, public affairs director for Navy Installations Command.

Participants begin the weekend session by getting a profile of their personalities, then attending sessions on marital communication, personality and family dynamics, and problems associated with military separation, Logan said.

While the Air Force does not have service-wide marital support programs, Air Force officials said individual bases offer a wide variety of programs to support military families and help them through separations, deployments, and the stresses relating to them.

Bloomstrom said he's optimistic about the emphasis the military services are putting on programs for married service members.

The goal, he said, is to help couples recognize and address danger signs before they escalate.

Another objective is to help military couples get more satisfaction out of their marriages by injecting a healthy dose of "fun and friendship" that he said builds up their "emotional bank account."

"We're talking about investing in the relationship in the good times," he said. "That way, when you have to make a withdrawal—as you do during a deployment—you still have enough left in the bank to cover it."

Stress is a response to signals called *stressors* that your brain interprets as a call to prepare for action. Adrenaline and stress hormones are released to activate your body ("fight or flight") and affect your actions, your thoughts, and your emotions. Stress helps to protect you, but it can be unhealthy if it continues for a long time. Too much stress can also interfere with your performance. Stress-related physical changes include:

- Increased blood pressure and heart rate
- Rapid breathing
- Sweating
- Stomach muscles contracting, causing "butterflies," cramps, diarrhea
- Muscle tension

Potential long-term effects of chronic stress include:

- Hypertension (high blood pressure)
- Heart disease
- Immune system suppression
- Increased risk for infectious disease
- Gastrointestinal disorders such as colitis
- Asthma
- Mental health problems

Quick Stress-Reduction Techniques

When you feel stressed, your breathing becomes fast and shallow and your muscles get tense. You can interrupt the stress response by:

- slowing your breathing and taking deep, slow breaths from your belly
- relaxing your muscles (e.g., by tensing and releasing muscles throughout your body)
- mental reframing

Everyone has a stream of private thoughts running through their minds. This is called *self-talk*. These thoughts reflect your beliefs and attitudes about the world, other people, and yourself, and they may be adding to your stress. To interrupt the automatic thought process:

- Become aware—monitor your thoughts and self-talk.
- Recognize that thoughts cause feelings and motivate behavior.

There is rarely a direct link between the stressful situation and your response. In fact, it's usually not the event or situation that leads to a stress reaction; *it's your interpretation of the event or situation* that causes you to respond in various ways.

The sequence of events that leads to feelings and behaviors in response to stressors is called the ***ABCs***:

- You experience the *Activating* event.
- Your *Beliefs* about the event lead to an interpretation of the event.
- Your interpretation of the event either increases or decreases the stress you feel—the *Consequences*.

A (*Activating* event) + *B* (*Beliefs*) = *C* (*Consequences*)

Check your thoughts and self-talk for these stress-promoting thinking patterns:

All-or-nothing thinking. Judging things as being all good or all bad, usually based on a single factor.

Exaggeration. Blowing the negative consequences of a situation or event way out of proportion.

Overgeneralization. Drawing conclusions about your whole life based on the negative outcome of a single incident.

Mind-reading. Believing you know what another person or group of people is thinking about you (usually bad) when you have no evidence.

Challenge your negative thoughts and self-talk by asking yourself whether there is evidence to support the way you are perceiving the situation.

Replace negative or stressful self-talk with more positive, useful, and realistic self-talk. Example: While on leave, you decide to take the bus to go visit your family and get stuck in traffic due to road construction. Change *negative self-talk* ("This will take forever. I will never get home. Why does this always happen to me?") to *positive and useful self-talk* ("I'm glad they are fixing this road. I can take this time to relax and listen to some music I enjoy.").

Controlling the Source of Stress by Solving Problems

Take action over stressors that you can control (your own habits, behavior, environment, relationships) by using the problem-solving process:

Step 1: Define the problem.

Step 2: Set a goal (for example, what would you like to see happen?).

Step 3: Brainstorm possible solutions.

Step 4: Evaluate the pros and cons of various possible solutions.

Step 5: Choose the best solution (weigh the pros and cons).

Step 6: Make a plan to implement the solution and try it!

Step 7: Assess how well it went.

Step 8: If the first solution doesn't work, try others.

If a Source of Stress Is beyond Your Control

Try an activity to distract or soothe yourself:

- Listen to music.
- Get together with a friend.
- Read a good book or watch a movie.
- Engage in physical exercise.
- Consider spiritual activity such as prayer.
- Perform yoga.
- Use humor (jokes or funny movies).
- Meditate.
- Take a nap.
- Write in a journal or diary.
- Take a hot bath or shower.
- Help others in need.
- Express your stress creatively.
- Take a "mental holiday."

Plan for Future Stressful Events

- *Create* a personalized "Stress Toolkit" by making a list of coping strategies that work for you when you're stressed, including deep breathing, muscle relaxation, and activities that you find soothing.
- *Visualize* potential future stressful situations.
- *Determine* if you will have some control in the situation.
- *Decide* how you will use the problem-solving process to reduce stressors.
- *Plan* to use various helpful activities to reduce the stress response.
- *Remember* to include friends and family for support.

Depression

Service members and their families experience unique emotional challenges.

Deployment and redeployment, single parenting, and long absences of loved ones are a stressful part of military life. At times, these events can lead to sadness, feelings of hopelessness, and withdrawal from friends, families, and colleagues. Parenting can feel more a burden than a joy. We may feel irritable and even neglectful of our children's needs. When these feelings and behaviors appear, depression may be present. Seeking care for depression, for ourselves or loved ones, takes energy and courage.

Depression is one of the most common and treatable mental disorders. Delay in identifying depression often leads to needless suffering for the depressed individual and his or her family. Depression is not uncommon during or after the holiday season. Preparing for the holidays, the increased expectations of family and friends, the sadness of not having a loved one present, or having to say good-bye after a holiday reunion can contribute to depression.

Depression is very treatable. Depression can be a part of chronic fatigue or unexplained aches and pains. The earlier depression is detected and treated, the less likely it is to develop into a more serious problem that can impact one's job, career, health, and relationships.

A primary care visit is an opportunity to explore concerns about the mental health of your spouse, yourself, or your children. What is depression? How does it appear in adults, adolescents, children, and the elderly? The following information might help you or someone you love identify and seek help for depression.

What Is Depression?

Depression is an illness that involves one's body, mood, and thoughts. It affects the way a person eats and sleeps, the way one feels about oneself, and the way one thinks about things. Depression is not a passing blue mood, nor is it a sign of personal weakness. Depression is a *medical* illness and a *treatable* illness just like diabetes or heart disease.

Individuals who are depressed often experience more difficulty in performing their job, caring for their children, and maintaining their personal relationships.

A family history of depression and negative life experiences such as loss, trauma, serious illness, and stress can also contribute to the onset of depression. There are effective treatments today for depression, including medications and therapy. Without treatment, symptoms can last for weeks, months, or years. Appropriate treatment, however, can help most people who suffer from depression.

The majority of people who are treated for depression will improve, even those with serious depression. Unfortunately, one-third of sufferers do not seek help, as they do not realize depression is a treatable illness.

Who Gets Depression?

Depression is one of the most common of mental disorders. Women are at a higher risk and experience depression about twice as often as men. Many women are also particularly vulnerable after the birth of a baby.

The hormonal and physical changes, as well as the added responsibility of a new life, can be factors that lead to postpartum depression. While the "blues" are common in new mothers and go away, a major depressive episode is not normal and requires active intervention.

Depression in men often shows up in the form of alcohol or drug use and working long hours. Men may act irritable, angry, and discouraged when they are depressed. Men are often less willing than women to seek help. Depression commonly affects people between the ages of thirty and forty-four. These are prime parenting years and prime working years.

Parenting is challenging in good health, but can be more so if one is depressed. As a parent, it is important to seek treatment for depression, as this condition affects everyone in your family.

In any given year, 9.5 percent of the population (about 18.8 million Americans) experience depression. The economic cost for this disorder is high, but the cost in human suffering cannot be estimated.

Factors That Contribute to Depression

Depression can seem to happen "out of the blue," with no specific cause. A person can get depressed even if everything seems to be going well. Many things can contribute to depression including:

- Dwelling on negative automatic thoughts about oneself, the world, and the future (such as job loss, divorce, illness or injury, trauma)
- History of feeling bad about oneself
- Changes in brain chemicals
- Using alcohol and/or illegal drugs to avoid or cope with emotional pain
- Use of certain prescribed and over-the-counter drugs (it is best to discuss the possible side effects of medications with a physician)
- The important role of family history and genetics
- Medical conditions, such as hypothyroidism, diabetes, or brain injury
- Anxiety disorders or other psychological problems

Traumatic or stressful life events that can bring on depression include:

- Combat experience
- Threat of death
- Death of another person or other major loss
- Physical, sexual, and/or emotional abuse
- A long period of stress at home and/or work

- Relationship problems or divorce
- Money problems
- Job loss
- Natural or man–made disasters

The good news is that no matter what causes or contributes to depression, depression can be resolved with appropriate treatment.

Negative *thoughts* (for example, "I'm a failure" or "things will never get better") often bring on depressed *feelings*. Feeling depressed in turn makes people less likely to do the things (*engage in behavior*) that might make them feel better. This leads to greater depression, which in turn leads to more negative thoughts, resulting in doing even fewer things that feel good. *Note:* War injuries and/or chronic pain may keep a person from doing enjoyable things.

Signs and Symptoms of Depression

There are some common signs that might indicate depression, but getting a doctor's opinion is the first step to evaluation. Signs and symptoms include:

SYMPTOMS OF ADULT DEPRESSION
- Persistent sad or empty mood
- Loss of interest or pleasure in ordinary activities
- Changes in appetite or sleep
- Decreased energy or fatigue
- Inability to concentrate, make decisions
- Feelings of guilt, hopelessness, or worthlessness
- Thoughts of death or suicide

SYMPTOMS OF ADOLESCENT DEPRESSION
- Loss of interest in school and regular activities; drop in school performance
- Withdrawal from friends and family
- Negative thoughts of self and future
- Difficulty making decisions

SYMPTOMS OF DEPRESSION IN PREADOLESCENT CHILDREN
- Physical symptoms, like chronic headaches or stomachaches that cannot be attributed to a physical illness
- Aggression and excessive crying

- Irritability, withdrawal, isolative behavior, loss of interest and/or pleasure in previously enjoyed activities
- Sleep disturbance (reduced or increased sleep), changes in appetite (reduced or increased appetite), and reduced energy

Children with other psychiatric disorders (ADHD, conduct disorder, eating disorders, and anxiety disorders) and those with general medical conditions (diabetes, asthma, cancers, and other chronic illnesses) may be prone to depression. The prevalence may also be higher among children with developmental disorders and mental retardation.

SYMPTOMS OF DEPRESSION IN THE ELDERLY Depression in older adults can be disabling and contribute to the inability to perform activities of daily living. Depression in the elderly is complex and difficult to diagnose due to other medical illnesses that may be present.

Clinicians need to differentiate between depression and problems such as dementia, stroke, and other types of brain injuries and illnesses.

Behavior and Depression

Negative Action, Negative Mood

People with the blues usually feel "down," tired, sad, and hopeless. The natural instinct when feeling down is to just go with the feelings. A person who is depressed might:

- Not do things that take energy or effort
- Decide that they will put off things they don't want to do until later, when they feel better
- Keep to oneself and not spend time with family or friends
- Sleep a lot or spend a lot of time trying to sleep
- Misuse alcohol and other substances (such as, drugs, nicotine, or caffeine)
- Overeat, or not eat enough or nutritiously
- Avoid feelings or others by keeping busy with habit-forming activities such as watching television or video-gaming

Here's an interesting point about depression: when a person just goes with depressed feelings and stays away from activities, it is those very activities that are being avoided that may help that person to feel better. Not doing things only makes the depression worse, because avoiding activities:

People who are feeling down or depressed can suffer from any of the following signs:

Physical Health
- Decreased energy, fatigue or tiredness, feeling "slowed down" or sluggish
- Physical problems that don't get better with treatment, such as headaches, stomach problems, and chronic pain
- Losing or gaining weight due to an unhealthy diet or lack of exercise

Thoughts
- Thoughts of death or suicide; past suicide attempts
- Hopelessness, excessive pessimism, negativity
- Thoughts of guilt, worthlessness, helplessness
- Negative thoughts about oneself, about the world, and about the future
- Problems paying attention and focusing
- Memory problems
- Negative thoughts that keep playing over and over again
- Being confused, finding it hard to make everyday decisions
- Poor judgment
- Racing thoughts that are difficult to slow down
- Thinking "I'm a loser," or harsh self-criticism

Behaviors
- Loss of interest or pleasure in hobbies and activities that were previously enjoyed
- Loss of interest or pleasure in sex
- Having a hard time getting started with activities
- Pulling away or isolating from others, or wanting to be alone
- Increased use of tobacco, alcohol, drugs, and/or caffeine
- Taking dangerous risks
- Laughing or crying at odd moments
- Sleeping too much or too little
- Eating more or less

Mood
- Always feeling sad, anxious, or "empty"
- Feeling restless, annoyed, or nervous
- Feeling anger, guilt, or regret

An actual depression may exist when some or several of the signs listed above:

- Occur together; for example, decreased energy *and* decreased appetite *and* sleep difficulty *and* poor concentration
- Last longer than two weeks
- Are very bothersome or are causing a lot of distress
- Get in the way of social, work, and family duties or other important areas or activities

When this is the case, it is best to seek out professional consultation with a primary care physician or mental health professional.

- Keeps a person from having fun and living a full life
- Puts off facing and solving problems
- Keeps a person from dealing with important feelings and issues (for example, grief when a loved one dies)
- Makes it harder to cope with painful feelings in the future
- Makes it more likely that the problems will get worse

Overall, when Bob is not doing things that are fun and rewarding, he is more likely to feel depressed. When Bob feels depressed, he doesn't enjoy or feels less satisfied doing things, and so he stops doing them. This creates the downward spiral. The less Bob does, the more depressed he feels, and the more depressed Bob becomes, the less he does.

Find Your Depression Traps

To get out of the downward spiral, it's first necessary to figure out the behavior that's making the problem worse. One way to do this is to look for depression TRAPs. A TRAP is a shorthand way to help determine the behavior or behaviors that might be making the depression worse. Usually a *situation* or *thought* brings on a *feeling*, like sadness, which then makes it more likely that the situation will be avoided. This is a problem because it means that a person may then avoid things that could help him or her to feel better. TRAP stands for:

T = **T**rigger (situation or thought)
R = **R**esponse (usually a feeling)
AP = **A**voidance **P**attern (avoidance behavior)

Example:

T = John's friends ask him to watch a football game with them. John thinks to himself, "I don't feel like it. It's pointless, I won't have fun anyway."

R = John feels irritated, tired, and more depressed.

AP = John decides to stay home and doesn't go out with his friends.

It can be difficult to figure out what behavior is causing the problem to worsen or not improve. In depression, often it's avoidance that causes problems.

Avoidance. Avoidance can be defined as a person doing or not doing something to get out of tough situations or to stop from feeling bad. Another example of avoidance is thinking, "I'm not in the mood," and then putting off doing things that should be done. Avoidance ends up making depression worse in the long run. For example, sleeping isn't avoidance behavior when it's during a set time period and needed rest is being obtained. On the other hand, feeling down and taking a long nap in the middle of the day when adequate rest was gotten the night before would probably be an avoidance behavior. Over the long run, using sleep to avoid activities means not getting the benefits that those activities might provide.

Positive Action, Positive Mood

Once the depression TRAPs have been determined, the behaviors that are contributing to the low mood will be better understood. When the behaviors that are *not* helpful are known, it becomes possible to choose to do something to pull out of the negative spiral.

Exactly what should a person do when he or she is feeling depressed? The key to finding the way out of depression is to *move toward what's important. Do things that are in line with individual goals and values even if there isn't a lot of motivation at first.*

TAKING POSITIVE ACTION DURING A DEPRESSION At this point, it's common to think that taking action toward goals is a lot easier said than done. If it were that easy to move toward goals when fatigue and

Consider individual goals in these terms: where would you like to be and what would you like to be doing in one month, one year, five years? When you know where you would like to be, and what you would like to be doing, think about some small, doable steps that you can take to reach these goals. Taking small steps toward your goals can help lift your depression.

feeling "down" have set in, then feeling better would be easy. But even though feeling better may be difficult at times, it's important to make the effort.

It's common to think that feeling better should come before taking positive action, but this is not a good idea. It's also common to think, "I have to *feel* like doing something positive before I do it." These ways of thinking are myths. Feelings shouldn't determine actions! In fact, acting in line with life values and goals is possible *even when there isn't much motivation.*

While feelings do influence decision making, *feelings don't cause behavior.* Here's an example: Instead of going out with friends, John decides to stay home. Walking into the kitchen, he notices that the sink is full of dirty dishes. He considers washing the dishes, but then realizes that he feels tired and depressed. He chooses to take a nap, thinking, "I'll wash the dishes later, when I feel like it."

In this example it seems like John's choice to take a nap was caused by feeling tired and depressed, but this isn't really the case. While John's feelings *influenced* his choice to take a nap, those feelings didn't *cause* him to take a nap. Here's another example: As John is walking to his bedroom to take a nap, his roommate says, "Hey John, I have a date coming over tonight. I'll pay you $100 to wash the dishes before she gets here." Even though John still feels tired and he doesn't want to wash the dishes, he decides to wash them before he takes a nap because he could really use the extra money.

In this example, while John's feelings of depression and tiredness made him *want* to take a nap, he still *chose* to wash the dishes when offered $100. His feelings didn't cause his actions. Remember: feelings don't control actions or behaviors.

So what causes and controls behaviors? *Thoughts* affect feelings and actions. A person can think it's a good idea to work toward life values and goals, and choose to do so even if there isn't much motivation to follow through. Learn more about this in the "Thinking and Depression" section of this chapter.

Moving toward Goals

Here are some ways to work toward personal goals even when there isn't much motivation to do so:

- Set small goals that are realistic and achievable. For example, rather than deciding to get a better-paying job by next week, a more achievable goal would be to start looking at job postings and update résumés and cover letters over the next week.

- Break big goals into smaller steps and set priorities. For example, instead of planning to clean the whole house, planning to clean for ten minutes at a time is probably more realistic.
- Create a to-do list with big tasks broken down into smaller tasks. This will help the big tasks seem less overwhelming. For example:
  o Pay Bills:
    - Gather all bills.
    - Write checks.
    - Put checks in envelopes and seal.
    - Place stamps on envelopes.
    - Put in mailbox.
- Go at a moderate pace. For example, clean for ten minutes a day for five days instead of trying to clean fifty minutes over the course of one day.
- Set up routines to get in the habit of taking positive action. For example, regularly walking the dog at eight o'clock every night will make a routine out of getting exercise.
- Don't worry about doing things perfectly. Just doing them is the important thing. For example, rather than assuming it's not worth it to mail a résumé that isn't perfectly written, it's more important to send the imperfect résumé than not sending it at all.
- Rewarding oneself for taking steps toward reaching goals by doing things that are fun, such as laughing at a funny movie, relaxing, eating good meals, seeing beautiful scenery, or playing games, is a great idea.
- Say yes to invitations to do things with friends and family or start doing the things that were once enjoyable (such as, fishing, hiking, shopping, socializing, and so on) even if the motivation isn't there.
- Give the activity a serious try before deciding that it won't help.

Now that we have shown how behaviors affect depression, let's take a look at how thinking affects depression.

Thinking and Depression

Role of Thoughts in Depression

People are always thinking, even if they're not aware of what they're thinking. As one thought passes, there's another one ready to take its place. Most of the thoughts people have are *automatic thoughts*—in other words, the thoughts pop up without a person even trying to think them. Automatic thoughts are usually about what's going on around a person. Automatic thoughts are often about what a person thinks about himself (or herself). Some automatic thoughts are negative. For example, "I'm not good enough." Or "I shouldn't have made that mistake." Automatic thoughts can also be positive; however, it's the negative thoughts that contribute to depression.

Fortunately, automatic thoughts are changeable. This is because *thinking is learned*, much like doing is learned. Much of what a person thinks and believes comes from what he or she has learned from others, and how others have related to the person. Influences in a person's life include:

- Parents
- Friends
- The media
- Society

This means that even negative thoughts are learned, and they may or may not be accurate or true. Since negative thinking can cause depression, some forms of depression can be thought of as a *learned thinking problem*. The good news is that because thoughts are learned, reducing depression is possible by learning new thoughts to take the place of unhelpful thoughts. It *is* possible to gain control over negative thoughts.

Remember: *thinking affects feelings and actions*. For example, if SPC Jones *thinks* that he will perform well on a mission, then he will probably feel excited about that mission and do a good job. If SPC Jones *thinks* that he won't do well, then he might feel upset or get distracted and not do such a great job. So, what SPC Jones thinks about his mission will affect how he feels about the mission and how he performs.

Often people blame others or an event for making them feel a certain way, such as happy, sad, or angry. For example, "My roommate makes me so mad." But *people and events don't cause thoughts or feelings*. Remember: it's how a person *thinks and interprets* an event or situation that affects feelings and actions. Feelings and behaviors are influenced by thoughts, by belief systems, and by how situations are interpreted.

Let's see how this works.

Depression tends to bring up thoughts that are negative and that focus more on the bad things that happened in the past or might happen in the future. Depressed people often have thoughts that they're worthless, helpless, and hopeless. It's important to realize that these negative thoughts are part of the depression and aren't necessarily true or useful.

During a depression, negative thoughts tend to get listened to because:

- The thoughts are automatic, so the person doesn't stop to check if they're true.

- A depressed person doesn't choose to have negative thoughts, and it's hard to make the thoughts just stop.
- The thoughts seem to be true, and the feelings connected with them are so strong and real that a depressed person doesn't even question or challenge them.
- Having negative thoughts over and over again makes them easier to believe and accept as the truth.

Negative thoughts often center on three ideas:

- *"I am the cause of _____ (bad event)."* For example, "I failed the training because I'm not good enough." Or "I caused all the bad things in my life because I'm a bad person."
- *One bad thing means everything is bad.* For example, "I failed my training, and so my whole life sucks." or "My girlfriend broke up with me, so all women are losers."
- *Things will always be bad.* For example, "I failed my training, so my future is hopeless" or "This is never going to get better."

Ten Common Types of Thinking Errors

Negative automatic thoughts often distort or twist the truth, making things seem worse than they really are. These kind of negative thoughts are called *thought distortions*, or *negative thinking patterns*, or *thinking errors*. Let's use the term "thinking errors." Errors in thinking happen when thoughts don't really fit all the facts. Thinking errors can be grouped into at least ten common types.

1. *All-or-nothing thinking.* Thinking in terms of either/or, black and white, good or bad, right or wrong.

A more healthy way to think is to look for a middle ground or look for the gray areas. Rarely in life is something all-or-nothing.

Example: Because Mack couldn't do enough sit-ups during a physical training test, he automatically thinks, "I failed so I must be a loser." Mack can challenge this thinking error by thinking, "I did well in other areas of the PT test, so I'm not a complete failure, and I'm not a loser."

2. *Exaggerating or minimizing.* Exaggerating means making too big of a deal out of a negative experience, or making things much more negative than they really are. Exaggerated thinking is often also called "making a mountain out of a molehill" or "blowing things way out of proportion." Minimizing means not giving oneself or others enough credit for doing something good. Too little is made out of something, such as a compliment or success.

A more healthy way to think is to stop blowing things out of proportion and recognize and value successes.

Example: Sheila completed her assigned mission faster and better than last time, but her commander told her that she made some mistakes. Sheila made a big deal out of what her commander told her and thought that she had blown her chance for promotion. Sheila can challenge this thinking error by reminding herself that mistakes can happen to anyone who is in training, that she is continuing to improve, and if she acts on her commander's feedback, there's no reason why she wouldn't have a chance for promotion.

3. *Overgeneralization.* Overgeneralization involves thinking that something that happened once or twice will keep happening again and again, especially if it is something bad.

A more healthy way to think is to recognize that just because something happened once or twice does not necessarily mean it will always happen.

Example: Because SPC Wynne lost her ID yesterday she thinks to herself, "I'm always doing stupid things like this! I'm never going to be organized!" Instead of this kind of overgeneralization, SPC Wynne could realize that just because she misplaced her ID once doesn't mean she always has or always will be disorganized.

4. *Mental filter.* Using a mental filter means seeing only the bad and not the good side of things. The positive is forgotten or ignored, and only the bad things are considered.

A more healthy way to think is to notice the good things and realize that they count as much if not more than the negative.

Example: Regina got an e-mail card from her friend on her birthday and thinks to herself, "My friend doesn't even care enough to send me an actual birthday card. I don't have any *real* friends." Regina can challenge this thinking error by thinking, "It was cool that my friend remembered and sent me birthday wishes."

5. *Not accepting the positive.* People with this thinking error reject anything positive, especially positive information about themselves.

A more healthy way to think is to accept the positive without thinking that it doesn't count for anything. Positive actions that have been taken, talents or skills, and comments about strengths from others are important and are a real part of who a person is. It's important to ask oneself why it's so easy to believe negative comments and reject positive compliments. Is that fair?

Example: Every time Marty's bosses praise him for doing a good job, he doesn't believe the praise. He thinks to himself, "They're just being nice. I really can't do anything right." Marty can challenge this thinking error by thinking, "My bosses really do believe I'm doing a good job, and I can be proud of my work."

6. *Reasoning with feelings instead of logic or facts.* Saying, "I feel like a loser, so I must be a loser," is an example of using feelings instead of facts as proof of truth.

A more healthy way to think is to question the feelings that are being used to make conclusions or decisions. It's a good idea to use negative feelings as a *signal* that it's necessary to look for facts to disprove the negative thought.

Example: Two of Joel's friends died after a bomb exploded as they drove under an overpass in Iraq. Ever since then, Joel feels nervous when he drives under an overpass. Now that he's back home, he uses his nervous feelings as proof that it's not safe to drive under overpasses. Joel can challenge this thinking error by reminding himself that his feelings don't prove that overpasses at home are dangerous, and instead he needs to remember real facts about overpasses (such as they are safe to drive under). Once he realizes this, he will likely begin to feel less nervous and stop reasoning with his feelings about driving under overpasses.

7. *Jumping to conclusions.* This type of thinking error happens when people think they know what will happen without first finding out the facts. Expecting something bad to happen usually goes along with this type of thinking. *Mind-reading* is another way of jumping to conclusions. An example of mind-reading is when a person thinks he knows what *others* are thinking, without finding out the truth first. Mind-reading often results in *incorrectly* believing what the other person is thinking.

A more healthy way to think is to check all the facts before jumping to any conclusions. No one knows what will happen in the future, and no one knows how to read minds.

Example: Jimmy thought that two guys in his unit were talking about him because they were whispering when he walked into his tent. Jimmy can challenge this thinking error by asking the guys what they were talking about. It turned out that the guys were talking about a personal problem that they didn't want other people to hear. It had nothing to do with Jimmy.

8. *Labeling.* A person can label herself, or label others, based on very little information or based on mistakes that were made. When people label themselves, they often do so harshly. This has the effect of making it harder to accept mistakes. And once the labels get "attached," they become difficult to remove.

When depressed, it is best not to attach labels, either to oneself or to others. It is preferable to find ways to accept mistakes and shortcomings and move on.

Example: PVT Roberts forgot to pass on a message to her Sergeant from the commander, so she labeled herself a "flake." PVT Roberts can challenge this label by accepting that she made the mistake, learning from it, forgiving herself, and moving on. She also can note that labeling only makes it worse because it brings up all the negative things associated with being a flake that aren't true for her.

9. *"Should" statements.* "Should" statements are based on rules or standards that people set up for themselves and others to follow, but are usually impossible to do all of the time. People sometimes set the standards so high that they set themselves and others up to fail, which only confirms the negative thoughts.

A more healthy way for individuals to think is to avoid beating themselves up with "shoulds" or "shouldn'ts." Remember: it's not always possible to get things done *exactly* as planned or expected.

Example: CPT Smith assigned SPC Gray to a duty that SPC Gray thinks is beneath him. He'd rather be leading the team and thinks CPT Smith should have given him that job. As he thinks about it more, he gets angrier and angrier. SPC Gray can challenge his thinking error by telling himself that even though he would have *liked* CPT Smith to have given him the job, it is CPT Smith's job to make that decision. His job is to do what CPT Smith decides for him, not to decide what CPT Smith should do.

10. *Taking it personally.* Taking things too personally involves the assumption that others do negative things on purpose. People who take things too personally may also tend to take responsibility for something that they're not responsible for.

A more healthy way to think is to look at the facts; most likely it will turn out that negative things are not done as a personal attack.

Example: SPC Gray might think that CPT Smith did not assign him the leader position because CPT Smith doesn't like him or that CPT Smith has something against him. SPC Gray gets angry thinking of reasons why CPT Smith doesn't like him. A healthier way to think is that CPT Smith has a lot of responsibilities and needs to get things done. It's nothing personal against SPC Gray.

Targeting Thoughts

Although everyone has negative thoughts at some point, negative thoughts become a problem when they happen on a regular basis and cause distress and when they are disruptive. Challenging negative thoughts means taking control, which often can help with mood problems. The best way to challenge negative thoughts is by:

- Thinking about what's going on in the moment that may be setting off any negative thoughts and feelings
- Playing "devil's advocate" with negative thoughts. Challenge those thoughts by looking at the actual facts

By learning to change thinking errors, how a person feels and acts can also be changed. No one is helpless to make some change, and it's not hopeless! People can use plenty of tools to help change their negative thinking. There is hope, because changing what and how we think allows us to get control over how we feel and act.

Sometimes life gets so tough, it's easy to think that there's no way to change thinking patterns. This is when some people may even start thinking about suicide.

General Health Tips for the Holidays

The following health tips are important for managing mild depression and for optimizing one's health, especially during the holiday season:

- Manage your diet.
- Get adequate rest.
- Avoid alcohol.
- Participate in regular exercise.
- Surround yourself with people who are important to you.
- Communicate your feelings to someone you trust.
- Join a social support group in your military community or in your local area.

Suicide

Suicide is when someone purposely takes his or her own life. Many people think about committing suicide at some time in their lives, especially in times of extreme stress or depression, but most don't follow through. Suicide, like depression, affects people of all ages and backgrounds.

Usually, people who commit suicide think their situation is totally hopeless. In this state of mind, death can seem like the only option. But *there are always other options and there is hope.* The quickest way to get help is to call one of the national suicide prevention hotlines available 24/7 at: 1-800-273-TALK (1-800-273-8255) or 1-800-SUICIDE (1-800-784-

2433). You can also seek help from your unit medic, corpsman, chaplain, or medical treatment facility.

Warning Signs of Suicide

While it's often hard to know who will commit suicide, there are warning signs that signal when a person is at high risk. These warning signs can include:

- Talking About and Planning One's Death
    - o Talking about dying and making plans to harm or kill oneself
    - o Having the means to carry out the suicide plan, such as owning a gun or having potentially dangerous pills available
- Previous Attempts
    - o Having attempted suicide in the past
- Depression
    - o Feeling depressed: most people who commit suicide are depressed; however, a person doesn't have to show signs of depression to commit suicide
- No Hope for the Future
    - o Thinking that one is all alone in the world, that no one likes him or her, that no one would care if he or she were dead, and/or feeling that the future is hopeless
- High Stress in Life
    - o Going through a very stressful time and feeling overwhelmed by problems in life
    - o Thinking that there are no other solutions to the problem except death.
    - o Having suffered a loss (such as loss of a relationships, job, or death of a friend or family member)
- Combat Trauma
    - o Having faced intense combat trauma
    - o Having combat-related guilt about acts carried out during times of war and/or upsetting thoughts about the war that feel overwhelming
- Changes in Personality
    - o Wanting to be alone all the time
    - o Feeling sad, tired, irritable, aggressive, anxious, and/or agitated
    - o Not interested in things that were once enjoyable or important in life
- Low Self-Esteem
    - o Feeling worthless, ashamed, guilty, and/or hating oneself

o Thinking, "The world would be better off without me," or "I'm a failure"
- Reckless or High-Risk Behavior
    o Reckless driving, gambling, threatening others' lives, or putting one's life at risk
- Changes in Behavior
    o Having no interest in work and other activities
    o Having more problems with one's leader, coworkers, family, and/or partner or spouse than usual
    o Sleeping more or less than usual and still feeling exhausted
    o Loss of appetite or overeating, and changes in weight not due to a healthy diet
    o Treating others poorly or rudely
    o Having a hard time concentrating on and finishing routine, everyday tasks
    o Giving away valued possessions
- Substance Abuse
    o Using alcohol and/or illegal drugs for a long period of time
    o Abusing prescribed medications as a way to deal with problems

Suicide hotlines are free and confidential, are staffed by trained counselors, and have information about support services that can be of assistance. Suicide hotlines should be contacted when:

- The sadness is overwhelming, or there are thoughts of hopelessness or suicide
- There is concern about someone who may be experiencing these feelings
- There is interest in suicide prevention, treatment, and service referrals

What to Do If Someone Says They Are Thinking about Suicide

When someone is at risk for suicide, take immediate action by doing the following:

- Tell someone immediately! Never promise to keep thoughts about suicide a secret.
- If there is a serious risk of suicide:
    o Take the person's concerns seriously, and listen without judging.

    o Tell the person what will be done to help, such as not
      discussing the issue with coworkers unless it's on a need-to-
      know basis. A need-to-know basis might include command or
      someone else who can help.
    o Limit the person's access to firearms or other lethal means of
      committing suicide (this may require getting additional assistance).

It may be necessary to involve others to help, such as military law enforcement, 911, or others that can help such as friends or family members.

Help the person get to a health care professional. Give him or her the number to a mental health professional, chaplain, or a counselor in your installation, or to the national suicide prevention hotlines at 1-800-273-TALK (1-800-273-8255) or 1-800-SUICIDE, or (1-800-784-2433). MilitaryOneSource (1-800-342-9647; www.militaryonesource.com) is another resource. Stay with the person until he or she has contacted help.

If the person refuses to get help, don't keep suicide thoughts a secret. Tell a friend, family member, professional, or supportive leader who can find the person help.

Loss and Grief

What Is Grief?

Grief is a normal and natural reaction to loss. It is also a natural and necessary part of healing after a loss. People usually grieve when someone they love dies. But a person can also feel grief after losing something meaningful or valuable.

People are often surprised by the reactions they have when they are grieving. For example, they may be in shock when first learning of the death of a loved one. They may be angry at God, themselves, the person who died, or someone who they think is responsible for the loss or death. They may also feel guilty about not having done something differently before the person died.

Major losses and death may cause some changes in life, sometimes very significant changes. These changes may include having to parent alone, getting use to single life after divorce, or going back to work. Going through these changes may add more stress, so it's important to have support from others. It's possible to find support by talking to a psychologist, chaplain, or other spiritual advisor, or to family members, friends, a health care professional, or other helpful people.

Losses can include:

• Divorce or breakup of an important relationship

- Death of a loved one
- Death of comrades (combat or non-combat related)
- Loss of a pet
- Loss of a sense of safety
- Loss of meaning and purpose in life
- Loss of physical health or a physical part of oneself
- Loss of ability to relate or connect with others
- Loss of identity
- Loss of self-esteem

Common thoughts, feelings, and reactions caused by loss and grief:

- Denial
- Disbelief or doubt
- Confusion
- Shock
- Sadness
- Yearning or longing
- Anger
- Shame
- Despair
- Guilt
- Regret
- Feeling empty and/or depressed
- Having a hard time relating to or connecting with others
- Thinking that a part of oneself has died
- Hopelessness about the future
- Thinking things aren't as important as they once were
- Getting tearful or crying easily
- Feeling restless or irritable
- Having upset stomach, headaches, or other physical pains
- Existing health problems become worse or new physical problems appear
- Loss of appetite
- Having a hard time sleeping or sleeping much more than usual
- Having little energy

How Long Does Grieving Last?

The grief period is different for everyone. A person's personality as well as family, cultural, spiritual, and religious beliefs and practices can influence how one responds to loss. It can take many months for the painful feelings and thoughts to go away. Grief has its own timeline. But over time, grief *will* begin to decrease. A grieving person will likely have good days and bad days. And it's normal and expected that the grief might return "out of the blue"; that's part of the grief process. Important dates, like anniversaries or birthdays, can bring back intense feelings of grief.

Grieving usually involves feeling sadness and other feelings related to the loss. It often involves talking about the loss with other people. However, sometimes people have a hard time grieving because:

- They don't deal with their grief because it's uncomfortable.
- They were raised to believe that they should never be sad and were told that "crying is for babies."
- They believe that feelings are a sign of weakness, or that grieving is okay only at funerals.
- Friends and family tell them, "You have to stay strong and move on with your life."

These are mistaken beliefs that get in the way of letting the grieving process happen naturally, and may result in even worse grief from which it's then harder to recover.

Coping with Grief

It is hard to accept and work through grief, but not dealing with it can lead to depression. Coping with loss and grief in healthy ways can prevent problems from getting worse. People can be hard on themselves following a loss. In fact, *it's okay to grieve*. It takes courage to grieve following the loss of someone important. Here are some things that can help the grieving process happen naturally, which will help avoid depression:

- Be patient. Take time to grieve. It may not feel like it at first, but with time the pain will ease and it will be easier to get on with normal activities.
- Join a support group where personal stories can be shared with others. It is often helpful to spend time with people who have gone through a similar loss.
- Seek helpful people, such as family or friends, or a chaplain or other spiritual advisor.
- Seek out professional consultation with a psychologist or social worker or other health care professional if the grieving persists.

Even though it can be hard to ask for help, it's important to know that no one has to experience grief alone. It's easy to feel alone and to think

Several warning signs may suggest that a person is having a severe grief reaction and needs help coping. Ignoring the warning signs may make the grief last longer and/or make the grieving more difficult. Professionals and groups with expertise can help. It is strongly recommended that a professional provider be contacted immediately if any of the following conditions or warning signs are present:

- Thinking about or planning to commit suicide or engage in self-harm
- After several days, the grief reaction is getting in the way of self-care, such as eating and taking a shower
- Finding distractions to avoid grieving, such as:
  o Not talking about the loss
  o Not being honest about the thoughts and feelings that are occurring since the loss
  o Not talking or thinking about memories related to the loss
  o Unable to function for weeks to months after the loss
  o Unable to carry out work, school, or family responsibilities

that no one else could possibly be going through the same thing. However, often other people *are* going through the same thing, or have had a similar experience coping with a loss, and they may be having the same thoughts and dealing with the same issues.

Talking about feelings, although uncomfortable, is an important step to getting past grief. Mental health care professionals can offer a private, safe place to talk about grief and assist with the grieving process.

Getting Support

When Stigma Gets in the Way

Depression and grief can get in the way of seeking help because depressed people tend to feel worn out and think that they are worthless, hopeless, and helpless. It's very common for depressed people to believe that nothing will help.

Often people have an incorrect view of what getting help means, or may be skeptical of treatment. For some, there is a stigma or shame attached to getting help, especially within the military. This type of thinking gets in the way of getting needed help. Effective treatment is available for depression. It takes courage to seek help for depression, and the earlier treatment is sought out, the better!

Those in the military are often hesitant to seek help for depression because of the following thoughts:

"GETTING HELP WILL AFFECT MY CAREER." Service members are more likely to get in trouble if they *don't* seek help, because not getting help can make problems worse. Not getting help for depression can result in negative behavior toward coworkers and poor work performance, which can cause other problems between a service member and others.

"MY LEADERS WILL HAVE ACCESS TO MY MENTAL HEALTH RE-CORDS." Information between a doctor and a service member *does* become part of the service member's medical record. Technically, the information is available to commanding officers upon their request. But in most cases, confidentiality is maintained between providers at a Military Treatment Facility and the person seeking help. Chaplains and other service providers should explain the limits of confidentiality or privacy to a service member. If they don't, just ask.

"MY SERVICE RECORDS WILL SHOW MY MENTAL HEALTH INFOR-MATION." Military service records don't contain mental health information unless the service member was officially ordered to get help or if they were found unfit or unsuitable for military duty.

"MY COMMAND DISCOURAGES ME FROM GETTING HELP." There are local community resources available to service members who don't feel comfortable going through the military. Service members and their unit will benefit if they seek and receive help for their problems before they get worse and risk lives and military readiness.

Some things that can be done *right now* to manage a depressed mood:

- Tune in to negative thinking and examine thoughts for thinking errors.
- Avoid the urge to be alone. Be with other people. Confide in someone—it's healthier than self-isolating.
- Know that a low mood can improve, even if not right away. Feeling better takes time and patience.
- Set small goals despite feeling depressed. Have a friend, family member, or mental health professional see if goals are realistic and reachable.
- Put off very important decisions or changes until the depression has lifted. Before deciding to make major changes such as changing

jobs or getting married or divorced, discuss it with others who have a more neutral view of the situation.

- Be around positive and supportive people.
- Don't use alcohol or drugs (unless the drugs are prescribed and taken as directed). Alcohol and/or drug use can increase depression in the long run.

Many people believe that they don't deserve to feel better or that they won't ever get better. Don't buy into these thoughts. They are just negative thoughts, and they aren't true! Everyone has the power and ability to change negative thinking. *Everyone deserves to get better, and they will if they keep working at it.*

Where to Get Help

No one should have to deal with grief or depression alone. It can be hard to ask for help, but health care professionals can provide a safe place to talk about feelings and help with the healing process. Here are a few resources:

An installation's support services can provide information and support. Support services include a chaplain, a Military Treatment Facility, and family advocacy programs and family centers. Phone numbers can be found in the installation's military directory.

Talk to command. Check in with a leader about how to handle a stressful situation before the situation gets out of control. Keeping leadership informed is good practice.

Make an appointment with a primary care provider (PCP). Ask the PCP about available treatment options, and a referral to a mental health practitioner if that is indicated.

MilitaryOneSource. MilitaryOneSource provides brief counseling to active duty military personnel and their families, including Reservists and the National Guard. (1-800-342-9647; www.militaryonesource.com)

T*A*P*S (The Tragedy Assistance Program for Survivors) is a nonprofit Veterans Service Organization that has a wide range of free services to all those affected by the death of a loved one in the armed forces. (1-800-959-TAPS [1-800-959-8277]; www.TAPS.org)

Vet Centers offer readjustment counseling for veterans and their families. Vet Center staff is available toll free at 1-800-905-4675 (Eastern) and 1-866-496-8838 (Pacific). www.vetcenter.va.gov

Veteran Affairs Resources. VA medical centers and Vet Centers provide veterans with affordable mental health services. Health insurance companies cover costs, or services cost little or nothing, according to a veteran's ability to pay. The VA Medical Center system's specialized PTSD clinics and programs can provide educational information and diagnostic evaluations concerning PTSD to eligible veterans. Following deployment to a combat zone after discharge, veterans who have enrolled for VA services are qualified for two years of care for conditions potentially related to their service. www.va.gov

Local community services can include crisis centers, mental health centers, or suicide prevention centers.

Find mental health providers locally. Check out http://therapists.psychology-today.com/ppc/prof_search.php.

Suicide hotlines. The national suicide prevention lifeline is available 24-hours. 1-800-273-TALK (1-800-273-8255) or 1-800-SUICIDE (1-800-784-2433). Both suicide hotlines will connect the caller to a certified crisis center nearest to the location from where the call is placed. www.suicidepreventionlifeline.org

Reaching Out to Others

The most important thing to do for someone who may be depressed is to assist him or her in getting help. Here are some suggestions:

- Offer understanding, patience, and encouragement.
- Listen carefully. It is best not to judge or mock what the person is going through; it is better to point out the positive, but realistic, aspects of their situation and offer hope that things will improve.
- Let the person know that even though he or she may have a strong urge to be alone, confiding in someone or being with other people is better than being alone and secretive.
- Let the person know that his or her mood will improve with help, that getting better takes time and patience, and he or she can feel better day-by-day.
- Help the person to stay with treatment until he or she gets better. If improvement is not evident, encourage the person to seek treatment from other sources.
- Help the person follow a treatment plan, such as going to appointments and taking medication, if prescribed. Offer to go with the person to his or her appointments.

Remember: when in doubt or when the symptoms are ongoing and serious, it is best to seek out in-person professional consultation with a primary care physician or mental health professional.

- Help the person stop drinking alcohol or using drugs that aren't prescribed. Substances may interact with prescribed medication and/or make depression worse.
- Encourage the person to go out for walks and pleasant outings (going to the movies or lunch), and other healthy activities (exercise). If he or she refuses, gently insist.
- Encourage the person to do some things that he or she once found fun, like hobbies or sports, or religious or cultural activities. Don't push him or her to take on too much too soon. The person needs company, but too many demands can increase stress and thoughts of failure.
- Ask the person if they have had thoughts about hurting themselves. Asking communicates that it's okay to talk about it.

Deployments 5

Predeployment Essentials: Documents

TAKING THE TIME TO GATHER AND PREPARE the proper documents in advance allows service members to choose people to act on their behalf, to make their wishes known to their loved ones, and, if they wish, to give legally binding instructions. While it may be uncomfortable to talk about certain possibilities, doing so in advance may help avoid conflict and allow for quick and decisive action in the event of an emergency.

Service members and their relatives should gather identification documents such as birth certificates, marriage certificates, and any other similar documents that can verify family relationships.

These documents may become important when dealing with insurance companies, financial institutions, and government agencies. It is a good idea to keep the originals of these documents in a safe place together with other important documents and to keep copies in a second, easily accessible place in case the service member or a relative needs access to them at any point. In addition, certain documents empowering others to act on a service member's behalf, such as a financial power of attorney, a health care advance directive, or a living will, should be made available in case the service member becomes unable to make decisions or to communicate his or her wishes to others.

Finally, all service members should make sure they have a legally valid will and should review the beneficiary designation forms for any life insurance policies they have to make sure they are current and accurate.

A financial power of attorney is a legal document by which one person gives another person the authority to act in his or her place regarding financial affairs. For example, a financial power of attorney empowers one person to sign a binding contract on behalf of another person. The person who signs the power of attorney is called the principal or grantor, and the person who gains rights to act under the power of attorney is called the attorney-in-fact. Service members are often encouraged to grant powers of attorney prior to deployment to enable a spouse or other family member to manage their affairs while they are away.

A financial power of attorney can be general—giving the attorney-in-fact unlimited authority over the principal's affairs—or limited to specific actions, such as filing tax returns or signing insurance forms. Powers of attorney may be limited to a specific period of time or may extend until the death of the principal or until revocation. A power of attorney must be "durable," however, in order to remain valid if the principal becomes incapacitated.

Creating these documents often involves making difficult personal decisions and also requires legal expertise. Service members who wish to create a will or sign a power of attorney, health care advance directive, or living will should consult a qualified legal professional.

The emotional cycle of an extended deployment, six months or greater, is readily divided into five distinct stages. These stages are composed as follows: predeployment, deployment, sustainment, redeployment, and postdeployment. Each stage is characterized both by a time frame and specific emotional challenges, which must be dealt with and mastered by each of the family members. Failure to adequately negotiate these challenges can lead to significant strife—both for family members and the deployed service member. Providing information early about what to expect, especially for families who have not endured a lengthy separation before, can go a long way toward "normalizing" and coping positively with the deployment experience. Furthermore, promoting understanding of the stages of deployment helps to avert crises, minimize the need for command intervention or mental health counseling, and can even reduce suicidal threats.

Predeployment

The onset of this stage begins with the warning order for deployment. This stage ends when the service member actually departs from home station. The predeployment time frame is extremely variable from several weeks to more than a year.

The predeployment stage is characterized alternately by denial and anticipation of loss. As the departure date gets closer, spouses often ask, "You don't really have to go, do you?" Eventually, the increased field training, preparation, and long hours away from home herald the extended separation that is to come. Service members energetically talk more and more about the upcoming mission and their unit. This "bonding" to fellow service members is essential to unit cohesion, which is necessary for a safe and successful deployment. Yet it also creates an increasing sense of emotional and physical distance for military spouses. In their frustration, many spouses complain, "I wish you were gone already." It is as if their loved ones are already "psychologically deployed."

As the reality of the deployment finally sinks in, the service member and family try to get their affairs in order. Long "honey-do" lists are generated to deal with all manner of issues including home repairs, security (door and window locks, burglar alarms, etc.), car maintenance, finances, tax preparation, child care plans, and wills, just to name a few. At the same time, many couples strive for increased intimacy. Plans are made for the "best" Christmas, the "perfect" vacation, or the "most" romantic anniversary. In contrast, there may be some ambivalence about sexual relations: "This is it for six months, but I do not want to be that close." Fears about fidelity or marital integrity are raised or may go unspoken. Other frequently voiced concerns may include "How will the children handle the separation? Can I cope without him or her? Will my marriage survive?" In this very busy and tumultuous time, resolving all these issues, completing the multitude of tasks, or fulfilling high expectations often falls short.

A common occurrence, just prior to deployment, is for service members and their spouses to have a significant argument. For couples with a long history, this argument is readily attributed to the ebb-and-flow of marital life and therefore not taken too seriously. For younger couples, especially those experiencing an extended separation for the first time, such an argument can take on "catastrophic" proportions. Fears that the relationship is over can lead to tremendous anxiety for both service member and spouse. In retrospect, these arguments are most likely caused by the stress of the pending separation. From a psychological perspective, it is easier to be angry than confront the pain and loss of saying goodbye for six months or more.

However, the impact of unresolved family concerns can have potentially devastating consequences. From a command perspective, a worried, preoccupied service member is easily distracted and unable to focus on essential tasks during the critical movement of heavy military equipment. In the worst-case scenario, this can lead to a serious accident or the development of a service member stress casualty who is mission ineffective. On the home front, significant spousal distress interferes with completing basic routines, concentrating at work, and attending to the needs of children. At worst, this can exacerbate children's fears that the parents are unable to adequately care for them or even that the service member will not return. Adverse reactions from children can include inconsolable crying, apathy, tantrums, and other regressive behaviors. In response, a downward spiral can develop—if not quickly checked—in which both service member and spouse become even more upset at the prospect of separating.

Although easier said than done, it is often helpful for military couples—in the predeployment stage—to discuss in detail their expectations of each other during the deployment. These expectations can include a variety of issues, to include freedom to make independent decisions, contact with the opposite sex (fidelity), going out with friends, budgeting, child-rearing, and even how often letters or care packages will be sent. Failure to accurately communicate these and other expectations is frequently a source of misperception, distortion, and hurt later on in the deployment. It is difficult at best to resolve major marital disagreements when face-to-face, let alone over six thousand miles apart.

Predeployment Checklist

_____Have you discussed your feelings on the deployment and your spouse's return?

_____Have the children been included in discussions on where you are going, when you are coming home, why you are leaving?

_____Have you reached an agreement on frequency of letter writing/phone calls?

_____Do you have current family snapshots?

_____Have you recorded your children's favorite bedtime stories/songs on cassettes?

_____Do both the deploying member and remaining parent or guardian understand what the Airman & Family Readiness Center, Family Services, Air Force Aid Society, American Red Cross, chaplain, and so on, can do for you and how to contact them?

SECURITY

_____Has the home been given a security check?

_____Do all window locks work?

_____Do the windows open or are they painted shut?

_____Do all door locks work properly?

_____Do you have keys for all doors or combinations for all padlocks?

_____Do the smoke alarms function and do you know how to test them?

_____Are all emergency numbers posted where they can easily be referred to?

_____Is there an appropriate message on the answering machine? (Having a male voice sometimes discourages crank phone calls.)

_____Do you need to change your phone number to an unlisted one?

MEDICAL
_____Do you know and understand how to use the medical facilities?

_____Do you know who your children's pediatrician is and what his/her phone number is?

_____Do you know your children's dentist/orthodontist and their schedule?

FINANCIAL
_____Have you determined who will pay the bills?

_____Do you have a spending plan?

_____Do you both understand the spending plan?

_____Does your spending plan consider the following?
  _____Rent/mortgage
  _____Utilities
  _____Food
  _____Automobile maintenance
  _____Insurance
  _____Loan payments
  _____Emergencies
  _____Long distance phone calls
  _____Postage
  _____Telegrams
  _____Travel (leave)
  _____Entertainment
  _____Presents
  _____Savings

_____Has an allotment been established?

_____Will the allotment be in effect in time?

_____Is there a "backup" plan if the allotment is late?

_____Have you established two checking accounts?

_____Have you decided upon a procedure for income taxes?

LEGAL
_____Do you know your spouse's Social Security number?

_____Have you provided for power of attorney?

_____Do you have current wills?

_____Have guardians for the children been named in the will?

_____Does everyone who qualifies have a government identification (ID) card?

_____Will any ID cards need renewing?

_____If ID needs renewing, has Form DD 1172 been completed?

_____Is the military member's record of emergency data on record and current?

_____Do you know the process for moving your household goods?

IMPORTANT PAPERS

Are the following important papers current and in an accessible safety deposit box?

_____Power of attorney

_____Wills

_____Insurance policies

_____Real estate (deeds, titles, mortgages, leases)

_____Bank account numbers

_____Charge account numbers

_____Savings bonds

_____Birth certificates

_____Marriage certificates

_____Naturalization papers

_____Citizenship papers

_____Family Social Security numbers

_____Inventory of household goods

_____Car title(s)

Do you each have the following phone numbers?

_____Police

_____Fire

_____Medical (hospital/doctor)

_____Service member's contact number

_____Service member's unit in local area

_____Spouses in unit/squadron

_____Reliable neighbors

_____Relatives

_____Children's school

_____Spouse's workplace

_____Utilities

_____Repair shops

_____Insurance company
_____Airman and family readiness center

HOUSEHOLD MAINTENANCE
_____Do you know who to call if something breaks?
_____Do you know how to operate the furnace?
_____Does the furnace have clean filters?
_____Does the furnace need periodic supplies of oil/gas?
_____Is the hot water heater operating properly?
_____Any pipes or faucets leaking?
_____Toilets operate correctly?
_____All drains operate correctly?
Are the following appliances operating correctly?
_____Stove
_____Refrigerator
_____Freezer
_____Dishwasher
_____Clothes washer
_____Clothes dryer
_____Television
_____Air conditioner
_____Does everyone know where the fuse box is?
_____Are the switches of the fuse box labeled?
_____Are there extra fuses?
_____Is there adequate outside lighting?
_____Is there a list of repair persons?
_____Are there tools in the house?
_____Is the lawn mower tuned?
_____Is there an adequate amount of firewood?

Deployment

This stage is the period from the service member's departure from home through the first month of the deployment.

A roller coaster of mixed emotions is common during the deployment stage. Some military spouses report feeling disoriented and overwhelmed. Others may feel relieved that they no longer have to appear brave and strong. There may be residual anger at tasks left undone. The service member's departure creates a "hole," which can lead to feelings of numbness, sadness, being alone, or abandonment. It is common to have difficulty sleeping and anxiety about coping. Worries about security issues may ensue, including "What if there is a pay problem? Is the house safe? How will I manage if my child gets sick? What if the car breaks down?" For many, the deployment stage is an unpleasant, disorganizing experience.

On the positive side, the ability to communicate home from Bosnia, or any other site, is a great morale boost. The Defense Satellite Network (DSN) provides service members the ability to call home at no cost, although usually for a fifteen-minute time limit. For some service members who are unwilling to wait on line, using commercial phone lines is an option. Unfortunately, it is common for huge phone bills to result, which can further add to familial stress. Another potential source of anxiety for families is that several weeks may pass before service members are able to make their first call home.

For most military spouses, reconnecting with their loved ones is a stabilizing experience. For those who have "bad" phone calls, this contact can markedly exacerbate the stress of the deployment stage and may result in the need for counseling. One possible disadvantage of easy phone access is the immediacy and proximity to unsettling events at home or in theatre. It is virtually impossible to disguise negative feelings of hurt, anger, frustration, and loss on the phone. For example, a spouse may be having significant difficulty (children acting out, car breaking down, finances, etc.) or a service member may not initially get along with peers or a supervisor. Spouse and soldier may feel helpless and unable to support each other in their time of need. Likewise, there may be jealousy toward the individual(s) whom the spouse or service member does rely on, or confide in, during the deployment. These situations can add to the stress and uncertainty surrounding the deployment. Yet military families have come to expect phone (and now even video) contact as technology advances. However, most report that the ability to stay in close touch—especially during key milestones (birthdays, anniversaries, etc.)—greatly helps them to cope with the separation.

Sustainment

The sustainment stage lasts from the first month through the fifth (penultimate) month of deployment.

Sustainment is a time of establishing new sources of support and new routines. Many rely on the Family Readiness Group (FRG), which serves as a close network that meets on a regular basis to handle problems and disseminate the latest information. Others are more comfortable with family, friends, church, or other religious institution as their main means of emotional support. As challenges come up, most spouses learn that they are able to cope with crises and make important decisions on their own. They report feeling more confident and in control. During the sustainment stage, it is common to hear military spouses say, "I can do this!"

One challenge during this stage is the rapid speed of information provided by widespread phone and e-mail access. In the near future, one can even expect that individual service members will have the ability to call home with personal cellular phones. Over long distances and without face-to-face contact, communications between husband and wife are much more vulnerable to distortion or misperception. Given this limitation, discussing "hot topics" in a marriage can be problematic and is probably best left on hold until after the deployment, when they can be resolved more fully. Obvious exceptions to this rule include a family emergency (such as the critical illness of a loved one) or a joyful event (such as the birth of a child). In these situations, the ideal route of communication is through the Red Cross so that the service member's command is able to coordinate emergency leave if required.

On a related note, many spouses report significant frustration because phone contact is unidirectional and must be initiated by the service member. Some even report feeling "trapped" at home for fear that they will miss a call. Likewise, service members may feel forgotten if they call—especially after waiting a long time on line to get to a phone—and no one is home. This can lead to anger and resentment, especially if an expectation regarding the frequency of calls is unmet. Now that Internet and e-mail are widely available, spouses report feeling much more in control, as they can initiate communication and do not have to stay waiting by the phone. Another advantage of e-mail, for both service member and spouse, is the ability to be more thoughtful about what is said and to "filter out" intense emotions that may be unnecessarily disturbing. This is not to say that military couples should "lie" to protect each other, but rather it helps to recognize that the direct support available from one's spouse is limited during the deployment.

The response of children to a parent's extended deployment is individualized and depends on their developmental age: infants, toddlers, preschool, school age, and teenagers. It is reasonable to assume that a sudden negative change in a child's behavior or mood is a predictable response to the stress of having a deployed parent.

Infants (less than one year) must be held and actively nurtured in order to thrive. If a primary caregiver becomes significantly depressed, then the infant will be at risk for apathy, refusal to eat, and even weight loss. Early intervention becomes critical to prevent undue harm or neglect. Pediatri-

Rapid communication is immensely helpful for military families, but it can also lead to unanticipated rumors, which then circulate unchecked within the Family Readiness Group (FRG). The most damning rumor involves an allegation of infidelity that is difficult to prove true or false. Other troubling rumors may include handling the deployment poorly, accidents or injuries, changes in the date of return, disciplinary actions, or even who calls home the most. Needless to say, such rumors can be very hurtful to service member, spouse, and the FRG. At its worst, unit cohesion and even mission success can suffer. Limiting the negative impact of such rumors is a constant challenge for unit leaders and chaplains. It is extremely important to keep service members and family members fully informed and to dispel rumors quickly. In fact, rumors lose their destructive power once the "secret" is exposed.

A commander's wife reported a rumor that a deployed service member was having an affair. Members of the FRG, who were very upset, related the details to their deployed spouses. Senior unit leaders decided not to tell the commander because the allegations were deemed too inflammatory. Unfortunately, unit morale and cohesion began to suffer greatly as the rumor spread throughout the ranks. A month later, the commander finally learned of this destructive rumor, which had been undermining his authority to lead. He immediately confronted his wife, senior leaders, and the service member about whom the allegation had been made. Evidence about the validity of these allegations, or how the rumor started in the first place, could not be found. In response, the commander issued a very firm policy regarding exposing all rumors—whether they be true or false. Unit morale and cohesion, although badly bruised, then began to recover.

cians can perform serial exams to ensure that growth continues as expected on height/weight charts. Army Community Services and Social Work can assist with parenting skills and eliciting family or community support. Lastly, the primary caregiver may also benefit from individual counseling.

Toddlers (one to three years) will generally take their cue from the primary caregiver. One issue is whether the mother or father is the service member leaving—especially when children are very young. If the "nondeploying" parent is coping well, they will tend to do well. The converse is also true. If the primary caregiver is not coping well, then toddlers may become sullen, tearful, throw tantrums, or develop sleep disturbance. They will usually respond to increased attention, hugs, and holding hands. The "nondeploying" parent may also benefit from sharing their day-to-day experiences with other parents facing similar challenges. In particular, it is important for the primary caregiver to balance the demands for caring for children alone with their own needs for time for self.

Preschoolers (three to six years) may regress in their skills (difficulty with potty training, "baby talk," thumb sucking, refusal to sleep alone) and seem more "clingy." They may be irritable, depressed, aggressive, prone to somatic complaints, and have fears about parents or others leaving. Caregivers will need to reassure them with extra attention and physical closeness (hugs, holding hands). In addition, it is important to avoid changing family routines such as sleeping in their own bed, unless they are "very" scared. Answers to questions about the deployment should be brief, matter-of-fact, and to the point. This will help to contain the free-floating anxiety of an overactive imagination.

School-age children (six to twelve years) may whine, complain, become aggressive, or otherwise "act out" their feelings. They may focus on the service member/parent missing a key event; for example, "Will you (the service member) be here for my birthday?" Depressive symptoms may include sleep disturbance or loss of interest in school, eating, or even playing with their friends. They will need to talk about their feelings and will need more physical attention than usual. Expectations regarding school performance may need to be a little lower, but keeping routines as close to normal is best for them.

Teenagers (thirteen to eighteen years) may be irritable and rebellious and fight or participate in other attention-getting behavior. They may show a lack of interest in school, peers, and school activities. In addition, they are at greater risk for promiscuity, alcohol, and drug use. Although they may deny problems and worries, it is extremely important for caregivers to stay engaged and be available to talk out their concerns. At first, lowering academic expectations may be helpful; however, return to their usual school performance should be supported. Sports and social activities should be encouraged to give normal structure to their life. Likewise, additional responsibility in the family, commensurate with their emotional maturity, will make them feel important and needed.

Unfortunately, some children may have great difficulty adapting to the stress of a deployed parent. If they are unable to return to at least some part of their normal routine or display serious problems over several weeks, a visit to the family doctor or mental health counselor is indicated. Children of deployed parents are also more vulnerable to psychiatric hospitalization—especially in single-parent and blended families.

Despite all these obstacles, the vast majority of spouses and family members successfully negotiate the sustainment stage and begin to look forward to their loved ones coming home.

Redeployment

The redeployment stage is essentially defined as the month before the service member is scheduled to return home.

The redeployment stage is generally one of intense anticipation. Like the deployment stage, there can be a surge of conflicting emotions. On the one hand, there is excitement that the service member is coming home. On the other, there is some apprehension. Some concerns include, "Will he [she] agree with the changes that I have made? Will I have to give up my independence? Will we get along?" Ironically, even though the separation is almost over, there can be renewed difficulty in making decisions. This is due, in part, to increased attention to choices that the returning service member might make. Many spouses also experience a burst of energy during this stage. There is often a rush to complete "to-do" lists before their mate returns—especially around the home. It is almost inevitable that expectations will be high.

Postdeployment

The postdeployment stage begins with the arrival to home station. Like the predeployment stage, the timeframe for this stage is also variable depending on the particular family. Typically, this stage lasts from three to six months.

This stage starts with the "homecoming" of the deployed service member. This can be a wonderfully joyous occasion with children rushing to the returning parent followed by the warm embrace and kiss of the reunited couple. The unit then comes to attention for one last time, followed by words of praise from the senior commander present. Lastly, weapons are turned in and duffel bags retrieved, and the family goes home.

Homecoming can also be an extremely frustrating and upsetting experience. The date of return may change repeatedly, or units may travel home piecemeal over several days. Despite best intentions, the spouse at home may not be able to meet the returning service member (short notice, the children might be sick, sitters cannot be found in the middle of the night, unable to get off work, etc.). Service members may expect to be received as "heroes" and "heroines" only to find that they have to make their own way home.

Typically, a "honeymoon" period follows in which couples reunite physically, but not necessarily emotionally. Some spouses express a sense of awkwardness in addition to excitement: "Who is this stranger in my bed?" For others, however, the desire for sexual intimacy may require time in order to reconnect emotionally first.

Eventually, service members will want to reassert their role as a member of the family, which can lead to tension. This is an essential task, which requires considerable patience to accomplish successfully. Service members may feel pressure to make up for lost time and missed milestones. Service members may want to take back all the responsibilities they had before. However, some things will have changed in their absence: spouses are more autonomous, children have grown, and individual personal priorities in life may be different. It is not realistic to return home and expect everything to be the same as before the deployment. During this period, spouses may report a lost sense of independence. There may be resentment at having been "abandoned" for six months or more. Spouses may consider themselves to be the true heroes (watching the house, children, paying bills, etc.) while service members cared only for themselves. At least one study (Zeff et al., 1997) suggests that the stay-at-home parent is more likely to report distress than the deployed service member. Spouses will also have to adapt to changes. Spouses may find that they are more irritable with their mates underfoot. They may desire their "own" space. Basic household chores and routines need to be renegotiated. The role played by the spouse in the marriage must be reestablished. Reunion with children can also be a challenge. Their feelings tend to depend on their age and understanding of why the service member was gone. Babies less than one year old may not know the service member and cry when held. Toddlers (one to three years) may be slow to warm up. Preschoolers (three to six years) may feel guilty and scared over the separation. School-age children (six to twelve years) may want a lot of attention. Teenagers (thirteen to eighteen years) may be moody and may not appear to care. In addition, children are often loyal to the parent that remains behind and do not respond to discipline from the returning service member. They may also fear the service member's return: "Wait till Mommy/Daddy gets home!" Some children may display significant anxiety up to a year later ("anniversary reaction"), triggered by the possibility of separation. In addition, the service member may not approve of privileges granted to children by the nondeployed parent. However, it is probably best for the service member not to try to make changes right away and to take time renegotiating family rules and norms. Not heeding this advice, the service member risks invalidating the efforts of his or her mate and alienating the children. Service members may feel hurt in response to such a lukewarm reception. Clearly going slowly and letting the child(ren) set the pace goes a long way toward a successful reunion.

Postdeployment is probably the most important stage for both service member and spouse. Patient communication, going slowly, lowering expectations, and taking time to get to know each other again is critical to the task of successful reintegration of the service member back into the family. Counseling may be required in the event that the service member is injured or returns as a stress casualty. On the other hand, the separation of deployment—unlike civilian couples—provides service member and spouse a chance to evaluate changes within themselves and what direction they want their marriage to take. Although postdeployment is a difficult as well as joyful stage, many military couples have reported that their relationship is much stronger as a result.

Lessons Learned

There are many challenges for military families to overcome during the five stages of deployment. Anticipating these challenges is important to minimize the emotional trauma caused by extended deployment. It is important not to overinterpret arguments, which are often caused by the pain and loss of separation. Resolving marital issues that precede deployment is very difficult to accomplish over long distances and is probably best left until the service member's return. Dates of departure and return often "slip" forward and backward. Establishing or maintaining a support network helps families cope. Rumors are hurtful and are best not repeated. If they cannot be resolved, then contact the chain of command to find out the truth or put a stop to them. Breaking up the time is a useful technique to prevent being overwhelmed. This can include weekly get-togethers with other families, monthly outings for the children (a favorite restaurant, the park, a picnic, etc.), and a visit to, or from, parents and in-laws around mid-deployment, just to name a few. In order to maintain their sanity, parents—now "single" because of the deployment—will need time without their children. Scheduling a regular "Mommy's (Daddy's) day out" can be achieved by daycare or sharing sitting with someone you trust. Overspending or increased alcohol use may provide short-term relief, but in the long term, they will only exacerbate the stress of deployment. Last, and most important, service member, spouse, and children will change and grow during the deployment. It is critical to go slow, be patient, and allow several months to reestablish family bonds.[1]

Reunion

The reunion of a family after a separation can be just as stressful as the separation itself. If your family has experienced some strain or tension during a reunion, you are not alone. You may have wondered why an occasion that is "supposed" to be so romantic and exciting should turn out less than perfect.

From the moment you are separated from the person you care about, you may begin to build up an image of that person in your mind. You may fantasize about how wonderful everything will be when you are together again.

You may remember the members of your family as they appear in the photograph in your wallet—the picture-perfect all-American family. A similar process is happening with the spouse and children. The missing member may be placed on a pedestal as the warrior out defending the country. Memories of everyday life such as making ends meet, occasional disagreements, and disciplining the children begin to fade from everyone's mind. The reunion is seen as the solution to all problems. "Once we are together again, everything will be perfect." However, reality rarely has a chance to live up to the high expectations you have set in your minds.

This is not meant to be a forecast of "doom and gloom." Homecomings can be very happy occasions as long as all family members make an effort to be as realistic as possible. If the tendency to not pick after oneself around the house occurred before the separation, that habit probably has not miraculously disappeared. If a weight problem existed prior to the separation, do not expect a fifty-pound loss to have occurred during the separation. If one of the children was experiencing problems at school, do not expect the problem to disappear at reunion time.

Talking to one another and working through the everyday challenges that family life presents is what is important. This does not all have to be accomplished on the day of the family reunion. Give yourselves some time to enjoy one another. Everyone needs to get reacquainted before problem-solving begins.

Returning from Deployment

It is normal to feel nervous and anxious about the homecoming. You may wonder whether your spouse will "like the way I look?" "like what I've done with the house?" "be proud of me for how I've handled things?" "still need me?" "still love me?"

Plan for homecoming day. After homecoming, make an agreement with your spouse on the schedule for the next few days or weeks. Where do the children, parents, extended family members, or friends fit in? Realize the day of homecoming is very stressful. You and your spouse may not have slept much and may be worn out from preparations.

Take time to get used to each other again. Reestablishing sexual intimacy will take patience, time, and good communication—some people need to be courted again.

Communicate! Tell your spouse how you feel—nervous, scared, happy, that you love and missed them. Listen to your spouse in return. The best way to get through the reacquaintance jitters, regain closeness, and renegotiate your roles in the family, is by talking and actively listening.

You've both been used to doing what you wanted during personal time. Feeling like you need some space is normal.

Your fantasies and expectations about how life will be upon return may be just fantasies. Be prepared to be flexible.

You or your spouse may be facing a change in job assignment or a move. Readjustment and job transition cause stress. This may be especially true for demobilizing Guard/Reservists who are transitioning back to civilian life.

Be calm and assertive, not defensive, when discussing decisions you have made, new family activities and customs, or methods of disciplining the children. Your spouse may need to hear that it wasn't the same doing these things alone, that you're glad he or she's back, and that you'd like to discuss problems and criticisms calmly.

Reassure your spouse that they are needed, even though you've coped during the deployment. Talk about keeping some of the independence you've developed. It's best not to "dump" all the chores—or only the ones you dislike—back on your spouse.

Your spouse may have seen or experienced some things that were very upsetting. Some normal reactions to these stressful situations are fear, nervousness, irritability, fatigue, sleep disturbances, startle reactions, moodiness, trouble concentrating, feelings of numbness, and frequent thoughts of the event. Talking with others and/or counselors trained in crisis stress reactions is very important.

Resist the temptation to go on a spending spree to celebrate the reunion. The extra money saved during deployment may be needed later for unexpected household expenses. Stick to your household budget. Show you care through your time and effort.

What to Expect from Your Children

Children may be feeling the same confusing things you and your spouse feel—worry, fear, stress, happiness, and excitement. Depending on their age, they may not understand how your spouse could leave them if he or she really loved them.

They may be unsure of what to expect from your spouse. They may feel uncomfortable or think of him or her as a stranger.

It's hard for children to control their excitement. Let them give and get the attention they need from the returning parent before you try to have quiet time alone with your spouse.

Children's reactions to the returning parent will differ according to their ages. Some normal reactions you can expect are:

- Infants—Cry, fuss, pull away from the returning parent, cling to you or the caregiver
- Toddlers—Be shy, clingy, not recognize the returning parent, cry, have temper tantrums, return to behaviors they had outgrown (no longer toilet trained)
- Preschoolers—Feel guilty for making parent go away, need time to warm up to returning parent, intense anger, act out to get attention, be demanding
- School-age—Excitement, joy, talk constantly to bring the returning parent up to date, boast about the returning parent, guilt about not doing enough or being good enough
- Teenagers—Excitement, guilt about not living up to standards, concern about rules and responsibilities, feel too old or unwilling to change plans to meet or spend extended time with the returning parent

Prepare children for homecoming with activities, photographs, participating in preparations, talking about Dad or Mom.

Children are excited and tend to act out. Accept and discuss these physical, attitudinal, mental, and emotional changes. Plan time as a couple and as a family with the children.

Stay involved with your children's school and social activities.

Take Time for Yourself

Look into ways to manage stress—diet, exercise, recreation—and definitely take care of yourself!

Make time to rest. Negotiate the number of social events you and your family attend.

Limit your use of alcohol. Remember, alcohol was restricted during your spouse's deployment, and tolerance is lowered.

Go slowly in getting back into the swing of things. Depend on family, your spouse's unit, and friends for support.

Remember . . .

- Go slowly—don't try to make up for lost time.
- Accept that your partner may be different.

- Take time to get reacquainted.
- Seek help for family members, if needed.
- If you feel like you are having trouble coping with adjustment, it is healthy to ask for help.

Many normal, healthy people occasionally need help to handle tough challenges in their lives. Contact a counseling agency or a minister, a Military Family Center, military chaplain, the Veterans Administration, or one of your community support groups that has been established in your area.

For the Returning Military

Even if you've been through a mobilization/deployment before, this one has been different because of the increased stressors of the time.

Regardless of your experience and assignment, you will have a natural period of adjustment.

Ease yourself back into the family gradually. If you come on like a "Sherman tank" and try to bulldoze your way back into your family's life, feelings of resentment will surface. See yourself as a "special guest" for a while.

Take some time to observe how the family has been running in your absence. You might be tempted to jump right in with "Now that I am home, there are going to be a few changes around here." You will see that some things will change naturally as a result of your presence in the family. If you disagree about the way other things have been handled, wait a few days and discuss it openly with your spouse.

Do not try to take over the finances immediately. A complete interrogation regarding the state of the checkbook as soon as you walk through the door is bound to create hostility. Set aside some time when things have calmed down to review the financial situation with your spouse.

Take it easy with the children in terms of discipline. For a while, stick with the rules your spouse has established during your absence. Immediately playing the "heavy" will not open up opportunities for you and the children to get to know one another again. It is not difficult to understand why some children are afraid of the returning parent if all they have to look forward to is "a changing of the guard."

On the other hand, sometimes it is easy to spoil your children. If you have not seen them for a long period of time, or you are home for only short periods of time, you may find yourself not wanting to discipline them. You are probably eager to make up for the time you were unable to spend with them. This is certainly understandable. But do not put your spouse in the position of constantly playing the "heavy" while you have all the fun with the children.

Do not be surprised if your spouse is a little envious of your travels. Your life may look very exciting compared to the job of "keeping the home fires burning." Surprise your spouse with a gift when you return from a new place. This way you can show off your "treasures" from different states or countries and cultures and share your experiences.

Expect your spouse to have changed. Neither of you is the same person you were a few months ago, or even a few weeks ago. The main adjustment for military families after a separation is the change in roles. Your spouse has learned to cope alone as a matter of survival. Out of necessity, some of your roles have been taken over in order to compensate for your absence. Try not to be threatened if you find an independent person when you return home. The fact that your spouse can cope without you does not necessarily mean that he or she cares about you any less.

You may find this tip sheet helpful in ensuring a successful homecoming and readjustment.

Reuniting with Your Spouse

- It is normal to feel nervous and anxious about homecoming. Often service members wonder whether their spouse will still "be proud of me?" "love me and need me?" "expect things from me?"
- Plan for homecoming day. After homecoming, make an agreement with your spouse on the schedule for the next few days or weeks. Where do the children, extended family members, or friends fit in?
- Realize the day of homecoming is very stressful. You and your spouse may not have slept much and may be worn out from preparations.
- Don't be surprised if your spouse is a bit resentful of your mobilization/ deployment. Others often think of the deployment as more fun and exciting than staying at home—even if you know otherwise.
- Take time to get used to each other again. Reestablishing sexual intimacy will take patience, time, and good communication—some people need to be courted again. Set aside "date" nights where you can do the things you did when you were courting and go to the places that have a special meaning for you both. Remember the rules about building strong relationships and stoke up that fire.
- *Communicate!* Tell your spouse how you feel—nervous, scared, happy, that you love and missed them. Listen to your spouse in return. The best way to get through the reacquaintance jitters, regain closeness, and renegotiate your roles in the family is by talking and actively listening.

- You've both been used to doing what you wanted during personal time. Feeling like you need some space is normal.
- Your fantasies and expectations about how life will be upon return may be just fantasies. Be prepared to be flexible.
- You and/or your spouse may be facing a change in job assignment or a move. Readjustment and job transition cause stress. This may be especially true for demobilizing Guard/Reservists who are transitioning back to civilian life.
- Resist the temptation to go on a spending spree to celebrate the reunion. The extra money saved during deployment may be needed later for unexpected household expenses. Stick to your budget. Show you care through your time and effort.

Reuniting with Your Children

- Children may be feeling the same confusing things you and your spouse feel—worry, fear, stress, happiness, excitement. Depending on their age, they may not understand how you could leave them if you really loved them.
- They may be unsure of what to expect from their returning parent. They may feel uncomfortable around you or think of you as a stranger.
- It's hard for children to control their excitement. Let them give and get the attention they need from you before you try to have quiet time alone with your spouse.
- Children's reactions to your return will differ according to their ages. Some normal reactions you can expect, and suggestions for handling them are:
  - o Infants: Cry, fuss, pull away from you, cling to your spouse or the caregiver they know. Talk to them while holding, hugging, bathing, changing, feeding, playing, and relaxing with them.
  - o Toddlers: Be shy, clingy, not recognize you, cry, have temper tantrums, return to behaviors they had outgrown (no longer toilet trained). Give them space and warm-up time. Be gentle and fun. Sit on floor at their level and play with them.
  - o Preschoolers: Feel guilty for making you go away, need time to warm up to you, intense anger, act out to get attention, be demanding. Reinforce that they are loved unconditionally, listen carefully, accept their feelings, find out new things they are interested in, play with them, control attention-getting behavior.

o School-age: Excitement, joy, talk constantly to bring you up to date, boast about you, guilt about not doing enough or being good enough. Review pictures, schoolwork, and family scrapbook. Praise for what they did during your deployment; do not criticize.

o Teenagers: Excitement, guilt about not living up to standards, concern about rules and responsibilities, feel too old or unwilling to change plans to meet you or spend extended time with you upon your return. Share what's happened during deployment, encourage them to share, do chores together, listen, respect privacy and friends, don't be judgmental.

- Reassure children and spouse and communicate your love to family.
- Children are excited and tend to act out. Accept and discuss these physical, attitudinal, mental, emotional changes.
- Get reinvolved with your children's school and social activities.

Single Service Members/Single Parents— Reuniting with Parents, Extended Family Members, and Friends

- You have certainly missed your family and friends, and they have missed you. Let them be a part of the reunion, but balance your needs with those you love and care about. You will have a period of readjustment when you return home.
- If you are single or live with your parent(s), family, or a friend, many of the above tips for a reuniting with spouses and children may apply. Changes in the house or routine may be stressful. Go slowly in trying to make the adjustment to being home again.
- Some things will have changed at home while you were gone— marriage in your family or friends, new babies born, new neighbors, changes in relationships.
- Some things will change with the people you've lived and worked with prior to deployment. Married friends will be involved with their families. Others may return to their old friends and you may feel left out.
- Your parents and family have been very worried about you over the past months. Give them time and special attention.
- You may be facing a change in job assignment or a move, or trying to meet new people, looking for a new relationship. All these things cause stress.

Take Time for Yourself

- You may have seen or experienced some things that were very upsetting. Some normal reactions to these abnormal situations are fear, nervousness, irritability, fatigue, sleep disturbances, startle reactions, moodiness, trouble concentrating, feelings of numbness, and frequent thoughts of the event. Talking with others who were there and/or counselors trained in crisis stress reactions is very important.
- Look into ways to manage stress—diet, exercise, recreation—and definitely take care of yourself!
- Make time to rest. Negotiate the number of social events to attend.
- Limit your use of alcohol. Remember alcohol was restricted during your deployment and your tolerance is lowered.
- Depend on family, your unit, and friends for support.

Remember . . .

Go slowly—don't try to make up for lost time.
Accept that your partner and loved ones may be different.
Take time to get reacquainted.
Seek help, if needed.

Becoming a Couple Again

How to Create a Shared Sense of Purpose after Deployment

Coming together as a couple after war deployment isn't always easy or something that happens naturally. It requires effort, and an understanding that each person has grown and changed during the separation. A positive way to think about this is that both of you, service person and spouse, have developed your own sense of purpose coping with new experiences while apart. What's important now is to come together and create a "shared sense of purpose" that is essential for your well-being as a couple, that of your children, and your life in the community. This won't happen overnight; it will take time, mutual compassion, and a desire to do so. Here are four steps to help you create a "shared sense of purpose."

STEP 1: UNDERSTAND EACH OTHER'S SENSE OF PURPOSE DURING SEPARA-TION. The returning service member's sense of purpose has been shaped by:

- Traumatic events that can be difficult to process and talk about
- Identification and closeness with their military unit and comrades who have shared similar experiences

Quick Tips for Keeping a
Strong Relationship during Deployment

Some ways to nurture your love through the ups and downs of deployment:

- Talk about your upcoming separation. Set aside some quiet time to talk about your feelings and plan how each of you will manage during your time apart.
- Discuss how you will stay in touch. Explore the available options, such as e-mail, phone calls, and regular mail.
- Keep busy and stay active if you are the at-home spouse. The more fulfilled you feel, the better you will handle separations and difficult times. (Of course, if you have children you won't have concerns about not being busy.)
- Share daily happenings from home. Hearing about your life (even the everyday routine) will help your deployed spouse feel closer to you.
- Learn about your spouse's job and other interests. Learning what your spouse's life is like will help you better understand his or her experiences while you are apart.
- Send care packages. Be sure to include special treats, funny notes, and items that have special meaning for the two of you.
- Record your thoughts in a journal to share with your spouse. You may want to keep an online journal with pictures for your spouse to access over the Internet.
- Record a tape or CD with songs that remind you of your spouse. Make a copy for each of you.
- Send handmade coupons to your deployed spouse. Your coupons might be for a special dinner or hour-long backrub when your partner returns home.
- Be realistic about communication. Keep in mind that your deployed spouse may be in an area with limited mail or e-mail service, or too busy to respond right away.

- Regimentation in the form of highly structured and efficient routines
- Heightened sensory experiences including sights, sounds, and smells
- Expanded self-importance and identity shaped by war

The spouse's sense of purpose has been shaped by:

- *New roles and responsibilities.* Many spouses have assumed new or more taxing employment, oversight of finances, and child-rearing.

- *Community support trade-offs.* Some spouses and children left the military base to stay with parents and in-laws for various reasons, but will have experienced loss of connection with their military community, its familiarity, and its support.
- *Emotional changes.* Some spouses may have experienced growing independence and thrived on it; others may have found this a difficult time leading to depression, anxiety, increased alcohol or substance use and abuse, and other symptoms of stress.

STEP 2: RECOGNIZE THAT THE FOLLOWING CONCERNS UPON RE-TURN ARE COMMON, OFTEN SHARED OR FELT INDIRECTLY, AND WILL REQUIRE MUTUAL ADJUSTMENTS AND TIME:

- *Home.* Life at home does not have the edge and adrenaline associated with wartime duty, which often leads to letdown, disappointment, and difficulty shifting gears.
- *Children.* Reconnecting with one's children is an anticipated event by service member and spouse. Children react differently depending upon their age, and can be shy, angry, or jealous as new bonds are reestablished. Discipline will now be shared, often resulting in conflicting opinions and styles.
- *Relationship.* Concern about having grown apart, growing close again without giving up individual growth and viewpoints, issues of fidelity, and being able to discuss these issues without raising more anxiety or anger challenge many couples.
- *Public.* While there has been widespread support of the service member, the public has mixed views of the war. Protracted deployment and an upcoming election may polarize the public, promoting media coverage that can undermine the pride and purpose military families feel about their involvement.

STEP 3: RELATIONSHIP BREAKERS: MOST COUPLES ARGUE ABOUT THREE THINGS: SEX, MONEY, AND CHILDREN. Understanding the potential of these issues to divide rather than unite is key to reestablishing a shared sense of purpose. These issues involve:

- *Intimacy.* Intimacy is a combination of emotional *and* physical togetherness. It is not easily reestablished after stressful separations creating an emotional disconnect. Partners may also experience high or low sexual interest, causing disappointment, friction, or a sense of rejection. In due time this may pass, but present concerns may include hoping one is still loved, dealing with rumors or concern about faithfulness, concern about medications that can affect desire and performance, and expected fatigue and alterations in sleep cycles.

- *Finances.* During the deployment, most service members and families received additional income from tax breaks and combat duty pay, as much as $1,000 extra per month. Some families may have been able to set aside appreciable savings; other families may have spent some or all of the money on justifiable expenses and adjusted family budgets. This may create disagreement that can hamper the important work of building *shared trust* and financial planning as a couple essential to moving forward.
- *Children.* Children have grown and changed during deployment. Some returning service members will see children for the first time. It is important to build upon the positive changes in your children and work as a couple to address issues of concern that need improvement or attention. Discipline of children will now be shared and should be viewed as something that can be built together rather than criticized or ignored.

STEP 4: RELATIONSHIP MAKERS: HERE ARE SOME THOUGHTS AND TIPS FOR BUILDING A SHARED SENSE OF PURPOSE AND STRONGER FAMILY.

- *Expectations.* Remember that fatigue, confusion, and worry, common during this transition, often lead to short tempers. In that frame of mind, it is easy to revert to the relationship breaker issues listed above. If this happens, suggest taking time out and return to discussions when both parties feel more relaxed.
- *Enjoy life.* Find and do activities that are pleasurable, such as a movie, a family picnic, bowling, or shopping. Create time in your weekly schedule to do something as a couple, as a family, and one-on-one activity that is shared between returning service member and his or her child or children.
- *Give thanks.* Together, thank those people, family, friends, coworkers, and new service member buddies who have helped you and your family during this deployment. Showing appreciation through writing notes together, calling people, or visiting them will bring a sense of fulfillment that reunites each other's experiences.
- *Communicate.* Talking together builds a shared sense of purpose. Desire to communicate is more important than details. Service members often prefer to discuss war stories with military buddies to

protect their spouse and family from traumatic memories. Spouses should not be offended. Other ways to communicate involve physical activity. Take walks, work out together, or engage in a sport. Healthy communication involves processing feelings, new information, and relieving stress. Read, draw, paint, dance, sing, play an instrument, volunteer at church or in the community to keep a sense of perspective.

- *Let time be your friend.* Time may not mend everything, but it is often one of the most important factors in healing and solving problems.
- *Be positive.* A positive attitude is one of the most important gifts you can bring to each other and your family during this time. Appreciating what one has gives strength and energy to a family and a couple. Special circumstances such as physical injury and psychological problems are not addressed here, and require additional support, information, and resources.
- *Know when to seek help.* Both service member and spouse have endured a level of stress, uncertainty, worry, and lonesomeness that can affect one's health and mental health. If either spouse or service member suspects he or she may be suffering from a health or mental health problem, it is essential to seek help. Many service members do not want to seek help for mental health problems from the military for fear of damaging their career. However, the consequences of letting a problem linger untreated can be much more damaging. There are excellent treatments, including medications, that can help people reclaim their lives and enjoy their families, as they should. You owe it to yourself and your family to be in good health.[2]

Notes

1. LTC Simon H. Pincus, USA, MC; COL Robert House, USAR, MC; LTC Joseph Christenson, USA, MC; and CAPT Lawrence E. Adler, MC, USNR-R, www.hoooah4.com.

2. Uniformed Services University of the Health Sciences, Bethesda, MD.

Resources

Zeff, K. N., Lewis, S. J., & Hirsch, K. A. (1997). Military family adaptation to United Nations operations in Somalia. *Military Medicine*, 162(6), 384–387.

Wounded Warriors   **6**

W HEN BATTLEFIELD INJURY OCCURS FAR from home, the road to recovery may be long and difficult to navigate. Even with the dedicated support of medical professionals, loved ones, military leadership, and brothers- and sisters-in-arms, this pathway from injury to home requires caring over time and over miles. Differences in the type of injury, in the nature of support available along the way, and the types of resources and responsibilities waiting at home may dictate different stops along the way for different service members.

Movement from care at the point of battlefield injury—physical, psychological, or combined—through levels of care abroad and within the United States and ultimately homeward is a complex process involving the interplay of personal endurance; military and medical leadership; technology and communications; and networks of civilian and military caregivers, supporters, and communities. The modern evacuation and movement of the injured provides new opportunities for care, necessary tracking and communications, and needs for protection from additional health burdens, both physical and administrative.

1. Over 75,000 service members have sustained combat injury in the wars in Iraq and Afghanistan. Approximately half of these have been serious enough that the service member has been unable to continue to function in theatre and has required a medical evacuation back to the continental United States. The injuries include but are by no means limited to traumatic amputations, loss of sight, and traumatic brain injury. The emotionally injured may also be evacuated. Importantly, even severe emotional injuries may not be readily apparent on the battlefield and occur in greater numbers

as home approaches and the challenges of return meet the worries of lost health and function.

2. The "invisibility" of psychological injury presents a complex medical situation in which denial, stigma, fear of reexposure to painful memories, and lack of knowledge of treatment options and efficacy impede help-seeking and strain an already stressed system of care resources. Administrative procedures can become part of secondary injury. On the other hand, when health systems create opportunities to miss care, the combination of fears, stigma, and emotional pain can enhance missed opportunities for psychological and behavioral care.

3. Most serious combat injuries powerfully impact the children and families of service members. Longitudinal data suggest that problems do not immediately resolve and commonly worsen during the course of the first year after hospitalization. Difficulty in readjusting to life back home may alter family relationships and support contributing to a vicious cycle of psychosocial challenges for both the injured service member and the family. The family should be seen as care collaborators in all health interventions and planning.

4. Returning combat veterans, even those not psychologically injured, experience a variety of behavioral and emotional responses secondary to their war experience. Distress symptoms are common and may include insomnia, nightmares, or other forms of sleep disorder; hypervigilance, jitteriness, or overexcitement; and avoidance or social withdrawal. Reintegration with family and life is a goal and can be a challenge.

5. Systems of care must address not only disorders but also the many emotional and behavioral manifestations of distress. They must incorporate health care provided by military, VA, and civilian treatment facilities; facilitate family participation in health care and treatment planning; and engage traditional community resources (e.g., churches and schools) as well as employee and local, state, and federal programs implemented specifically to provide assistance to returning veterans.

6. Secondary injury can result from the induced helplessness, overwhelming stress, and indignities resulting from administrative delays, errors, and omissions, which may unnecessarily complicate recovery.

7. Variability in the time and emotional availability and responsiveness of family members requires resources and flexibility in order to identify and establish care advocates for each injured service member.

8. People returning from combat deployment can sometimes initiate or increase the frequency of risk behaviors that compromise their health and the health and safety of those around them. Excessive alcohol use may

develop as a misguided attempt to reduce stress. Irritability or anger (common symptoms on return home) may turn into violence, at times directed to one's family, in the context of excessive alcohol use or the decreased emotional control that can accompany traumatic brain injury.

9. Medical advances and current practice have altered the amount of time an individual may remain in a specific care environment. Rarely in the modern world of war is the injured now in theatre or even overseas for long periods of time. Yet healing and administrative processes still take time and hold patients in new settings where family may or may not be present and resources have to be constantly adjusted to meet needs. Resources have to be sufficient and flexibly assigned to meet each level of care in order to sustain the recovery process and be responsive to the cultural context of the injured and geographical considerations (i.e., those residing in rural or remote locations).

10. Current processes of medical evacuation generally provide for superb initial stabilization and management of physical and psychosocial injuries to service members within the military medical system. However, they do not well address the longer-term challenges associated with care across boundaries of community, family, and VA and civilian medical services. The care of injured from battlefield to home must be reengineered to incorporate the new health care available, the technology and transport, the varied effects of injury on family members, the subsequent impact on the nature and availability of family resources to the injured service member, and the range in available resources during evacuation and at home station over time.

11. Navigating the complexities of ongoing medical care and disability evaluation is in and of itself a health challenge and a health burden. It can be an impediment to the intrinsically human process of adaptation to serious physical or emotional injury. Navigating this complex road requires acknowledging the injury's impact on one's identity, one's future, one's family, and one's livelihood. Such knowledge changes how we view ourself and our family, and can change how our family and friends view us and our future. This adaptation, recovery, and return requires time and community to sustain the process.

Injured service members are often treated at medical facilities a great distance away from their homes. The military recognizes the benefits of a family's visit while a service member recuperates and often provides assistance in transporting family members to the facility where the service member is recuperating. In addition, a number of private organizations provide further travel assistance to qualified family members. These organizations include the Fisher House Foundation, which provides free or low-cost lodgings at Fisher Houses located on the grounds of military and VA medical centers throughout the country, as well as free airline tickets through its Hero Miles program. In addition, family members who need time off from work to be with a recuperating service member may benefit from the Family and Medical Leave Act (FMLA), a federal law that guarantees many workers up to twelve weeks of unpaid leave during a twelve-month period to care for family members suffering from serious medical conditions.

The financial consequences of an injury are generally not the first concern for service members and their families. However, understanding the various benefits available to assist with financial needs is an important part of the recovery process. Service members, including reservists, may continue to receive full pay while recovering from injury and awaiting a medical evaluation. In addition, program called Traumatic Servicemembers' Group Life Insurance (TSGLI) provides qualified service members with assistance in the direct aftermath of a severe injury. Coverage is retroactive to qualifying service members who suffered traumatic injuries in Iraq and Afghanistan on or after October 7, 2001. For more details about TSGLI see the insurance section in chapter 1.

Casualty Status

According to the Department of Defense (DoD), a casualty is "any person who is lost to the organization by reason of having been declared beleaguered, besieged, captured, dead, diseased, detained, duty status whereabouts unknown, injured, ill, interned, missing, missing in action, or wounded."

When a service member is injured, gets sick, or is hospitalized, he or she becomes a "casualty." The service member is then further categorized according to his or her casualty type and the casualty status.

The military now categorizes casualties as dead, wounded, ill, or injured with subdivisions such as very seriously ill or injured, seriously ill or injured, and not seriously ill or injured. Originally the DoD categories only covered combat casualties, but these have now been expanded to cover all injuries and illnesses. The new categories now take into account many other conditions, including psychological and traumatic injuries as a result of the wars,

Federal Recovery Coordinators

Federal recovery coordinators ensure that appropriate oversight and coordination is provided for care of active duty service members and veterans with major amputations, severe traumatic brain injury, spinal cord injury, severe sight or hearing impairments, and severe multiple injuries. The coordinators also work closely with family members to take care of services and needs. The aim is to ensure that lifelong medical and rehabilitative care services and other federal benefits are provided to seriously wounded, injured, and ill active duty service members, veterans, and their families.

The coordinators have a background in health care management and work closely with the clinicians and case management teams to develop and execute plans of services needed across the continuum of care, from recovery through rehabilitation to reintegration to civilian life.

These federal recovery coordinators ensure a smooth transition of wounded service members through VA's health care system, while also cutting red tape for other benefits.

Your Support Team

Wounded service members have case managers assigned to work with them during their recovery period. The job of these individuals is to provide information and help assist the service member and family during the recovery period and the Physical Evaluation Board (PEB) and Medical Evaluation Board (MEB) process. These individuals also provide information on Veteran Service Organizations (VSOs). Many military hospitals serving wounded or injured service members also have Family Assistance Centers. Liaison officers also serve in hospitals acting as the advocate for the patient and the link between the wounded warriors and their units and families. The liaison officer also works with patient administrative teams who help gather patient treatment information, make travel arrangements, liaise with the families, and act as link with charitable organizations.

Families can also seek assistance from the installation chaplains, social workers, and family center: Army Community Services, Marine Corps Community Services, Air Force Family Support Center, Navy Fleet and Family Support Center, and Coast Guard Work Life Offices.

Important note: The wars in Iraq and Afghanistan have resulted in tens of thousands of wounded warriors, and this has put additional pressures and strains on military marriages. In many cases this has also brought about a significant change in the spousal role. Partners who used to stay at home are

---

Military bodies responsible for assisting injured service members and wounded transitioning veterans:

Army—Wounded Warrior Transition Brigades
Navy—Safe Harbor Program
Marine Corps—Marine for Life and Wounded Warrior Regiment
Air Force—Palace HART (Helping Airmen Recover Together)

now caregivers as well, but may have to consider becoming the breadwinner. While the wounded warrior is entitled to a whole range of benefits and help, it may still not be enough to pay all the bills. In such cases, spouses may have to consider getting a job or going back to school to get new qualifications. If you have been out of the workforce some time, it can be very challenging searching out new jobs, doing the rounds of interviews, getting your résumé up to date, and so on. Fortunately help is available for all of these things with guidance on job hunting, available work, and even résumé writing.

Please also see *The Wounded Warrior Handbook* by Don Philpott, Janelle Hill, and Cheryl Lawhorne (Government Institutes, 2008). It is an easy-to-use, comprehensive reference guide for wounded warriors, as well as for their families and loved ones.

A huge and growing amount of literature is available from the military and others; scores of support organizations are involved in this arena, and hundreds of websites offer information and help. All of these do a magnificent job in their respective areas, but it can be a daunting task to pull together all this information, especially at a time of crisis. The information in this handbook was gathered from hundreds of these sources and resources in the public domain and elsewhere and includes the most up-to-date information about health services and benefits from the Department of Veterans Affairs. The handbook also deals with other critical issues such as important financial, legal, and tax matters, although this information is provided purely as guidance.

The handbook provides a comprehensive framework that will allow wounded warriors and their families to quickly access information that they need regarding medical treatment, rehabilitation, counseling, support, and transition.

A Family Member's Trauma

From the moment you were informed that your service member was deploying into a combat zone, your life altered. The normal routine shifted to include the underlying concern felt when a loved one is in harm's way. The day you received notification that your service member was wounded, you were wounded as well. Families are connected: what happens to one member affects all the other members of the family. While attention is focused on supporting your service member, time needs to be spent as well acknowledging your own traumatic experience, and the ongoing effects this experience will have on you and your life.

Notification can be a traumatic experience in and of itself. Even when you know that your service member is in a combat zone and anything can happen, it is still a shock when you receive a phone call stating that something has. That phone call triggered a series of events that eventually led you to travel from the comfort of your home to the unfamiliar hospital bedside of your service member. Travel, even under the best of circumstances, is a stressful event. When combined with reuniting with your seriously wounded service member, it becomes even more so. All these experiences in such a short amount of time can be overwhelming, and then you begin to factor in the reality of the injuries and condition of your service member. Life can suddenly feel out of control.

Whether you are a spouse, parent, child, or other relative of the service member, your life has been irrevocably changed by the events that brought you here. Change is a challenging thing and often uncomfortable while you adapt to the new reality the change has brought to your life. With change, something of the old way of life is lost, and as with all loss, there is a normal period where grieving occurs. No one can know what your loss is. Each of us is unique, and what may be significant to one person may not be to another. Your grieving process is personal. Take some time to think about what you have lost.

Acknowledge your own loss and grieve for it. Understand that the extent of your own loss is not fully apparent now. It will take time to realize how much your life will be changed by this experience. Be patient with yourself while you come to grips with the shift in your life.

Your trauma is real. While you might tell yourself it is nothing compared to what your service member is enduring, it will have an effect on you. Being aware of that gives you some measure of control to lessen that effect. You have the right to feel pain and sorrow. Take care of yourself. Focus on what you have the power to do: that is, to change your own actions or reactions. Actively pursue stress management. Utilize the resources available to you. Seek out and utilize support services for yourself and your children. The social worker assigned to your service member is there for you as well. Your entire family has been wounded along with your service member, and it deserves the same care and concern as you are giving your service member.

War-Zone-Related Stress Reactions: What Families Need to Know

A National Center for Posttraumatic Stress Disorder (PTSD) Fact Sheet

Military personnel in war zones frequently have serious reactions to their traumatic war experiences. Sometimes the reactions continue after they return home. Ongoing reactions to war-zone fear, horror, or helplessness are connected to posttraumatic stress and can include:

- Nightmares or difficulty sleeping
- Unwanted distressing memories or thoughts
- Anxiety and panic
- Irritability and anger
- Emotional numbing or loss of interest in activities or people
- Problem alcohol or drug use to cope with stress reactions

How Traumatic Stress Reactions Can Affect Families

- Stress reactions may interfere with a service member's ability to trust and be emotionally close to others. As a result, families may feel emotionally cut off from the service member.
- A returning war veteran may feel irritable and have difficulty communicating, which may make it hard to get along with him or her.
- A returning veteran may experience a loss of interest in family social activities.
- Veterans with posttraumatic stress disorder may lose interest in sex and feel distant from their spouses.
- Traumatized war veterans often feel that something terrible may happen "out of the blue" and can become preoccupied with trying to keep themselves and family members safe.
- Just as war veterans are often afraid to address what happened to them, family members are frequently fearful of examining the traumatic events as well. Family members may want to avoid talking about the trauma or related problems. They may avoid talking because they want to spare the survivor further pain or because they are afraid of his or her reaction.
- Family members may feel hurt, alienated, or discouraged because the veteran has not been able to overcome the effects of the trauma. Family members may become angry or feel distant from the veteran.

The Important Role of Families in Recovery

The primary source of support for the returning service member is likely to be his or her family.

Families can help the veteran not withdraw from others. Families can provide companionship and a sense of belonging, which can help counter the veteran's feeling of separateness because of his or her experiences. Families can provide practical and emotional support for coping with life stressors.

If the veteran agrees, it is important for family members to participate in treatment. It is also important to talk about how the posttrauma stress is affecting the family and what the family can do about it. Adult family members should also let their loved ones know that they are willing to listen if the service member would like to talk about war experiences. Family members should talk with treatment providers about how they can help in the recovery effort.

What Happens in Treatment for PTSD?

Treatment for PTSD focuses on helping the trauma survivor reduce fear and anxiety, gain control over traumatic stress reactions, make sense of war experiences, and function better at work and in the family. A standard course of treatment usually includes:

- Assessment and development of an individual treatment plan
- Education of veterans and their families about posttraumatic stress and its effects
- Training in relaxation methods, to help reduce physical arousal/ tension
- Practical instruction in skills for coping with anger, stress, and ongoing problems
- Detailed discussion of feelings of anger or guilt, which are very common among survivors of war trauma
- Detailed discussions to help change distressing beliefs about self and others (e.g., self-blame)
- If appropriate, careful, repeated discussions of the trauma (exposure therapy) to help the service member reduce the fear associated with trauma memories
- Medication to reduce anxiety, depression, or insomnia
- Group support from other veterans, often felt to be the most valuable treatment experience

Mental health professionals in VA medical centers, community clinics, and Readjustment Counseling Service Vet Centers have a long tradition of working with family members of veterans with PTSD. Couples counseling and educational classes for families may be available. Family members can encourage the survivor to seek education and counseling, but should not try to force their loved one to get help. Family members should consider getting help for themselves, whether or not their loved one is getting treatment.

Self-Care Suggestions for Families

- Become educated about PTSD.
- Take time to listen to all family members and show them that you care.
- Spend time with other people. Coping is easier with support from others, including extended family, friends, church groups, or other community groups.
- Join or develop a support group.
- Take care of yourself. Family members frequently devote themselves totally to those they care for and, in the process, neglect their own needs. Pay attention to yourself. Watch your diet and exercise, and get plenty of rest. Take time to do things that feel good to you.
- Try to maintain family routines, such as dinner together, church, or sports outings.
- If needed, get professional help as early as possible, and get back in touch with treatment providers if things worsen after treatment has ended.

For more information about PTSD please visit the VA website at www .va.gov. A PTSD guide for families can be found at the following Web address: http://ncptsd.va.gov/ncmain/ncdocs/manuals/GuideforFamilies.pdf.

Families

One huge advantage of being married to someone in the military is the wealth of resources available to you through your new extended family, and this is especially true when you have children. There are family support services (see box below for their military branch–specific names), spouses clubs, mentoring organizations, child care facilities, "respite care" for wounded families, volunteer networks, and many other licensed and professional services all aimed at providing you and your family with the support you need, particularly if you have wounded love ones or children with special needs. All the branches have dedicated, trained, and professional

Remember, each branch of the military has its own name for Family Support Centers and their own programs for new spouses. These are:

Army Community Service Center—Family Team Building
Airman and Family Readiness Center—Heartlink
Marine Corps Community Services Center—LINKS (Lifestyle, Insights, Networking, Knowledge, and Skills)
Navy Fleet and Family Support Center—COMPASS

family support advisors who are available to help you. In the USMC, for instance, these advisors are known as family readiness officers and work with Marine Corps Community Services. Your Family Support Center can put you in touch with the right people. You should never feel alone or helpless. There is always someone to turn to for help.

Starting a Family

I<span></span>F YOU ARE THINKING OF STARTING A FAMILY, ensure that your health insurance covers you as the mother throughout your pregnancy for prenatal care and delivery and then covers you and your child thereafter. Consult with your health benefits advisor.

You should start taking care of yourself *before* you start trying to get pregnant. This is called preconception health. It means knowing how health conditions and risk factors could affect you or your unborn baby if you become pregnant. For example, some foods, habits, and medicines can harm your baby—even before he or she is conceived. Some health problems also can affect pregnancy.

Talk to your doctor before pregnancy to learn what you can do to prepare your body. Women should prepare for pregnancy before becoming sexually active. Ideally, women should give themselves at least three months to prepare before getting pregnant.

The five most important things you can do before becoming pregnant are the following.

- Take 400 micrograms (400 mcg or 0.4 mg) of folic acid every day for at least three months before getting pregnant to lower your risk of some birth defects of the brain and spine. You can get folic acid from some foods, but it's hard to get all the folic acid you need from foods alone. Taking a vitamin with folic acid is the best and easiest way to be sure you're getting enough.
- Stop smoking and drinking alcohol. Ask your doctor for help.

- If you have a medical condition, be sure it is under control. Some conditions include asthma, diabetes, depression, high blood pressure, obesity, thyroid disease, or epilepsy. Be sure your vaccinations are up to date.
- Talk to your doctor about any over-the-counter and prescription medicines you are using. These include dietary or herbal supplements. Some medicines are not safe during pregnancy. At the same time, stopping medicines you need also can be harmful.
- Avoid contact with toxic substances or materials at work and at home that could be harmful. Stay away from chemicals and cat or rodent feces.

You Are Pregnant

You will probably want to tell everyone that you are having a baby, but as the wife of a serving military member you may also tell his command. If you are serving in the military and become pregnant, it is even more important that you notify command so they can adjust your duties. For the father it is also a good time to put in a request for paternity leave.

Prenatal Care

Prenatal care can help keep you and your baby healthy. Babies of mothers who do not get prenatal care are three times more likely to have a low birth weight and five times more likely to die than those born to mothers who do get care.

Doctors can spot health problems early when they see mothers regularly. This allows doctors to treat them early. Early treatment can cure many problems and prevent others. Doctors also can talk to pregnant women about things they can do to give their unborn babies a healthy start to life.

Health Care Dos and Don'ts

Get early and regular prenatal care. Whether this is your first pregnancy or third, health care is extremely important. Your doctor will check to make sure you and the baby are healthy at each visit. If there are any problems, early action will help you and the baby.

Take a multivitamin or prenatal vitamin with 400 micrograms (400 mcg or 0.4 mg) of folic acid every day.

Ask your doctor before stopping any medicines or starting any new medicines. Some medicines are not safe during pregnancy. Keep in mind that even over-the-counter medicines and herbal products may cause side effects or other problems. But not using medicines you need could also be harmful.

Avoid x-rays. If you must have dental work or diagnostic tests, tell your dentist or doctor that you are pregnant so that extra care can be taken.

Get a flu shot if your baby's due date is between March and July. Pregnant women can get very sick from the flu and may need hospital care.

Food Dos and Don'ts

Eat a variety of healthy foods. Choose fruits, vegetables, whole grains, calcium-rich foods, and foods low in saturated fat. Also make sure to drink plenty of fluids, especially water.

Get all the nutrients you need each day, including iron. Getting enough iron prevents you from getting anemia, which is linked to preterm birth and low birth weight. Eating a variety of healthy foods will help you get the nutrients your baby needs. But ask your doctor if you need to take a daily prenatal vitamin or iron supplement to be sure you are getting enough.

Protect yourself and your baby from foodborne illnesses, including toxoplasmosis and listeria. Wash fruits and vegetables before eating. Don't eat uncooked or undercooked meats or fish. Always handle, clean, cook, eat, and store foods properly.

Don't eat fish with lots of mercury, including swordfish, king mackerel, shark, and tilefish.

Lifestyle Dos and Don'ts

Gain a healthy amount of weight. Your doctor can tell you how much weight gain you should aim for during pregnancy.

Don't smoke, drink alcohol, or use drugs. These can cause long-term harm or death to your baby. Ask your doctor for help quitting.

Unless your doctor tells you not to, try to get at least two hours and thirty minutes of moderate-intensity aerobic activity a week. It's best to spread out your workouts throughout the week. If you worked out regularly before pregnancy, you can keep up your activity level as long as your health doesn't change and you talk to your doctor about your activity level throughout your pregnancy. Learn more about how to have a fit pregnancy.

Don't take very hot baths or use hot tubs or saunas.

Get plenty of sleep and find ways to control stress.

Get informed. Read books, watch videos, go to a childbirth class, and talk with moms you know.

Ask your doctor about childbirth education classes for you and your partner. Classes can help you prepare for the birth of your baby.

Environmental Dos and Don'ts

Stay away from chemicals like insecticides, solvents (like some cleaners or paint thinners), lead, mercury, and paint (including paint fumes). Not all products have pregnancy warnings on their labels. If you're unsure if a product is safe, ask your doctor before using it. Talk to your doctor if you are worried that chemicals used in your workplace might be harmful.

If you have a cat, ask your doctor about toxoplasmosis. This infection is caused by a parasite sometimes found in cat feces. If not treated, toxoplasmosis can cause birth defects. You can lower your risk by avoiding cat litter and wearing gloves when gardening.

Avoid contact with rodents, including pet rodents, and with their urine, droppings, or nesting material. Rodents can carry a virus that can be harmful or even deadly to your unborn baby.

Take steps to avoid illness, such as washing hands frequently.

Stay away from secondhand smoke.

Your doctor will give you a schedule of all the doctor's visits you should have while pregnant. Most experts suggest you see your doctor:

- about once each month for weeks 4 through 28
- twice a month for weeks 28 through 36
- weekly for weeks 36 to birth

If you are older than thirty-five or your pregnancy is high risk, you'll probably see your doctor more often.

What Happens during Prenatal Visits?

During the first prenatal visit, you can expect your doctor to ask about your health history including diseases, operations, or prior pregnancies; ask about your family's health history; do a complete physical exam, including a pelvic exam and Pap test; take your blood and urine for lab work; check your blood pressure, height, and weight; calculate your due date; and answer your questions.

At the first visit, you should ask questions and discuss any issues related to your pregnancy. Find out all you can about how to stay healthy.

Later prenatal visits will probably be shorter. Your doctor will check on your health and make sure the baby is growing as expected. Most prenatal visits will include checking your blood pressure; measuring your weight gain; measuring your abdomen to check your baby's growth (once you begin to show); and checking the baby's heart rate.

While you're pregnant, you also will have some routine tests. Some tests are suggested for all women, such as blood work to check for anemia, your blood type, HIV, and other factors. Other tests might be offered based on your age, personal or family health history, your ethnic background, or the results of routine tests you have had.

First Trimester (Week 1 to Week 12)

During the first trimester your body undergoes many changes. Hormonal changes affect almost every organ system in your body. These changes can trigger symptoms even in the very first weeks of pregnancy. Your period stopping is a clear sign that you are pregnant. Other changes may include:

- Extreme tiredness
- Tender, swollen breasts; your nipples might also stick out
- Upset stomach with or without throwing up (morning sickness)
- Cravings or distaste for certain foods
- Mood swings
- Constipation (trouble having bowel movements)
- Need to pass urine more often
- Headache
- Heartburn
- Weight gain or loss

As your body changes, you might need to make changes to your daily routine, such as going to bed earlier or eating frequent, small meals. Fortunately, most of these discomforts will go away as your pregnancy progresses. And some women might not feel any discomfort at all! If you have been pregnant before, you might feel different this time around. Just as each woman is different, so is each pregnancy.

Second Trimester (Week 13 to Week 28)

Most women find the second trimester of pregnancy easier than the first. But it is just as important to stay informed about your pregnancy during these months.

You might notice that symptoms like nausea and fatigue are going away. But other new, more noticeable changes to your body are now happening. Your abdomen will expand as the baby continues to grow. And before this trimester is over, you will feel your baby beginning to move!

As your body changes to make room for your growing baby, you may have:

- Body aches, such as back, abdomen, groin, or thigh pain
- Stretch marks on your abdomen, breasts, thighs, or buttocks
- Darkening of the skin around your nipples

- A line on the skin running from belly button to pubic hairline
- Patches of darker skin, usually over the cheeks, forehead, nose, or upper lip. Patches often match on both sides of the face. This is sometimes called the mask of pregnancy.
- Numb or tingling hands, called carpal tunnel syndrome
- Itching on the abdomen, palms, and soles of the feet *(Call your doctor if you have nausea, loss of appetite, vomiting, jaundice, or fatigue combined with itching. These can be signs of a serious liver problem.)*
- Swelling of the ankles, fingers, and face *(If you notice any sudden or extreme swelling or if you gain a lot of weight really quickly, call your doctor right away. This could be a sign of preeclampsia.)*

Third Trimester (Week 29 to Week 40)

You're in the home stretch! Some of the same discomforts you had in your second trimester will continue. Plus, many women find breathing difficult and notice they have to go to the bathroom even more often. This is because the baby is getting bigger and is putting more pressure on your organs. Don't worry—your baby is fine, and these problems will lessen once you give birth.

Some new body changes you might notice in the third trimester include:

- Shortness of breath
- Heartburn
- Swelling of the ankles, fingers, and face *(If you notice any sudden or extreme swelling or if you gain a lot of weight really quickly, call your doctor right away. This could be a sign of preeclampsia.)*
- Hemorrhoids
- Tender breasts, which may leak a watery pre-milk called colostrum
- Your belly button may stick out
- Trouble sleeping
- The baby "dropping," or moving lower in your abdomen
- Contractions, which can be a sign of real or false labor

As you near your due date, your cervix becomes thinner and softer (called effacing). This is a normal, natural process that helps the birth canal (vagina) to open during the birthing process. Your doctor will check your progress with a vaginal exam as you near your due date. Get excited—the final countdown has begun!

Your New Baby

Once your baby is placed into your arms, your gaze will go right to his or her eyes. Most newborns open their eyes soon after birth. Eyes will be brown or bluish gray at first. Looking over your baby, you might notice that the face is a little puffy. You might notice small white bumps inside your baby's mouth or on his or her tongue. Your baby might be very wrinkly. Some babies, especially those born early, are covered in soft, fine hair, which will come off in a couple of weeks. Your baby's skin might have various colored marks, blotches, or rashes, and fingernails could be long.

Spending time with your baby in those first hours of life is very special. Although you might be tired, your newborn could be quite alert after birth. Cuddle your baby skin-to-skin. Let your baby get to know your voice and study your face. Your baby can see up to about two feet away. You might notice that your baby throws his or her arms out if someone turns on a light or makes a sudden noise. This is called the startle response. Babies also are born with grasp and sucking reflexes. Put your finger in your baby's palm and watch how she or he knows to squeeze it. Feed your baby when she or he shows signs of hunger.

Right after birth babies need many important tests and procedures to ensure their health. Some of these are even required by law. But as long as the baby is healthy, everything but the Apgar test can wait for at least an hour. Delaying further medical care will preserve the precious first moments of life for you, your partner, and the baby. A baby who has not been poked and prodded may be more willing to nurse and cuddle. So before delivery, talk to your doctor or midwife about delaying shots, medicine, and tests.

Going Home

The first few days at home after having your baby are a time for rest and re-covery—physically and emotionally. You need to focus your energy on your-self and on getting to know your new baby. Even though you may be very excited and have requests for lots of visits from family and friends, try to limit visitors and get as much rest as possible. Don't expect to keep your house perfect. You may find that all you can do is eat, sleep, and care for your baby. And that is perfectly okay. Learn to pace yourself from the first day that you arrive back home. Try to lie down or nap while the baby naps. Don't try to do too much around the house. Allow others to help you and don't be afraid to ask for help with cleaning, laundry, meals, or with caring for the baby.

Your doctor will check your recovery at your postpartum visit, about six weeks after birth. Ask about resuming normal activities, as well as eating and fitness plans to help you return to a healthy weight. Also ask your doc-tor about having sex and birth control. Your period could return in six to eight weeks, or sooner if you do not breastfeed. If you breastfeed, your

Postpartum Depression

Postpartum depression is a biological illness caused by changes in brain chemistry that can occur following childbirth. During pregnancy, hormone levels increase considerably, particularly progesterone and estrogen, and fall rapidly within hours to days after childbirth. Also, the amount of endorphins, the feel-good hormones that are produced by the placenta during pregnancy, drops significantly after delivery. Even the thyroid gland can be affected by the enormous hormonal changes that are associated with pregnancy and childbirth, leaving women more at risk for depression.

Experts identify three broad types of postpartum mood disorders that are classified according to the severity and the duration of symptoms. The "baby blues" affects approximately 50 to 75 percent of new mothers and generally surfaces within a few days of delivery. Women with the maternity blues describe more tearfulness, irritability, and anxiety than usual with an overall sense of being overwhelmed. Because these symptoms usually decrease by two weeks without medical or psychological help, most women do quite well with added rest and extra help caring for their infant, along with reassurance and emotional support that their feelings are normal and temporary.

Psychosis is an extreme form of postpartum depression. Although it is rare, psychosis is a life-threatening emergency that requires immediate medical treatment to protect both you and your child. If you have psychosis, you may be experiencing some of the following symptoms:

- Hearing sounds or voices when no one is present
- Feeling afraid that you might harm yourself to escape the pain
- Having thoughts about harming your baby
- Rapid weight loss and refusal to eat
- Going without sleep for forty-eight hours or more
- Feeling as though your thoughts are not your own
- Feels like you are "going through the motions" of taking care of your baby without feeling much love

About one out of ten women who give birth will develop a postpartum depression. If you think that you are one of them, you might be:

- Crying more than usual
- Feeling sad much of the time
- Unable to concentrate and feeling in a fog
- Finding it difficult to remember where you've put things
- Unable to enjoy the things that you used to enjoy
- So exhausted but still unable to sleep even when your baby sleeps

- Tired most of the day
- Feeling like you will always feel this way
- Afraid to be alone
- Wishing you were dead instead of having to feel this way any longer

Frequently, symptoms go unrecognized because you may think they are part of the stress of caring for a new baby. You might delay asking for help out of embarrassment, guilt, and a mistaken belief that a "good mother" should be capable of handling the overwhelming adjustment of caring for a new baby with little or no need for help. Also, weaning a baby from the breast and the return of menstruation are significant hormonal events that can alter the biochemical balances in the body and affect the timing of a depression.

Although a postpartum depression might not always be preventable, it certainly is possible to diminish the severity of symptoms, should they occur. Even before delivery, locate the stressors in your life and eliminate them. Put a support system in place during pregnancy so that you will feel less alone and overwhelmed after the baby arrives. In the months following childbirth, plan for free time, get plenty of rest, and do not deny your feelings or feel guilty for having them. Educating yourself about postpartum mood disorders is one of the best ways to ensure early diagnosis and proper treatment. Postpartum mood disorders are treatable, and seeking the help of a qualified therapist is essential.*

Resources: www.aamft.org, www.postpartum.net, and www.depressionafterdelivery.com

---

* American Association for Marriage and Family Therapy.

period might not resume for many months. Still, using reliable birth control is the best way to prevent pregnancy until you want to have another baby.

Both pregnancy and labor affect a woman's body. After giving birth you will lose about ten pounds right away and a little more as body fluid levels decrease. Don't expect or try to lose additional pregnancy weight right away. Gradual weight loss over several months is the safest way, especially if you are breastfeeding. A healthy eating plan along with regular physical fitness might be all you need to return to a healthy weight. But talk to your doctor before you start any type of diet or exercise plan.

If you want to diet and are breastfeeding, it is best to wait until your baby is at least two months old. During those first two months, your body needs to recover from childbirth and establish a good milk supply. Then when you start to lose weight, try not to lose too much too quickly. This can be harmful to the baby, because environmental toxins that are stored in your body fat can be released into your breast milk. Losing about one pound per week (no more than four pounds per month) has been found to be a safe amount and will not affect your milk supply or the baby's growth.

After childbirth you may feel sad, weepy, and overwhelmed for a few days. Many new mothers have the "baby blues" after giving birth. Changing hormones, anxiety about caring for the baby, and lack of sleep all affect your emotions.

Be patient with yourself. These feelings are normal and usually go away quickly. But if sadness lasts more than two weeks, go see your doctor. Don't wait until your postpartum visit to do so. You might have a serious but treatable condition called postpartum depression. Postpartum depression can happen any time within the first year after birth.

Some women don't tell anyone about their symptoms because they feel embarrassed or guilty about having these feelings at a time when they think they should be happy. Don't let this happen to you! Postpartum depression can make it hard to take care of your baby. Infants with mothers with postpartum depression can have delays in learning how to talk. They can have problems with emotional bonding. Your doctor can help you feel better and get back to enjoying your new baby.

If this is your first baby, you might worry that you are not ready to take care of a newborn. You're not alone. Lots of new parents feel unprepared when it's time to bring their new babies home from the hospital. You can take steps to help yourself get ready for the transition home.

Taking a newborn care class during your pregnancy can prepare you for the real thing. But feeding and diapering a baby doll isn't quite the same. During your hospital stay, make sure to ask the nurses for help with basic baby care. Don't hesitate to ask the nurse to show you how to do something more than once! Remember, practice makes perfect. Before discharge, make sure you—and your partner—are comfortable with these newborn care basics:

- Handling a newborn, including supporting your baby's neck
- Changing your baby's diaper
- Bathing your baby
- Dressing your baby
- Swaddling your baby
- Feeding and burping your baby
- Cleaning the umbilical cord
- Caring for a healing circumcision

- Using a bulb syringe to clear your baby's nasal passages
- Taking a newborn's temperature
- Tips for soothing your baby

Before leaving the hospital, ask about home visits by a nurse or health care worker; many new parents appreciate somebody checking in with them and their baby a few days after coming home.

Many first-time parents also welcome the help of a family member or friend who has "been there." Having a support person stay with you for a few days can give you the confidence to go at it alone in the weeks ahead. Try to arrange this before delivery.

Your baby's first doctor's visit is another good time to ask about any infant care questions you might have. Ask about reasons to call the doctor. Also ask about what vaccines your baby needs and when. Infants and young children need vaccines because the diseases they protect against can strike at an early age and can be very dangerous in childhood. This includes rare diseases and more common ones, such as the flu.

Tips for New Dads

It is important for the father to be involved in every stage of the pregnancy to support and encourage you and to learn what his responsibilities are. For first-time parents it is a time of great happiness but also apprehension, which is quite normal and understandable. Never forget, however, that help is always on hand. Most bases have a new parent support program, which provides free advice and guidance from the moment you know you are pregnant. On many bases, a "Baby Boot Camp" program is offered to help prepare expecting parents. The support then continues through the early years of your child's life.

A great way to bond with your wife is to sign up for parenting classes with her. Your base might also offer childbirth classes.

Because you are in the military, you cannot guarantee that you will be available to be with your wife when she delivers, so together choose someone who will be available to help her, drive her to the hospital, and so on.

As the big day approaches, make a checklist of what your wife will need to take with her and what is the quickest way to the hospital, and get into the habit of making sure that you always have enough gas in your car!

It is also a good idea to discuss with your doctor and the hospital the birth itself. This is sometimes called a birth plan and can specify the preferred method of delivery, the family and friends who can be with you during labor, as well as any special religious requirements.

If you have been to birthing classes, it will be a great help to your wife during labor. Your role is to support and encourage her and also to act as her advocate. And remember to take your camera or video to record the magical moments when your child is born.

In most cases paternity leave, although discretionary, is granted, and it is important to be home for the first few days after your wife and child are home. This is when they will really need you. Your wife will be tired and she will need loving, and the baby will need near round-the-clock attention for feeding, cleaning, and caring. Work out a roster that works for you both. Many new mothers like to have their own mother around for a few days, but as the new dad, don't let her do all the work. It will take time to get into a routine and the new baby may not cooperate, but be patient.

Remember that child care is also available on most bases.

Returning to Work

No matter how long your maternity (or paternity) leave, you might not feel ready to return to work when the time has come. Although the idea of working again might appeal to you, you might wonder how you will juggle work and home life. As a mother you might wonder how you will be able to keep up with the demands of motherhood. If you are breastfeeding, you might worry about finding a private space to pump. You might feel guilty that you are leaving your new baby under the care of somebody other than yourself.

Many new mothers know exactly what you're going through. Nowadays, more than half of all mothers with infants work. And even more mothers with older babies and children are working. Their advice and lessons learned can help you through the transition.

As a new father you may feel a little guilty about leaving your wife at home alone to cope with looking after the household and a new baby.

For both parents, help is at hand. Many bases have Department of Defense–sponsored Child Development Centers. These child care facilities are popular, so they may have a waiting list. You can also check out local child care resources at www.militaryonesource.com.

If you are serving in the military and a mother, you need to make special plans in case you are deployed. You can greatly reduce the emotional strain of having to leave your child or children by preparing for such an eventuality. You can make videos of yourself and record stories on tape that can be played back when you are not there. You can put together a photo album that you can take with you, and you can ask family and friends to act as a support group to help your husband while you are away.

Breastfeeding

Breastfeeding is a personal decision, but one you should discuss with your doctor. Many studies show that breastfeeding has many benefits and does provide the baby with protection against a number of infections. It also helps many women return to their normal weight sooner. However, baby formulas also provide complete nutritional diets.

Breastfeeding in public is now widely accepted, which has enabled many breastfeeding mothers to return to work earlier.

Breastfeeding keeps you connected to your baby, even when you are away at work, and your baby will continue to receive the best nutrition possible.

After you have your baby, arrange with your employer to take as much time off as you can, since it will help you and your baby get into a good breastfeeding routine and help you make plenty of milk.

If you can't breastfeed your baby directly during your work breaks, plan to leave your expressed or pumped milk for your baby. The milk can be given to your baby by the caregiver with a bottle or cup. Some babies don't like bottles; they prefer to breastfeed. So be patient and give your baby time to learn this new way of feeding. Babies may better learn other ways of feeding from their dad or another family member.

You can help your baby practice bottle-feeding by giving him or her a bottle occasionally after he or she is around four weeks old and well used to breastfeeding. During these practice times, offer just a small amount (an ounce or two) of milk once a day.

Before you deliver, talk with your employer about why breastfeeding is important, why pumping is necessary, and how you plan to fit pumping into your workday, such as during lunch or other breaks. You could suggest making up work time for time spent pumping milk. If your day care is near your workplace, try to arrange to go there to breastfeed your baby during work time.

Request a clean and private area where you can pump your milk, preferably some place other than the bathroom. You also need a place to wash your hands and your pump parts.

You can start pumping and storing your milk before you go back to work so that you have lots of milk stored and ready for the first week when you are away from your baby. It is helpful to copy your baby's feeding schedule when coming up with your pumping schedule. Pumping patterns are affected by your breast size and milk storage capacity, so pay attention to your breasts. When they start to feel full, pump until your milk stops spraying and then for a few more minutes each time. Don't wait until they are very full and swollen. Expect each breast to make about one ounce of milk every hour.

Some states have laws that require employers to allow you to breast-feed at your job, set up a space for you to breastfeed, and/or to allow paid or unpaid time for breastfeeding or pumping. See the resources section to see if your state has a breastfeeding law for employers. Even if your state does not have breastfeeding laws, most employers support breast-feeding employees when they explain their needs.

Note: The following all provide support to new parents—Fleet and Family Support Center, Marine Corps Community Services, Airman and Family Readiness Center, and Army Community Service Center.

New Parent Support

Having a baby means lots of changes to your lives and lifestyle. You will probably already have converted a bedroom into a nursery and bought all the things your new child will need. And it probably came as a shock just how much everything cost—and that's just the beginning!

According to the U.S. Department of Agriculture's report "Expenditures on Children by Families," a couple earning between $56,870 and $98,470 will spend $221,190 on a child up until age seventeen.

That is why it is so important to have your finances in order. As soon-to-be parents, you need to take a hard look at your financial situation and start to plan for the future.

Conduct a financial audit—what are your monthly outgoings, what other financial commitments do you have, what is your credit card debt, and so on. If your wife is working and will have to give up work, how will that impact your finances? Once you know exactly what your financial situation is, you can decide if cuts need to be made in some areas to free up money to pay for the baby's upkeep. In the short term you may have to find extra money to pay for child care, and in the long term you may want to put money aside for your child's college education. Even a small amount put aside every week or month will mount up over the years, and you can let family and friends know in case they want to make a gift in lieu of birthday or Christmas presents.

Check health and life insurance to ensure you have adequate cover. While most young couples don't think about life insurance, it is exactly the right time to take it out, because the younger you are, the lower the premiums you pay. While the serving member of the marriage will have some coverage, it is a good idea for both partners to have life and disability coverage. Make sure you apply for and receive all the benefits and leave you are entitled to.

As soon as possible after the delivery, get a Social Security number for your baby and update your will to include your new child as a beneficiary if that is your wish.

You will find that family and friends will buy lots of clothes and toys for the new baby that will save you money, but other costs such as diapers, crib, baby seat for the car, and so on will have to be met.

Join a young mother's club and start swapping baby clothes and other items. Babies grow so fast they don't wear their clothes out, so why not pass them on? You can also find great bargains at garage sales, thrift shops, and the like.

Blanketing Military Children with Security By Stephen J. Cozza, M.D. COL, U.S. Army, Chief Department of Psychiatry, WRAMC

Military life is inherently one of great accomplishments and benefits, but it also presents significant risks and dangers to active duty personnel. Injury or death are possibilities that can be faced by military personnel and their families at any time. If something does happen to a military service member, it affects everyone in his or her family; no family member is immune to the impact of such an incident. Even when children are too young to be able to speak and clearly reveal their thoughts and feelings, research and experience reveals that they are profoundly influenced by these significant events. Some experts refer to these as "transforming" experiences. While powerless to protect military children from difficult life experiences, there are many ways we can work together to help children through these challenges and make transformations as positive as possible.

Below are some simple steps that might be taken by families facing uncertainty or grief.

Keep lines of communication open. Parents and educators are both members of the child's support team. Since teamwork is more effective when communication is direct, talk and keep talking about what is happening in the child's life. Every team member is responsible for this activity. Parents need to let educators know about changes that may affect their child. Teachers need to ask about any changes they observe in a child's understanding. Parents may be so overwhelmed by the events and critical decisions they have to make that they forget to communicate important information to the school in a timely manner.

Limit disruption to routines as much as possible. Continuity represents stability. A predictable schedule can be extremely comforting. Children know what to expect at school, making it a potential haven for children who feel that their life has been turned upside-down. Keeping to a routine can also help adults see how a child is doing, since they know how the child used to behave in the same situation.

Talk about changes in the way that works best for your child. Children of different ages and abilities will require different amounts of information, explained in various ways. A thirteen-year-old will have more questions and want more information than a three-year-old. A child who has special needs may need to discuss or express his or her reactions to the changes in a different way. A verbal child may want to talk about what has happened more than a visual child, who would be better served by drawing pictures. Tailor your reactions and responses to the needs of that individual child.

Discuss feelings. Just as children have to learn the names of colors and shapes, they also have to learn the names of feelings. They need to understand that everyone has all kinds of feelings, and that even grown-ups feel scared or alone at times. Children are also incredibly perceptive. If they think an adult is sad or worried, it can be confusing if the adult denies those emotions and says that he or she is not. Talk about how they feel, how you feel, and what you can each do to cope with those feelings. Show children that all feelings are okay; it is what you do about them that is most important.

Tap into existing resources. The military has a host of resources to help military members and their spouses. Communities also have sources of support for families.

Schools are a great place to learn about community resources. Remember that the Internet can link you to supportive people no matter where you live.

Engage children in creating coping mechanisms. The most effective ways to support children are the ones that they take part in creating. Rather than pitying children, honor their sacrifices and their courage in expressing their feelings, and involve them in creating coping mechanisms that work for them. In this way, you will be supporting their strength and encouraging their courage, while helping them feel more in control.

Provide extra time and support whenever possible. Children, just like adults, may not react to changes in the way that those around them may expect. Special events, such as Father's Day and Mother's Day, may reveal grief that had been hidden from view. Day-to-day activities may be abandoned because they are difficult to face at first—for example, the book that was always shared at bedtime may be shelved for a while. Since grief is such an intensely personal experience, make sure that those grieving have access to support for a while instead of confining your support to the period just after the change.

Knowing that someone else is thinking of their mother on her birthday may be just what a family needs. Support should be there any time grieving is detected or suspected.

Growing as a Couple

Never Stop Saying "I Love You"

A successful and lasting marriage is based on love, friendship, and communication. Hopefully the love remains as strong as ever, and with time your relationship develops into a much deeper friendship.

We have already talked about how important communications is to a successful relationship, and it doesn't become any less important just because you have been married for a few years. You may get to a state where you instinctively know what your partner is thinking, but you should still talk to one another—to share your thoughts and feelings.

We have talked before about "never assume anything," and this is a great motto for a marriage. Don't assume that just because something is not said, everything is fine. It may be that one of you has an issue but doesn't know how to talk about it, so you are bottling it up inside. Never do this. If you have a concern, talk to your partner and resolve it. There is almost nothing that can't be resolved by talking.

When couples stop speaking to each other on a regular basis, they tend to drift apart. If they are not talking to each other, they turn to doing their own thing rather than doing things together. This can lead to a disconnect, which, if allowed to continue, may lead to estrangement.

One of the things you should talk about on a regular basis is, are you both getting everything you want out of the marriage? Are you on track to realizing your mutual goals? Are you doing enough to save for your retirement years together?

It is good to take stock every now and then and make little adjustments and tweaks—look on it as fine-tuning your relationship so that it runs even better than before.

As you approach middle age, these talks take on a new dimension because your lives will change. Your children may be leaving home to go to college. You may be close to paying off your mortgage and have lots of new money to play with or save. You may have elderly parents or relatives that need looking after. And you are both getting older, and retirement, which may have seemed such a long way off when you were younger, is now just around the corner.

It is a good time to sit down and discuss all these issues. Many people feel that they have not achieved all they set out to do, or they may be dissatisfied with their jobs. These feelings of disconcert can lead to midlife crises and decisions taken in haste. This is not the time to quit your job or go and blow the family savings on a sports car. It is the time, however, to talk over these feelings with your partner.

If you are unhappy at work and feel a career change might be a good thing, see what your partner thinks about it. You may both agree that going back to school would be a good thing and open new doors for you. However, it is much better to come to this decision after a realistic discussion with your partner and know that he or she is supportive.

Another great reason to talk is to express your feelings about each other. Many people hate getting old because of what it does to their looks and their body. That is why you should both reassure each other all the time that you find your partner attractive and desirable and still love them.

If you are having feelings of low-esteem and are not getting support from your partner, it is easy to get tempted if someone at work starts to flirt with you. That is often how these quickie romances start, but they are rarely successful and usually in the end everyone gets hurt.

If you have a close, loving relationship, you should be able to tell your partner that someone made a flattering comment about you at work. Your partner should immediately respond by saying that they can understand why, because you are still a very desirable person.

Close couples are also better equipped to cope with a crisis, because they will be able to talk to each other about it, and both partners know they can count on the other for support.

Talking to each other as lovers and best friends will keep the marriage on track. Doing things together will enable you to spend quality time together and prepare you for retirement when you will have so much more time to fill. There are lots of things you can do together on a regular basis. You could go for a daily walk, which allows you to talk and get healthy at the same time. If you both enjoy the same thing, you can join a club and meet other people who share your interests, and thus increase your circle of friends.

There are all sorts of volunteer opportunities that can be enjoyable and also allow you to give back to the community. If you each have different hobbies, take an interest in what your partner likes. You don't have to go bird-watching together, but when he or she comes home, ask about what he or she saw—show that you are interested and care about what he or she does.

Intimacy

For many couples the frequency of lovemaking decreases as they get older. That doesn't mean that you love your partner any less, and in fact, your relationship might be stronger and more intimate than ever before. You both know how to pleasure each other—if you don't, talk about it—and there are many ways of doing this without physically making love.

The important thing is to talk to your partner honestly and openly about your sexual activities and your own needs. Be more spontaneous. If you have a routine that you make love on the third Wednesday of every month, you need a new routine. Don't set a time and date, especially if you are empty nesters. It is surprising how a little spontaneity will spice up your sex life. Get some aromatherapy oils and give each other a massage or share a hot bath together with a glass of wine.

Show affection with a caress, a hug, holding hands, or a kiss—and you can never, ever say "I love you" too much.

Finances   8

Budget and Financial Support

Taxes

EDERAL TAXES MUST BE PAID ON ALL income, including wages, interest earned on bank accounts, and so on. However, some tax benefits may arise as a result of a service member serving in a combat zone, while other benefits—such as exclusions, deductions, and credits—may arise as a result of certain expenses incurred by the service member. The Combat Zone Exclusion, for instance, is tax-free and does not have to be reported on tax returns.

The deadline for filing tax returns and paying any tax due is automatically extended for those serving and those hospitalized as a result of injuries incurred while serving in the Armed Forces in a combat zone, in a qualified hazardous duty area, or on deployment outside of the United States while participating in a contingency operation.

Combat zones are designated by an executive order from the president as areas in which the U.S. Armed Forces are engaging or have engaged in combat. There are currently three such combat zones (including the airspace above each):

Arabian Peninsula Areas, beginning January 17, 1991—the Persian Gulf, Red Sea, Gulf of Oman, the part of the Arabian Sea north of 10° North latitude and west of 68° East longitude, the Gulf of Aden, and the countries of Bahrain, Iraq, Kuwait, Oman, Qatar, Saudi Arabia, and the United Arab Emirates.

Kosovo area, beginning March 24, 1999—Federal Republic of
Yugoslavia (Serbia and Montenegro), Albania, the Adriatic Sea, and the
Ionian Sea north of the 39th Parallel.
Afghanistan, beginning September 19, 2001.

In general, the deadlines for performing certain actions applicable to taxes
are extended for the period of the service member's service in the combat
zone, plus 180 days after the last day in the combat zone. This extension applies
to the filing and paying of income taxes that would have been due April 15.

Members of the U.S. Armed Forces who perform military service in an
area outside a combat zone qualify for the suspension of time provisions if
their service is in direct support of military operations in the combat zone,
and they receive special pay for duty subject to hostile fire or imminent
danger as certified by the Department of Defense.

The deadline extension provisions apply not only to members serving
in the U.S. Armed Forces (or individuals serving in support thereof) in the
combat zone but to their spouses as well, with two exceptions. First, if you
are hospitalized in the United States as a result of injuries received while
serving in a combat zone, the deadline extension provisions would not apply to your spouse. Second, the deadline extension provisions for a spouse
do not apply for any tax year beginning more than two years after the date
of the termination of the combat zone designation.

Filing individual income tax returns for your dependent children is not
required while your husband is in the combat zone. Instead, these returns
will be timely if filed on or before the deadline for filing your joint income
tax return under the applicable deadline extensions. When filing your children's individual income tax returns, put "COMBAT ZONE" in red at the
top of those returns.

Tax Exclusions

The Combat Zone Exclusion

If you serve in a combat zone as an enlisted person or as a warrant officer
(including commissioned warrant officers) for any part of a month, all your
military pay received for military service that month is excluded from gross
income. For commissioned officers, the monthly exclusion is capped at the
highest enlisted pay, plus any hostile fire or imminent danger pay received.

Military pay received by enlisted personnel who are hospitalized as a
result of injuries sustained while serving in a combat zone is excluded from
gross income for the period of hospitalization, subject to the two-year

limitation provided below. Commissioned officers have a similar exclusion, limited to the maximum enlisted pay amount per month. These exclusions from gross income for hospitalized enlisted personnel and commissioned officers end two years after the date of termination of the combat zone.

Annual leave payments to enlisted members of the U.S. Armed Forces upon discharge from service are excluded from gross income to the extent the annual leave was accrued during any month in any part of which the member served in a combat zone. If your wife is a commissioned officer, a portion of the annual leave payment she receives for leave accrued during any month in any part of which she served in a combat zone may be excluded. The annual leave payment is not excludable to the extent it exceeds the maximum enlisted pay amount for the month of service to which it relates less the amount of military pay already excluded for that month.

The reenlistment bonus is excluded from gross income although received in a month that you were outside the combat zone, because you completed the necessary action for entitlement to the reenlistment bonus in a month during which you served in the combat zone.

A recent law change makes it possible for members of the military to count tax-free combat pay when figuring how much they can contribute to a Roth or traditional IRA. Before this change, members of the military whose earnings came from tax-free combat pay were often barred from putting money into an IRA, because taxpayers usually must have taxable earned income. Taxpayers choosing to put money into a Roth IRA don't need to report these contributions on their individual tax return. Roth contributions are not deductible, but distributions, usually after retirement, are normally tax-free. Income limits and other special rules apply.

Thrift Savings Plan (TSP)

The TSP is a retirement savings plan with special tax advantages for federal government employees and service members. Participation is optional, and service members must join TSP while they are still serving in the military. TSP is similar to traditional 401(k) plans often sponsored by private employers; contributions to TSP accounts are not taxed at the time they are made, but distributions from the accounts generally are subject to income tax at the time the distributions are withdrawn. Veterans who did not sign up for TSP while in service cannot join the plan after leaving the military. Contributions to TSPs are subject to certain limitations. Detailed information about TSP is available at www.tsp.gov.

There are three basic ways for service members to access funds in their TSP accounts: in-service withdrawals, TSP loans, and postseparation withdrawals.

IN-SERVICE WITHDRAWALS Most service members can borrow against the contributions and earnings made to their TSP accounts. These loans generally have no tax consequences. However, the loan must be paid back with interest, usually within five years. Payments usually take the form of payroll deductions. Therefore, service members who do not receive monthly pay (e.g., reservists with irregular training intervals) may not be eligible for TSP loans.

Service members may also withdraw money from their TSP account under what is known as a financial hardship withdrawal. Financial hardship withdrawals generally are subject to a 10 percent penalty tax, in addition to the income tax on the withdrawal. However, this 10 percent penalty generally does not apply if the withdrawal is made because of a permanent and total disability or if the money is used to pay for deductible medical expenses that exceed 7.5 percent of the service member's adjusted gross income.

The 10 percent penalty does not apply to any portion of a distribution that represents tax-exempt contributions from pay earned in a combat zone. Also, Combat Zone Exclusion pay contributed to a TSP account is not taxable when withdrawn, unlike regular pay. However, the interest earned on amounts contributed to a TSP account that were exempt from tax because of the Combat Zone Exclusion is taxable. If a service member receives a distribution from an account that has both Exclusion and non-Exclusion contributions, the distribution will be paid in the same proportions as the service member's Exclusion and non-Exclusion contributions.

TSP participants may withdraw money from their accounts if either they are at least fifty-nine-and-a-half years old or they have a verifiable financial hardship. For instance, a disabled service member may face financial hardship in connection with his or her medical condition. In such a case, a financial hardship withdrawal may be permitted.

Financial Counseling

Money issues probably cause more arguments between married couples than anything else. Often the issues are so serious and cause such friction that they lead to the breakup of the marriage. It is often not how much money the couple has but how it should be spent that causes the rows.

It used to be that a married couple could get by with one partner working and the other staying at home. Unfortunately times and the economic climate have changed, and now both partners usually have to work in order to earn enough to pay all the bills. If one partner then loses his or her job, there is a serious financial crunch. Many other situations can get out of hand.

One partner may run up a massive credit card debt. One may want to save every penny while the other wants to spend. Some may insist on having his or her own bank account and be secretive about how much is in it even though that partner pays his or her share of the bills. As a couple you may enjoy eating out and not realize just how much it is costing you every month. All of these cases can quickly become a recipe for disaster,

Two things are essential for sound financial management as a couple—communication and budgeting. You must talk honestly about your financial situation and shared expectations, then work out an appropriate agreed budget—and stick to it. If you can't you probably need to seek financial counseling.

Married couples shouldn't have secrets, especially over money. Sit down and work out a financial road map for your future. Do you want to buy a house? Where do you want to be in ten, twenty, or thirty years' time? Do you want to have money set aside for the children's college fund? Do you want a retirement nest egg? Then try to work out a time frame to achieve this. That will determine how much you have to save in order to do this.

Then write down all your household expenses. Compare that with how much is coming in. Do you have any money left over to save? If not, where can cuts be made, and what changes can you make to your lifestyle to reduce spending in order to achieve your long-term goals?

That is where budgeting comes in. Budgeting is not just managing your money but introducing ways to make it go further. Cut coupons and use them—it can add up to grocery savings of hundreds of dollars over a year. Commissaries overseas will even accept coupons up to six months after their expiration date. You can join a discount warehouse and buy in bulk. You may not want to buy twenty-four toilet paper rolls at a time, so split your shopping with friends so that you all save.

Pay your bills early rather than wait until the last minute and run the risk of incurring late penalties.

Another great way of budgeting is to plan your week, decide what meals you are going to eat each day, and buy only those items when you do your weekly shopping. This prevents impulse purchases and the temptation to eat out. Packed lunches are cheaper than eating lunch out. Remember, it is all the small savings that add up to big savings.

Another important element of budgeting is to ensure that you both have your own spending money to do with as you wish. This does not have to be a huge amount, but you should agree between you how much you each get—and then how you spend it is up to you.

Sound financial management is an ongoing process. Revisit your financial strategy every year or so—are you still on track? Have your circumstances changed? And if so, how has this impacted your budget planning and what changes need to be made to get you back on track?

While both of you must know what bills and other expenses need paying, it makes sense for one person to manage this and be responsible for writing checks and so on. If one of the partners is deployed, it is even more important that the other partner does this. Keep all the bills and other financial documents together in a secure place. A separate file can be kept for all items that you will need for your annual tax filing—this will save a lot of trouble later on.

Discuss upcoming expenditures and jointly agree that they are justified. If you need to consult a financial advisor or tax preparer, go as a couple so you can both ask questions and express opinions,

If you still have issues over finances, you should seek help. In the first instance you can speak to a financial advisor on base, your bank manager, or your tax preparer or go to www.consumer.gov and click on the "Money" page, which has advice and publications you can download on a wide range of financial issues. If you still need help, there are many resources you can turn to, from financial and marriage counselors to non-profit financial and credit counseling organizations.

Financial Aid

Veterans of Foreign Wars (VFW) Unmet Needs Program
With the help of corporate sponsors, the VFW Foundation receives funding to establish, administer, and promote the Unmet Needs Program. Funds from donations are available to the five branches of service (Army, Navy, Air Force, Marines, and Coast Guard), as well as members of the Reserves and National Guard. Funds awarded by the program are offered in the form of grants—not loans—so recipients don't need to repay them.

ELIGIBILITY CRITERIA The service member has to have been active duty or discharged from active duty within thirty-six months prior to applying.

- Can receive funds only once every eighteen months
- The hardship must be primarily due to deployment or military service.
- Hardships caused by civil, legal, or domestic misconduct are not eligible for the grant.

Useful Tips from MilSpouse.com:
Dealing with Debt by Joseph Montanaro

If you have more than one credit card, focus your biggest payments on the card with the highest interest rate. This will minimize the amount of money you're wasting on interest charges. Typically, credit cards from department stores have the highest rates.

As another way to minimize interest charges, you might look into transferring your balance to a new card with a lower annual percentage rate. Read the fine print carefully to make sure you're getting a good deal.

Once you've successfully banished that monstrous debt, make sure it stays away for good. As soon as possible, establish a "holiday fund" and begin stashing away a small amount from each paycheck. Many banks and credit unions offer interest-bearing "Christmas Club" accounts specifically for this purpose. But stuffing $10 a week into a shoebox can work if you have the discipline not to touch it.

When gift-buying season rolls around, start with a firm budget and a detailed shopping list. If Santa can stick to his list, so can you! Start early to give yourself plenty of time for comparison shopping. You may be able to find better deals online if you have a few weeks to spare for shipping. Don't exceed your budget, and if it's not on your list, don't buy it—even if it's on sale. Ideally, you should be able to make most of your purchases with the cash you saved throughout the year.

Joseph Montanaro is a certified financial planner practitioner with USAA Financial Planning Services, a member of the USAA family of companies. He served in the U.S. Army for six years on active duty and is currently a lieutenant colonel in the U.S. Army Reserve. His article appeared on www.milspouse.com. Used with permission.

- Hardships caused by financial mismanagement by self or others, or due to bankruptcy, are not eligible for the grant. Applicants with these situations will be provided with resource information and referrals to other agencies.

The applicant must be the service member, or the applicant must be currently listed or eligible to be listed as a dependent of the service member under DEERS. Persons eligible to apply on behalf of the military family in need:

- Personnel
- Military Unit point of contact—Family Assistance Center Coordinator, commanding officer, medical hold case worker

- VA Representative or VFW service officer assisting with a VA claim

Expenses eligible for payment:

- Housing expenses—mortgage, rent, repairs, insurance
- Vehicle expenses—payments, insurance, repairs
- Utilities, includes the primary phone
- Food and personal items.
- Children's clothing, diapers, formula, school, or child-care expenses
- Medical bills, prescriptions, and eyeglasses—the patient's portion for necessary or emergency medical care only
- Appliance repair

Ineligible expenses:

- Credit cards, military charge/debt cards, retail store credit cards
- Personal, student, or payday loans
- Negative bank accounts
- Cable, Internet, secondary phone, or cell phone
- Cosmetic or investigational medical procedures and expenses
- Taxes—property or otherwise
- Child support or alimony
- IRS or military debt, or debt owed to a friend/family member
- Legal or educational expenses
- Furniture, electronic equipment, and vehicle rentals
- Down payments on homes or vehicles
- Reimbursements for items already paid for
- Bills obviously due to excessive use or personal mismanagement

Relationships and Distance

Many other nonprofit organizations offer similar support. These include the Navy USMC Relief Society, Operation Homefront, Injured Marine Semper Fi, Hope for the Warriors, Americasheroesatwork.gov, and Americasupportsyou.com. Your family support center can provide a full list of all such organizations available to you.

Jobs   9

Finding a Job as a Military Spouse

FINDING A JOB IS DIFFICULT AT THE BEST of times with the current state of the economy, and it poses even more problems if you keep relocating because of permanent changes of station (PCSs). If you work for a national or multinational company with lots of offices, you may be able to continue working with them at your new location. While some jobs are almost recession-proof—teaching, nursing, and so on—getting hired for other jobs can be a challenge. One of the challenges is deployment. Many employees might be reluctant to hire you if they think your partner is likely to be deployed, leaving you to look after the home and family and unable to continue with your job. The fact that your partner may suddenly be posted to another base is also a handicap because some employees feel it is a waste of time training you for a job if you are not likely to be with them very long.

However, if you want to find work, a lot of resources are at your disposal. There are opportunities to work on base, which is more convenient. There are also jobs off base, but many bases are in remote areas, and transport could be a problem. The more remote the area, the fewer the jobs available in any case.

For jobs on base contact the Family Support Center for how to get in touch with the employment assistance program office. It will have information on job opportunities on and off base, as well as how to apply for federal positions. Let everyone know you are looking for a job. Your friends may hear about an opportunity and can then pass it on. For off-base jobs contact the local labor office and scan the local newspapers—their websites often post jobs before they appear in print—and send your résumé around to prospective employers. One way to test the water is to register with a temp agency. Lots of temp jobs lead to permanent employment; it gives you an opportunity to decide whether you like working for the company, and it gives them the chance to test your competencies.

Depending on your skill sets, there are lots of work-from-home jobs provided you have a computer and Internet connection. Opportunities in this area include translation and transcription services, bookkeeping, data entry, call center services, and so on. Be careful, though, as there are many scams involving working from home; check your prospective employer out carefully.

Consider going back to school or taking training courses to qualify for more jobs. The Department of Defense (DoD) offers tuition assistance for military spouses, and there are many online and offline training and further-education opportunities.

If you are relocating, start the job search before you move. Make sure your résumé and references are up to date. Don't wait until you have moved to do this—that is the time you need to be settling into your new home and available to respond to any job opportunities that arise. For that reason, it is a good idea to carry your résumés with you when you move rather than packing them.

If you hold a license or certificate to practice in a particular state, see what is needed to get that transferred to the state you are moving to.

Finding a Job Overseas

Finding a job overseas can be even more challenging because of language, U.S. qualifications not being recognized, and just different ways of doing things.

Do your homework carefully to discover what is available and what you think you are qualified to do, and be flexible. If the job you would like is not available, consider other options—either a career change or going back to school.

Talk to other spouses about what is available; join discussion groups and the spouses club if there is one.

Most overseas bases have commissaries or exchanges as well as civilian and defense contractors who may have positions open. There may be other U.S. bases nearby run by other branches of the military, but don't let that stop you from applying if there is a job.

Check out the Office of Personnel Management website at www .usajobs.opm.gov. You'll be amazed how by how many federal jobs are posted and how many of them are overseas.

My Career Advancement Account (MyCAA.com)

The DoD remains strongly committed to helping military spouses find employment in high-demand, high-growth portable career fields.

The DoD MyCAA program provides a lifetime benefit of up to $6,000 of financial assistance (FA) for military spouses who are pursuing licenses, certificates, credentials, or degree programs leading to employment in portable career fields.

Spouses of DoD active duty members and activated members of the National Guard and Reserve Components who are on Title 10 orders are eligible to receive MyCAA FA.

Military spouses who are legally separated under court order or statute are ineligible. Spouses who are active duty or activated Guard or Reserve members themselves are ineligible. Coast Guard spouses are ineligible.

MyCAA FA pays tuition for education and training courses and professional licenses, certifications, and credentials. This includes state certifications for teachers, medical professionals, and other occupations requiring recognized certifications; licensing exams and related prep courses; continuing education unit (CEU) classes including those offered through professional associations; and degree programs leading to employment in portable career fields. MyCAA also pays for high school completion courses, GED tests, and English as a second language (ESL) classes.

MyCAA does not pay for electronic devices or computers of any kind (CPUs, laptops, iPods, etc.); college entrance exams and related prep courses (SAT, LSAT, GRE, etc.); application, graduation, or membership fees; student activity cards; child care; lodging; parking; transportation; or medical services. MyCAA does not pay separate costs for books, supplies, or equipment.

Eligible spouses can establish a MyCAA account at https://aiportal.acc.af.mil/mycaa. Once spouse profile information is provided, MyCAA will verify spouse DEERS benefit eligibility. Eligible spouses will be allowed to create their career and training plan and request FA when they are within thirty days of course start dates. Additionally, spouses are responsible for applying to their selected school or program and enrolling in each course included in their approved MyCAA career and training plan.

If you do get a job, make sure you comply with that country's tax laws. If you are employed by a U.S. company, you might be paid in dollars that are exempt from federal taxes. If you are employed by a local company and paid in that country's currency, you will probably be subject to their tax laws.

Military Spouse Preference Program

The Military Spouse Preference (MSP) Program is derived from Title 10, United States Code, Section 1784, "Employment Opportunities for Military Spouses," and applies to spouses of active duty military members of the U.S. Armed Forces (including Coast Guard) who relocate to accompany their sponsor on a permanent change of station (PCS) move. The program is intended to lessen the career interruption of spouses who relocate with their military sponsors. MSP is a DoD program. Consequently, it applies only to DoD vacancies. Military spouses are eligible to request MSP regardless of current employment status.

If you are a spouse of an active duty military member, you may be eligible for MSP. The MSP Program applies only if:

- the spouse was married to the military sponsor prior to the reporting date to the new assignment;
- the relocation was based on a PCS move and not for separation or retirement;
- the vacancy is within the commuting area of the sponsor's permanent new duty station; and
- the spouse is among the "best qualified" group and is within reach for selection.

MSP applies if you are ranked among the best qualified for this vacancy, and the list established from this announcement is used to fill the vacancy. To be rated best qualified, MSP applicants must attain an eligibility rating on this examination of 80 or higher, not including points for veteran's preference. MSP does not apply, however, when preference would violate statutes or regulations on veteran's preference or nepotism.

Note: Applicants claiming MSP will be required to produce a copy of the military sponsor's PCS orders to substantiate eligibility prior to appointment in the federal service. Failure to provide these orders may result in the cancellation of any pending appointment to a federal service position.

If you can't find employment consider working from home, either working for yourself or for an employer. You could give English language lessons, or if you have special skills, you could offer music lessons or coaching in math, science, and so on. As mentioned earlier, there are also opportunities to work from home for a company that requires you to do translating, transcription, data entry, and so on. Before embarking on this, however, make sure that you have the necessary permissions and licenses.

Job-Related Websites

General

https://aiportal.acc.af.mil/mycaa/default.aspx
www.military.com/spouse
www.msccn.org
www.milspouse.org
www.dod.mil/mapsite/spousepref.html
www.milspouse.org/Job
www.msvas.com

Air Force

www.afcrossroads.com
www.usafservices.com

Army

www.myarmylifetoo.com
www.armymwr.com

Marine Corps

www.usmc-mccs.org/fmeap
www.usmc-mccs.org/employ

Navy

www.lifelines.navy.mil
www.mwr.navy.mil

Training and Education Opportunities

The Military Spouse Career Advancement Initiative (pilot program) provides assistance to military spouses seeking to gain the skills and credentials necessary to begin or advance their career. Career Advancement Accounts (CAA) cover the costs of training and education, enabling participants to earn a degree or credential in in-demand, portable fields in almost any community across the country.

CAA can be used to pay up to $3,000 in fees for one year and may be renewed for one additional year, for a total two-year account amount of up to $6,000 per spouse.

Who Is Eligible?

You are eligible for a CAA if you:

• have a high school diploma or GED;

- are not currently receiving training assistance funded by the U.S. Department of Labor; and
- are married to any active duty service member/sponsor who:
    - o is assigned to one of the installations participating in the pilot site *or* is deployed or on an unaccompanied military tour from the participating installation and
    - o has a minimum of one year remaining at the current installation duty assignment (unless affected by a BRAC closure).

Eligible or potentially eligible spouses are encouraged to contact the local installation's Education Center, Family Support Center, or One-Stop Career Centers nearest to their installation for more information.

Which Installations Are Participating in the Pilot Program?
Camp Pendleton Marine Corps Base, California
Eglin Air Force Base, Florida
Fort Benning Army Installation, Georgia
Fort Bragg Army Installation, North Carolina
Fort Carson Army Installation, Colorado
Fort Lewis Army Installation, Washington
Hickham Air Force Base, Hawaii
Hurlburt Field Air Force Base, Florida
Marine Corps Base Kaneohe Bay, Hawaii
McChord Air Force Base, Washington
Naval Air Station Brunswick, Maine
Naval Air Station Jacksonville, Florida
Naval Station Kitsap, Washington
Naval Station Pearl Harbor, Hawaii
Peterson Air Force Base, Colorado
Pope Air Force Base, North Carolina
San Diego Naval Station, California
Schofield Barracks Army Installation, Hawaii

If you are not located at one of the above installations, visit www .military.com/spouse for employment, education, and training opportunities.

How Can I Get Started?
Make an appointment with your local installation's Education Center. They can assist with career counseling, finding education and training resources,

and starting the application process, including determining whether you are eligible for a CAA.

What Can I Use the CAA to Pay For?

FIELDS OF STUDY You may use CAAs to receive training or education in one of these fields:

- Health care (including jobs such as nurses, radiology technicians, dental hygienists, pharmacy technicians, and more)
- Education (teachers, child care workers, teacher's assistants, and more)
- Financial services (claims adjusters, real estate sales agents, credit analysts, bookkeeping clerks, bank tellers, and more)
- Information technology (computer support specialists, network analysts, database administrators, and more)
- Skilled trades (carpenters, electricians, plumbers, and more)

RECENTLY ADDED FIELDS OF STUDY The program is limited to selected degree/certificate areas for these new fields of study:

- Human resources
- Business management
- Hospitality management
- Homeland security

The Entrepreneurial Spirit

A recent article in the *Wall Street Journal* talked about a wife's career experiences. Her husband, an Air Force officer, was transferred to New Jersey, a move that required her to quit a retail management position. Her experience indicated what many spouses already know: if you are in a profession where you have a fast track to success, it will be cut short upon marriage to a member of the military. Now a business owner, she is in a better position to handle frequent moves, remote locations, and related challenges. Actually, she said, her military connection promotes automatic trust in base-dependent areas.

Difficulty finding jobs is a common problem among the 700,000-plus spouses of active duty military service people. Unemployment tends to be much higher than for the general public. In a 1995 study at an air base, 16 percent of spouses were unemployed, four times the then-national rate. Recent estimates find the current unemployment rate among military spouses at 25 percent overall and—at some bases—as high as 65 percent.

Military spouses are starting their own businesses as a way to cope with the lifestyle demands of military marriage. The DoD pays Staffcentrix to give three-day on-base seminars about self-employment. This organization has trained over 1,500 military spouses who solicit work as administrative assistants, graphic designers, legal researchers, database managers, and so on. These roles are called virtual assistants. Being outside the base also commands a higher wage than local employment.

A retired Air Force crew chief who married an Air Force officer started working as a self-employed virtual assistant. In two months he was commanding an average of thirty dollars an hour. His clients came from four states. This geographic spread reassures him that he'll be able to take his business with him when his wife is transferred.

Business ownership provides entrepreneurs with opportunities to find interesting work in various locations. However, it doesn't solve all military spouse challenges. Business activities on base are heavily regulated. Entrepreneurs must secure permission to start their enterprises. Operations that might generate significant traffic onto the base are likely to be prohibited. State laws are also an issue.

Military spouse entrepreneurs report that they are happy beneficiaries of the new wave of patriotism. Many customers seek to patronize military-connected businesses. Word of mouth among a highly mobile military community provides unexpected marketing exposure. Your reputation often precedes you.

When you transition from the military to civilian life, you might want to start your own business.

Do you have the entrepreneurship spirit? Entrepreneurial thinking generates innovation. Are you innovative? Taking risks adds excitement to your career. Are you a risk taker? Can you treat your career like a business?

Here's how to get in touch with your inner entrepreneur:

- *Work for a small company or seek out an innovative division or manager at a larger firm.* "If you're an entrepreneurial person by nature, you're better off in a place where you don't have to wait your turn," says Michael Kempner, president and CEO of The MWW Group. "If I did good and worked hard, I wanted to get noticed. I wanted to rise on my merits, not stay in place based on politics, size, or because I'm waiting my turn."
- *Be ready to jump.* Put yourself in your boss's position. He needs to know he can rely on you to get the job done. That often means going beyond the minimum amount of work required and the time

allotted. When you agree to stay late that night, you are letting your boss know you are committed to providing the highest-quality product to the client.

- *Write a career plan.* If you want to be truly entrepreneurial, you need to treat your career like a business. Curt Tueffert recommends writing a career plan modeled after traditional business plans. The national sales director for Digital Consulting and Software Services in Houston, he teaches an advanced professional selling course at the University of Houston. He tells his students to incorporate themselves. "The final assignment is to turn in a blueprint for your sales career, everything that you've learned in class and all of your abilities and outside experiences," Tueffert says.

Franchises

Would you love to run a business, but want a template to work from? The following franchises are top rated by *Entrepreneur* magazine and *Success* magazine:

Pillar to Post (home inspection)
Kumon Math (tutoring)
American Leak Detection (gas/water leaks)
Great Clips (haircuts)
Handyman Connection (residential repairs)
We the People (paralegals helping people complete basic legal documents)
Jackson Hewitt (computerized tax prep)

WHAT YOU COULD DO TODAY Before you decide to do any investing, be sure to carefully check out franchises. Talk with a half-dozen randomly selected franchisees before investing.

Avoid Burnout

One of the biggest threats to the long-term success of a home-based business is burnout. To avoid burnout, stay passionate about what you're doing, set regular business hours, and work just those times. Don't allow yourself to get into the habit of working every evening and weekend, too.

The long-term economics of your solo business should influence how you parcel out your energy supplies. Adopt a matching component to your to-do list—it's a won't-do list. Consider it an umbrella classification for things you've decided you won't do any longer, won't tolerate anymore, or have just outgrown. It helps clarify boundaries and reinforce understanding that your energy as an entrepreneur is a limited and valuable resource.

As projects get added to the to-do list, the won't-do list should also continue to grow. What might be on this list? Two credit cards you rarely use—cancel. Subscriptions to magazines that keep ending up piled on the floor—eliminate. Office furnishings no longer needed—donate. Books that are outdated—recycle. You will find that the streamlining is energizing. Before you add anything to your to-do list, contemplate what might balance it by being added to the won't-do list. If you haven't created a won't-do list yet, do so. (I guess that means putting "make a won't-do list" on your to-do list!)

The Small Business Administration (www.sba.gov) offers a wealth of information about starting and running a small business.

The person who goes farthest is generally the one who is willing to do and dare. The sure-thing boat never gets far from shore.

—DALE CARNEGIE (SOURCE: DORIS APPELBAUM, WWW.APPELBAUMRESUMES.COM)

Resources

General

American Red Cross

While providing services to 1.4 million active duty personnel and their families, the Red Cross also reaches out to more than 1.2 million members of the National Guard and the Reserves and their families who reside in nearly every community in America. Red Cross workers in hundreds of chapters and on military installations brief departing service members and their families regarding available support services and explain how the Red Cross may assist them during the deployment.

Both active duty and community-based military can count on the Red Cross to provide emergency communications that link them with their families back home and give access to financial assistance, counseling, and assistance to veterans. Red Cross Service to the Armed Forces personnel work in 756 chapters in the United States, on 58 military installations around the world, and with our troops in Kuwait, Afghanistan, and Iraq.

www.redcross.org

America Supports You

This website has links to hundreds of other websites specific to your needs.

www.americasupportsyou.mil

Angels 'n Camouflage

A cooperative initiative with various organizations across the country, Angels 'n Camouflage, Inc., reinforces the importance and advantages of supporting our veterans and deployed service members. Since its inception in 2002, Angels 'n Camouflage, Inc., has helped thousands of veterans and troops through "Mail Call," and emergency assistance for those veterans homeless or injured from combat.

> www.angelsncamouflage.org

Army National Guard Websites

Army National Guard
National Guard Website
www.1800goguard.com

Army Reserve Websites

U.S. Army Reserves
www.armyreserve.army.mil
Army Reserve Family Programs Online
Army Reserve Family and Readiness Program
www.arfp.org

Deployment Health Clinical Center

Health Clinical Center of the Department of Defense: Health information for clinicians, veterans, family members, and friends.

> www.pdhealth.mil

Guard Family Program

One stop to find information on programs, benefits, and resources on National Guard family programs.

> www.guardfamily.org
> ESGR (Employment Support for the Guard and Reserve)
> www.esgr.org

Iraq War Veterans Organization

Website created by the Iraq War Veterans Organization to provide information and support for Iraq veterans, active military personnel, and family members. All aspects of predeployment, deployment, and postdeployment are included.

> www.iraqwarveterans.org

Marine Corps League

The Marine Corps League was founded by Maj. Gen. Commandant John A. Lejeune in 1923 and chartered by an Act of Congress on August 4,

1937. Its membership of 51,500 comprises honorably discharged, active duty, and reserve marines with ninety days of service or more, and retired marines. Contact the Marine Corps League at 1-800-625-1775, 703-207-9588, or fax at 703-207-0047.

www.mcleague.org

Military OneSource

Military OneSource is a "one-stop shop" for information on all aspects of military life.

From information about financial concerns, parenting, relocation, emotional well-being, work, and health, to many other topics, Military OneSource can provide a wealth of information. There are many informative topics on the website specific to wounded service members and families. For example, by clicking on "Personal & Family Readiness" and selecting "Severely Injured Service Members," you can access topics such as "Coping with Compassion Fatigue," "Finding Temporary Work during a Loved One's Extended Hospitalization," and "Re-establishing Intimacy after a Severe Injury."

In addition to the comprehensive information available online, twenty-four-hour-a-day, seven-day-a-week representatives are available at the 800 number provided below.

Calling will provide you with personalized service specific to answering your needs. You can call the same representative back for continuity of service, as each person has their own extension. Military OneSource is closely aligned with the Military Severely Injured Center. You can call Military OneSource as a parent, spouse, or service member. The information you need is a phone call away.

1-800-342-9647

www.militaryonesource.com

The Military Order of the Purple Heart

The Military Order of the Purple Heart provides support and services to all veterans and their families. This website includes information on VA benefits assistance, issues affecting veterans today, and links to other key websites for veterans.

703-642-5360

www.purpleheart.org

Noncommissioned Officers Association (NCOA)

NCOA was established in 1960 to enhance and maintain the quality of life for noncommissioned and petty officers in all branches of the Armed

Forces, National Guard, and Reserves. The Association offers its members a wide range of benefits and services designed especially for current and former enlisted service members and their families. Those benefits fall into these categories: Social Improvement Programs to help ensure your well-being during your active military career, your transition to civilian life, and throughout your retirement; Legislative Representation to serve as your legislative advocate on issues that affect you and your family, through our National Capital Office in Alexandria, Virginia; and Today's Services to help save you money through merchant program discounts. Contact NCOA at 1-800-662-2620.

> www.ncoausa.org

Returning Veterans Resource Project NW

Provides free counseling for veterans and families in Oregon.

> www.returningveterans.com

Soldiers to Veterans

Soldiers to Veterans is a community of disabled veterans and their families coming together to turn struggles and pain into positive action. It is a safe place to ask frank questions and speak openly of experiences. Nondisabled veterans, active duty, their spouses, and professionals are welcome to join the forum to mentor and empower the families struggling with life after the war.

> www.soldierstoveterans.com

Veterans Health Information

A list of links to civilian and military health care information.

> www.va.gov/vbs/health

Veterans of Foreign Wars (VFW)

The VFW has a rich tradition of enhancing the lives of millions through its legislative advocacy program that speaks out on Capitol Hill in support of service members, veterans and their families, and through community service programs and special projects. From assisting service members in procuring entitlements, to providing free phone cards to the nation's active duty military personnel, to supporting numerous community-based projects, the VFW is committed to honoring our fallen comrades by helping the living. Contact the VFW at 202-453-5230, or fax at 202-547-3196.

> www.vfw.org

Veterans Outreach Center (VOC)

The VOC proactively seeks out veterans in need who continue to suffer in silence—battling personal wars that can be won, with our help. VOC's collaborative approach to treatment cares for the whole person; veterans receive the breadth of services needed to regain their mental, physical, and economic health, reconnect with themselves and the community, and resume productive lives.

www.veteransoutreachcenter.org

Vets 4 Vets

Outreach support groups run by vets for Iraq-era vets.

www.vets4vets.us

Women Veterans Health Program

Provides full range of medical and mental health services for women veterans.

www.va.gov/wvhp

Documents

Air Force

The Community College of the Air Force (CCAF) automatically captures your training, experience, and standardized test scores. Transcript information may be viewed at the CCAF website: www.au.af.mil/au/ccaf.

Army

For everything you want to know about the free AARTS transcript (Army/ American Council on Education Registry Transcript System), go to http:// aarts.army.mil. This free transcript includes your military training, your Military Occupational Specialty (MOS), and college-level examination scores with the college credit recommended for those experiences. It is a valuable asset that you should provide to your college or your employer and it is available for Active Army, National Guard, and Reserve Soldiers. You can view and print your own transcript at this website.

Save time and money: Unless you know for sure that you need to take a particular course, wait until the school gets all your transcripts before you sign up for classes. Otherwise you may end up taking courses you don't need.

Coast Guard

The Coast Guard Institute (CGI) requires each service member to submit documentation of all training (except correspondence course records), along with an enrollment form, to receive a transcript. Transcript information can be found at the Coast Guard Institute website: www.uscg.mil/hq/cgi/forms.htm.

Navy and Marine Corps

Information on how to obtain the Sailor/Marine American Council on Education Registry Transcript (SMART) is available at www.navycollege.navy.mil. SMART is now available to document the American Council on Education (ACE) recommended college credit for military training and occupational experience. SMART is an academically accepted record that is validated by ACE. The primary purpose of SMART is to assist service members in obtaining college credit for their military experience. Additional information on SMART can also be obtained from your nearest Navy College Office or Marine Corps Education Center, or contact the Navy College Center.

Advocacy

American Bar Association

The mission of the ABA Standing Committee on Legal Assistance for Military Personnel is to help the military and the Department of Defense improve the effectiveness of legal assistance provided on civil matters to an estimated nine million military personnel and their dependents.

www.abanet.org/legalservices/lamp/home.html

The American Legion

Since its founding in 1919, The American Legion has been an advocate for America's veterans, a friend of the U.S. military, a sponsor of community-based youth programs, and a spokesman for patriotic values. It is the nation's largest veterans organization with nearly 2.7 million members and about 15,000 local "posts" in most communities and six foreign countries. The Legion provides free, professional assistance—for any veteran and any veteran's survivor—in filing and pursuing claims before the VA; it helps deployed service members' families with things ranging from errands to household chores to providing someone to talk to; and offers Temporary Financial Assistance to help families of troops meet their children's needs. Contact the American Legion at 202-861-2700, ext. 1403, or fax at 202-833-4452.

www.legion.org

American Legion Auxiliary

The women of the American Legion Auxiliary educate children, organize community events, and help our nation's veterans through legislative action and volunteerism. It is the world's largest women's patriotic service organization with nearly 1 million members in 10,100 communities.

www.legion-aux.org

AMVETS

As one of America's foremost veteran's service organizations, AMVETS (or American Veterans) assists veterans and their families. A nationwide cadre of AMVETS national service officers (NSOs) offers information, counseling, and claims service to all honorably discharged veterans and their dependents concerning disability compensation, VA benefits, hospitalization, rehabilitation, pension, education, employment, and other benefits.

1-877-726-8387

301-459-9600

www.amvets.org

Hope for the Warriors

The mission of Hope for the Warriors™ is to enhance quality of life for U.S. service members and their families nationwide who have been adversely affected by injuries or death in the line of duty. Hope for the Warriors actively seeks to ensure that the sacrifices of wounded and fallen warriors and their families are never forgotten nor their needs unmet, particularly with regard to the short- and long-term care of the severely injured.

On their own, our service members and their families are awe inspiring in the face of their disabilities and hardships—courageous and resolute. But it is with the support of a grateful nation that they remain unfaltering in their determination and find hope and purpose beyond recovery. As a united support network, all individuals, whether of great or small means, can find an opportunity to honor those who have willingly sacrificed to defend and protect our freedom. They have designed special projects and programs that allow and encourage community involvement.

www.hopeforthewarriors.org

Military Order of the Purple Heart of the USA (MOPH)

The MOPH represents combat wounded veterans in the nation's capitol. This means that the voice of the combat wounded veteran is heard in Congress, at the Department of Defense, and at the Veterans Administration.

The MOPH is constantly alert to any legislation that affects its members. The MOPH also works on combat wounded veterans' behalf. Contact MOPH at 703-642-5360.

www.purpleheart.org

National Veterans Foundation

Serves the crisis management, information, and referral needs of all U.S. veterans and their families through management and operation of the nation's only toll-free helpline for all veterans and their families; public awareness programs that shine a consistent spotlight on the needs of America's veterans; and outreach services that provide veterans and families in need with food, clothing, transportation, employment, and other essential resources.

1-888-777-4443

www.nvf.org

Veteran Service Officers Organizations

American Legion—www.legion.org
American Veterans—www.amvets.org
Disabled American Veterans—www.dav.org
Military Coalition Members—www.themilitarycoalition.org/Members.htm
Military Order of the Purple Heart—www.purpleheart.org
National Association of State Directors of Veterans Affairs—www.nasdva.net
Paralyzed Veterans of America—www.pva.org
Veterans of Foreign Wars—www.vfw.org

TRICARE

TRICARE—www.tricare.mil
TRICARE Dental—www.tricaredentalprogram.com
TRICARE Retiree Dental—www.trdp.org
TRICARE Pharmacy—www.express-scripts.com
TRICARE North Region—www.healthnetfederalservices.com
TRICARE South Region—www.humana-military.com
TRICARE West Region—www.triwest.com
Active Duty Dental Program—www.addp-ucci.com
Guard and Reserve Web portal to access for signing up for TRICARE

Reserve Select—www.dmdc.osd.mil/appj/esgr/privacyaAction.do
Military Medical Support Office (MMSO)—www.tricare.mil/tma/
MMSO/index.aspx

Wounded Warrior Service Programs

Army Wounded Warrior Program—www.aw2.army.mil
Marine for Life—www.m4l.usmc.mil
Navy Safe Harbor—Wounded, Ill, and Injured Support—www.npc
.navy.mil/CommandSupport/SafeHarbor

INJURED SUPPORT
Air Force Wounded Warrior Program—www.woundedwarrior.af.mil

Organizations Specific to Disability

Blind Veterans Association—www.bva.org
Colorado Traumatic Brain Injury Trust Fund Program—www.cdhs
.state.co.us/tbi/definition_of_tbi.htm
Defense and Veterans Brian Injury Center—www.dvbic.org
Denver Options—Operation TBI Freedom—www.
operationtbifreedom.org
Helping Hands—www.monkeyhelpers.org
National Amputation Foundation—www.nationalamputation.org

Vacations for Wounded Service Members

Vacations for Veterans is to enable veterans of the U.S. Armed Forces recently wounded in combat operations, and who have received the Purple
Heart Medal in the Afghanistan or Iraq campaigns, to receive free lodgings
donated by vacation homeowners.
www.vacationsforveterans.org

Counseling

Art of Redirection Counseling—www.artofredirection.com
Give an Hour—www.giveanhour.org
Lost and Found Inc.—www.lostandfoundinc.org
One Freedom—www.onefreedom.org
People House—www.peoplehouse.org
Pikes Peak Behavioral Health Group—www.ppbhg.org
Sleep Recover and Reintegration—www.annewein.com

Soldiers Project—www.thesoldiersproject.org

Sunrise Seminars—www.sunriseseminars.com

Veterans and Families Coming Home—www.veteransandfamilies
.org

Veterans Helping Veterans Now—www.vhvnow.org

Vets 4 Vets—www.vets4vets.us

Special Programs for OEF/OIF Wounded

Angels of Mercy—www.supportourwounded.org

Bob Woodruff Foundation—http://remind.org

Cadence Riding—www.cadenceriding.org

Challenge Aspen—www.challengeaspen.com

Challenged Athlete Foundation—www.challengedathletes.org

Coalition to Salute America's Heroes—www.saluteheroes.org

Disabled Sports USA—www.dsusa.org

Family & Friends for Freedom Fund, Inc.—www.injuredmarinesfund
.org

Fisher House—www.fisherhouse.org

Hearts and Horses—www.heartsandhorses.org

Hope for the Warriors—www.hopeforthewarriors.org

Independence Fund—www.independencefund.org

Lakeshore Foundation—www.lakeshore.org

Military OneSource Wounded Warrior Resource Center—www
.woundedwarriorresourcecenter.com

Northrop Grumman (assisting with employment)—http://
operationimpact.ms.northropgrumman.com

Operation Family Fund—www.operationfamilyfund.org

Operation First Response—www.operationfirstresponse.org

Outdoor Buddies—www.outdoorbuddies.org

Pentagon Foundation—www.pentagonfoundation.org

Pikes Peak Therapeutic Riding Center—www.pptrc.org

Project Victory—www.tirrfoundation.org

Rebuild Hope—www.rebuildhope.org

Semper Fi Fund (must be a marine or have been attached to a marine unit
on deployment when injuries took place)—www.semperfifund.org

Sentinels of Freedom (scholarships)—www.sentinelsoffreedom.org

Strikeouts for Troops—www.strikeoutsfortroops.org

Sun Valley Adaptive Sports—www.svasp.org

Therapeutic Riding and Education Center—www.trectrax.org

Wounded, Ill, and Injured Compensation and Benefits Handbook—
www.transitionassistanceprogram.com

Wounded Heroes Fund—www.woundedheroesfund.net

Wounded Marine Careers Foundation—www.woundedmarinecareers
.org

Wounded Warrior Project—www.woundedwarriorproject.org

Families

Army Families Online

The well-being liaison office assists the Army leadership with ensuring the effective delivery of well-being programs in the Army.

www.armyfamiliesonline.org

Army Morale Welfare and Recreation

Army recreation programs.

www.armymwr.com

Azalea Charities

Provides comfort and relief items for soldiers, sailors, airmen, and marines sick, injured, or wounded from service in Iraq and Afghanistan. It purchases specific items requested by Military Medical Centers, VA Medical Centers, and Fisher House rehabilitation facilities each week. It also provides financial support to *CrisisLink*, a hotline for wounded service members and their families, and *Hope for the Warriors*, special projects for wounded service members.

www.azaleacharities.com/about/mission.shtml

Blue Star Mothers of America

A nonprofit organization of mothers who now have, or have had, children honorably serving in the military. Their mission is "supporting each other and our children while promoting patriotism."

www.bluestarmothers.org

Heroes for Heroes

Heroes for Heroes supports injured military members and their families, and the Armed Services YMCA, at the Naval Medical Center San Diego and Camp Pendleton.

www.heroesforheroes.net

Military Connection
Comprehensive military directory providing information on job postings, job fairs, and listings.

www.militaryconnection.com

The Military Family Network
One nation, one community, making the world a home for military families.

www.emilitary.org

Military Homefront
Website for reliable quality of life information designed to help troops, families, and service providers.

www.militaryhomefront.dod.mil

My Army Life Too
Website of choice for Army families providing accurate, updated articles and information on various topics.

www.myarmylifetoo.com

National Military Family Association (NMFA)
Serving the families of those who Serve, the NMFA—"The Voice for Military Families"—is dedicated to serving the families and survivors of the seven uniformed services through education, information, and advocacy. NMFA is the only national organization dedicated to identifying and resolving issues of concern to military families. Contact NMFA at 1-800-260-0218, 703-931-6632, or fax at 703-931-4600.

www.nmfa.org

The National Remember Our Troops Campaign
The National Remember Our Troops Campaign works to recognize military service members and their families by providing an official U.S. Blue or Gold Star Service Banner. The Star Service Banner displayed in the window of a home is a tradition dating back to World War I.

www.nrotc.org

Strategic Outreach to Families of All Reservists (SOFAR)
SOFAR helps Reservist families reduce their stress and prepare for the possibility that their Reservist or Guard member may exhibit symptoms of

trauma from serving in a combat zone. The goal of SOFAR is to provide a flexible and diverse range of psychological services that fosters stabilization, aids in formulating prevention plans to avoid crises, and helps families to manage acute problems effectively when they occur.

www.sofarusa.org

Family Assistance

American Red Cross—www.redcross.org

Armed Forces Foundation—www.armedforcesfoundation.org

Army Long Term Family Case—www.hrc.army.mil/site/active/tagd/ cmaoc/altfcm/index.htm

Army OneSource—www.myarmyonesource.com

Assistance with résumés, job readiness training, etc.—www .chooselifeinc.org

Cell phones/calling cards for soldiers—www.cellphonesforsoldiers.com

Freedom Calls—www.freedomcalls.org

Freedom Hunters—www.freedomhunters.org

Grand Camps for kids and grandparents—www.grandcamps.org

Hero Salute—www.herosalute.com

Homes for Our Troops—www.homesforourtroops.org

The Military Family Network—www.emilitary.org

Military Homefront—www.militaryhomefront.dod.mil

Military OneSource—www.militaryonesource.com

Military news with benefit information—www.military.com

Military Spouse Career Center—www.military.com/spouse

Military Spouse Resource Center (assist with employment, education, scholarships)—www.milspouse.org

Military Students on the Move—www.militarystudent.org

National Association of Child Care Resource and Referral Agencies— www.naccrra.org

National Military Family Association—www.nmfa.org

National Resource Directory—www.nationalresourcedirectory.org

Our Military—www.ourmilitary.mil/index.aspx

Our Military Kids—www.ourmilitarykids.org

Project Focus—www.focusproject.org

Project Sanctuary—www.projectsanctuary.us

Rebuilding Together—www.rebuildingtogether.org

Snowball Express—www.snowballexpress.org

Social Security—www.ssa.gov

Soldiers Angels—www.soldiersangels.com

Specific to Illinois—www.operationhomefront.org

Swords to Plowshares (employment, training, health, and legal)—www
.swords-to-plowshares.org

Tragedy Assistance Program for Survivors—www.taps.org

United Services Organization—www.uso.org

Veterans Holidays (discounted rates)—www.veteransholidays.com

Women, Infants, and Children (WIC)—www.fns.usda.gov/wic

Financial Assistance

Get your W-2 from myPay: https://mypay.dfas.mil/mypay.aspx

American Legion Temporary Financial Assistance (TFA)—www
.legion.org/veterans/family/assistance

American Military Family—www.AMF100.org

American Soldier Foundation—www.soldierfoundation.org

AnnualCreditReport.com—www.annualcreditreport.com

Elks Lodge (have financial assistance available)—www.elks.org

Equifax Credit Information Service—www.equifax.com

Experian National Consumer Assistance—www.experian.com

Home Front Cares—www.thehomefrontcares.org

Impact a Hero—www.impactahero.org/index.php

Military Installation Finder—www.militaryinstallations.dod.mil/
ismart/MHF-MI

Military OneSource—http://militaryonesource.com/skins/MOS/
home.asps

National Veterans Foundation—www.nvf.org/contact/rfs/index.php

Operation Helping Healing—www.helpingheal.org/guidelines.html

Operation Home Front—www.operationhomefront.net

Reserve Aid—www.reserveaid.org

Salute Heroes for Wounded Warriors—www.saluteheroes.org

Transunion—www.transunion.com

Unmet Needs—www.unmetneeds.com

USA Cares—www.usacares.org

VA Form 26-1880, Request for Certificate of Eligibility—www.vba
.va.gov/pubs/forms/26-1880.pdf

VA Home Loan Resources—www.homeloans.va.gov/veteran.htm

Education

Application Pell Grants or Federal Stafford Loans (FAFSA)—www
.fafsa.ed.gov

Air Force (CCAF) Transcript—www.au.af.mil/au/ccaf

Army (AARTS) Transcript—http://aarts.army.mil

Coast Guard Institute Transcript—www.uscg.mil/hq/cgi/forms.html

The Defense Activity for Non-Traditional Education Support (DANTES)—www.dantes.doded.mil/dantes_web/danteshome.asp

Department of Defense Voluntary Education Program—www.voled .doded.mil Federal Financial Student Aid—www.federalstudentaid .ed.gov

Navy and Marine Corps (SMART) Transcript—www.navycollege .navy.mil

VA Education Services (GI Bill)—www.gibill.va.gov/

VA Regional Office Finder—www1.va.gov/directory/guide/home .asp

VA 22-1990 Application for Education Benefits—www.vba.va.gov/ pubs/forms/22-1990.pdf

Veterans' Upward Bound—www.veteransupwardbound.org/vetub.html

Education Resources

AHEAD—Association on Higher Education and Disability—www .ahead.org

American Council on Education—www.acenet.edu

Comprehensive Development Center—http://dcwi.com/~cdc/ Welcome.html

National Center for Learning Disabilities—www.ncld.org/content/ view/871/456074

On-line Disability Information System (ODIS)—www.ume.maine .edu/~cci/odis

OSERS: National Institute on Disability & Rehabilitation Research (NIDRR)—www.ed.gov/offices/OSERS/NIDRR/index.html

Rehabilitation Counseling Web Page—http://pages.prodigy.com/ rehabilitation-counseling/index.htm

Students Seeking Disability Related Information—www.abilityinfo .com

University Resources

Centennial Colleges' Centre for Students with Disabilities (CSD)— www.cencol.on.ca/csd

Coalition of Rehab Engineering Research Organizations—http:// trace.wisc.edu/CRERO

Curry School of Education—http://curry.edchool.virginia.edu

George Washington University Rehabilitation Counselor Education Programs—www.gwu.edu/~chaos

Iowa State University Disabled User Services Homepage—www.public.iastate.edu/~dus_info/homepage.html

Johns Hopkins University Physical Medicine and Rehabilitation—www.med.jhu.edu/rehab

Nebraska Assistive Technology Project—www.nde.state.ne.us/ATP/Techhome.html

Northwestern University Rehab Engineering, Prosthetics and Orthotics—www.repoc.nwu.edu

Ohio State University—Disability Services—www.osu.edu/units/ods

Oklahoma State University National Clearing House of Rehabilitation Training Material—www.nchrtm.okstate.edu

Tarleton State University—www.tarleton.edu

Thomas Edison State College—Distance Learning—www.tesc.edu

University of California at Berkeley School of Psychology—www-gse.berkeley.edu/program/SP/sp.html

University of California at Los Angeles Disabilities and Computing Program (DCP)—www.dcp.ucla.edu./

University of Delaware—SEM—www.ece.udel.edu/InfoAccess

University Of Georgia—Disability Services—www.dissvcs.uga.edu

University of Illinois at Urbana-Champaign—www.uiuc.edu

University of Kansas Medical Center, School of Allied Health—www.kumc.edu/SAH

University of Minnesota, Disability Services—http://disserv.stu.umn.edu

University of New Hampshire, Institute on Disability—http://iod.unh.edu

University of Virginia, Special Education Website—http://special.edschool.virginia.edu

University of Washington, Department of Rehabilitation Medicine—http://depts.washington.edu/rehab

Victoria University, TAFE Services—www.adcet.edu.au

West Virginia University Rehabilitation Research and Training Center (WVRTC)—www.adcet.edu.au

Wright State University Rehabilitation Engineering Information and Training—www.engineering.wright.edu/bie/rehabengr/rehabeng.html

Relocation
Chamber of Commerce Locator—www.chamberofcommerce.com
"Plan My Move"—www.militaryhomefront.dod.mil/pls
.htmsdb/f?p=107:1:3267731230074301
Relocation Assistance Office Locator—www.militaryinstallations.dod
.mil/smart/MHF-MI

Military Personnel Portals
Air Force Portal—www.my.af.mil
Army Knowledge Online (AKO)—www.army.mil/ako
The "It's Your Move" pamphlet—www.usapa.army.mil/pdffiles/p55_2
.pdf
Navy Knowledge Online (NKO)—www.nko.mil
Travel and per diem information—https://secureapp2.hqda.pentagon
.mil.perdiem
"Special needs" resources—www.militaryhomefront.dod.mil
USA Travel Source—www.relo.usa.com

Transition

Sentinels of Freedom
Sentinels of Freedom's mission is to provide life-changing opportunities
for service members who have suffered severe injuries and need the support of grateful communities to realize their dreams. Unlike any other
time in history, many more severely wounded are coming home faced
with the challenges of putting their lives back together. Sentinels of Freedom provides "life scholarships" to help vets become self-sufficient. Sentinels succeeds because whole communities help. Local businesses and
individuals not only give money, but also time, goods and services, housing, and transportation.
www.sentinelsoffreedom.org

Veterans and Families Coming Home
Provides resources for vets to ease their transition from military to civilian
life.
www.veteransandfamilies.org
Air Force Airman and Family Readiness Center—www
.militaryinstallations.dod.mil
Army Career and Alumni Program (ACAP)—www.acap.army.mil

Civilian Assistance and Re-Employment (CARE)—www.cpms.osd
.mil/care

Coast Guard Worklife Division—Transition Assistance—www.uscg
.mil/hq/g-w/g-wk/wkw/worklife_programs/transition_assistance
.htm

Department of Labor—www.dol.gov

Department of Veterans Affairs (DVA)—www.va.gov

Department of Veterans Affairs Locations—www1.va.gov/directory/
guide/home.asp?isFlash=1)

DoD Transportal—www.dodtransportal.org

Family Center, Chaplain's Office, and Related Resources Finder—
www.nvti.cudenver.edu/resources/militarybasestap.htm

Marine for Life—www.mfl.usmc.mil

Marines Career Resource Management Center (CRMC)/Transition
& Employment Assistance Program Center—www.usmc-mccs
.org/tamp/index.cfm

Military Family Network—www.emilitary.org

Military Home Front—www.militaryhomefront.dod.mil

Military Installation Locator—www.militaryinstallations.dod.mil/
ismart/MHF-MI

Military OneSource—www.militaryonesource.com/skins/MOS/
home.aspx

National Guard Transitional Assistance Advisors—www.guardfamily
.org/Public/Application/ResourceFinderSearch.aspx

Navy Fleet and Family Support Center—www.fssp.navy.mil

Operation Transition website—www.dmdc.osd.mil/ot

A Summary of Veteran's Benefits—www.vba.va.gov/bln/21/index.htm

Temporary Early Retirement Authority (TERA) Program—www
.dmdc.osd.mil/tera

Veterans Affair Programs

CHAMPVA for dependents—www.va.gov/hac/forbeneficiaries/
champva/champva.asp

Transition Assistant Advisor—www.taapmo.com

Veteran Affairs—www.va.gov

Veteran Business—www.vetbiz.gov

Transportation

Air Ambulance Service—www.aircompassionamerica.org

Air Charity Network—www.aircharitynetwork.org
Angel Flight West—www.angelflightwest.org
Mercy Medical—www.mercymedical.org/helpful-links
Operation Hero Miles—www.heromiles.org
Veterans Airlift Command—www.veteransairlift.org

Employment

5 Star Recruitment Careers—www.5starrecruitment.com
American Corporate Program (veterans mentoring)—http://acp-usa
.org
America's Heroes at Work—www.americasheroesatwork.gov
Buckley AFB NAF Human Resource Office—www.460fss.com/460_
FSS/HTML/HRO.html
Colorado Department of Labor and Employment—www.
coloradoworkforce.com
Colorado Springs Help Wanted—http://regionalhelpwanted.com/
colorado-springs-jobs
Colorado State Government Job Announcements—www.gssa.state.co
.us/announce/Job+Announcements.nsf/$about?OpenAbout
Enable America—www.enableamerica.org
Helmets to Hardhats—www.helmetstohardhats.org
Hire a Hero—www.hireAhero.com
Hire America's Heroes—www.hireamericasheroes.org
Hire Vets First—www.hirevetsfirst.gov
Job Bank—www.jobsearch.org
Recruit Air Force—www.recruitairforce.com
Recruit Army—www.RecruitArmy.com
Recruit Marines—www.recruitmarines.com
Recruit Navy—www.recruitnavy.com
Return 2 Work—www.return2work.org
Military Connection—www.militaryconnection.com
Military Officers Association of America—www.MOAA.org
USA Jobs—www.usajobs.gov
Veterans Green Jobs—www.veteransgreenjobs.org
Veteran Job Fairs—www.VetsJobs.net
Vet Jobs—www.vetjobs.com

Military

DEERS/RAPIDS Locator—www.dmdc.osd.mil/rsl/owa/home

Military Audiology—www.militaryaudiology.org
Military Coalition—www.themilitarycoalition.org
National Archives and Records Administration—www.archives.gov
To Transfer Military Occupation Specialty to Civilian—www
    .OnetCenter.org
Transition Assistance Program Turbo Tap—www
    .transitionassistanceprogram.com

Education/Scholarships

Air Force Aid Society
The Air Force Aid Society provides need-based grants of up to $1,500 to selected sons and daughters of current, former, and deceased Air Force personnel. The Air Force Aid Society website provides information on and applications for the education grants offered by the Society.
  1-800-429-9475
  703-607-3072
  www.afas.org/body_grant.htm

Army Emergency Relief
In addition to providing information on and applications for scholarships provided by the Army Emergency Relief to the spouses and children of deceased Army personnel, the Army Emergency Relief also maintains a listing of general financial aid links and scholarship search engines.
  1-866-878-6378
  703-428-0000
  www.aerhq.org/education.asp
  Children of Fallen Heroes—www.cfsrf.org
  Fish House Foundation—www.fishhouse.org
  Freedom Alliance—www.freedomalliance.org
  Scholarships for military children—www.militaryscholar.org
  Troops to teachers—www.dantes.doded.mil

Hope for the Warriors
The mission of Hope for the Warriors™ is to enhance quality of life for U.S. service members and their families nationwide who have been adversely affected by injuries or death in the line of duty. It has developed a number of advocacy, support, and educational programs.

Hope for the Warriors
PMB 48
1335 Suite E, Western Blvd.
Jacksonville, NC 28546
1-877-2HOPE4W
910-938-1817
info@hopeforthewarriors.org

Marine Corps Scholarship Foundation

The Marine Corps Scholarship Foundation website provides information on and applications for scholarships offered by the Foundation to the sons and daughters of current or former U.S. marines, and to the children of current or former U.S. Navy corpsmen who have served with the U.S. Marine Corps.

New Jersey Office: 1-800-292-7777
Virginia Office: 703-549-0060
www.marine-scholars.org

Military.com

Military.com is a commercial, service-related organization that maintains a website offering a scholarship search function for dependents of service members as well as state-by-state education benefits listings.

www.military.com

Navy-Marine Corps Relief Society

The Navy-Marine Corps Relief Society maintains a website for information on and applications for educational grants offered and administered by the Navy-Marine Corps Relief Society.

703-696-4960
www.nmcrs.org

Reserve Officers Association

In addition to offering scholarship and loan programs to the families of its members, the Reserve Officers Association maintains a list of military dependent scholarships and scholarships for the children of deceased service members generally.

1-800-809-9448
www.roa.org/roal/roal_detail.asp?id=806

Scholarships for Military Children

Scholarships for Military Children is a scholarship program that was created by the Defense Commissary Agency. Scholarships for Military Children maintains a website that provides information on and applications for scholarships funded through the manufacturers and suppliers whose products are sold at military commissaries around the globe.

   1-888-294-8560
   www.MilitaryScholar.org
   www.fallenheroesfund.org 37

Society of Daughters of the U.S. Army (DUSA)

SCHOLARSHIP AWARDS PROGRAM

The DUSA website provides information on applications for DUSA scholarships, which are offered to daughters or granddaughters of CWOs or officers of the U.S. Army who died on active duty.

   www.dodea.edu/students/dusa.htm

Service Specific

   Air Force Cross Roads—www.afcrossroads.com
   Marines—www.marines.mil/Pages/Default.aspx
   Navy Personnel Command—www.npc.navy.mil
   U.S. Army Human Resource Command—www.hrc.army.mil/
      indexflash.asp
   U.S. Coast Guard—www.uscg.mil

Service Specific Financial Assistance

   Air Force Aid Society (AFAS)—www.afas.org
      They also have a loan called the Falcon loan, which is $500 or less
      for emergency needs.
   Army Emergency Relief—www.aerhq.org
   Coast Guard Mutual Assistance (active, reserve, and retired)—www
      .cgmahq.org
   Navy-Marine Corps Relief Society Financial Assistance—www.nmcrs
      .org

Housing

   Building Homes for Heroes—www.buildinghomesforheroes.com

Homes for Our Troops (they will build you a house at no cost if accepted)—www.homesforourtroops.org

Operation Forever Free—www.operationforeverfree.org

Rebuilding Together—www.rebuildingtogether.org

Rebuilding Together believes we can preserve affordable homeownership and revitalize communities by providing free home modifications and repairs, making homes safer, more accessible, and more energy efficient.

Legal

American Bar Association, Pro Bono Programs (information on free legal services)—www.abanet.org

National Veterans Legal Services Program—www.nvlsp.org

Index

About the Authors

Janelle Hill is the president and lead consultant of PBS Marketing/Federal Concierge LLC, a consulting provider supporting a variety of project and program needs to businesses, contractors, and the federal government. She is also a United States Marine Corps Key Volunteer and an advocate for special needs children. Her husband is a major in the USMC. She is the coauthor of *The Wounded Warrior Handbook* (2008).

Cheryl Lawhorne is an original plank holder in the Wounded Warrior Battalion West at Camp Pendleton, California. She now serves as the deputy project manager for the Recovery Care Coordination Program with the Wounded Warrior Regiment in Quantico, Virginia, under the guidance of Headquarters Marine Corps and the Office of the Secretary of Defense. She was a contributing author to *The Wounded Warrior Handbook* (2008).

Don Philpott is the editor-in-chief of *International Homeland Security: The Quarterly Journal for Homeland Security Professionals*, and the author of more than 5,000 articles in various publications and over 90 books, including *Is America Safe: Terrorism, Homeland Security, and Emergency Preparedness* (2009) and *The Wounded Warrior Handbook* (2008).